thomson●com

changing the way the world learns℠

To get extra value from this book for no additional cost, go to:

http://www.thomson.com/wadsworth.html

thomson.com is the World Wide Web site for Wadsworth/ITP
and is your direct source to dozens of on-line resources.
thomson.com helps you find out about supplements,
experiment with demonstration software, search for a job,
and send e-mail to many of our authors. You can even
preview new publications and exciting new technologies.

thomson.com: *It's where you'll find us in the future.*

Texas Politics
Economics, Power, and Policy SIXTH EDITION

James W. Lamare

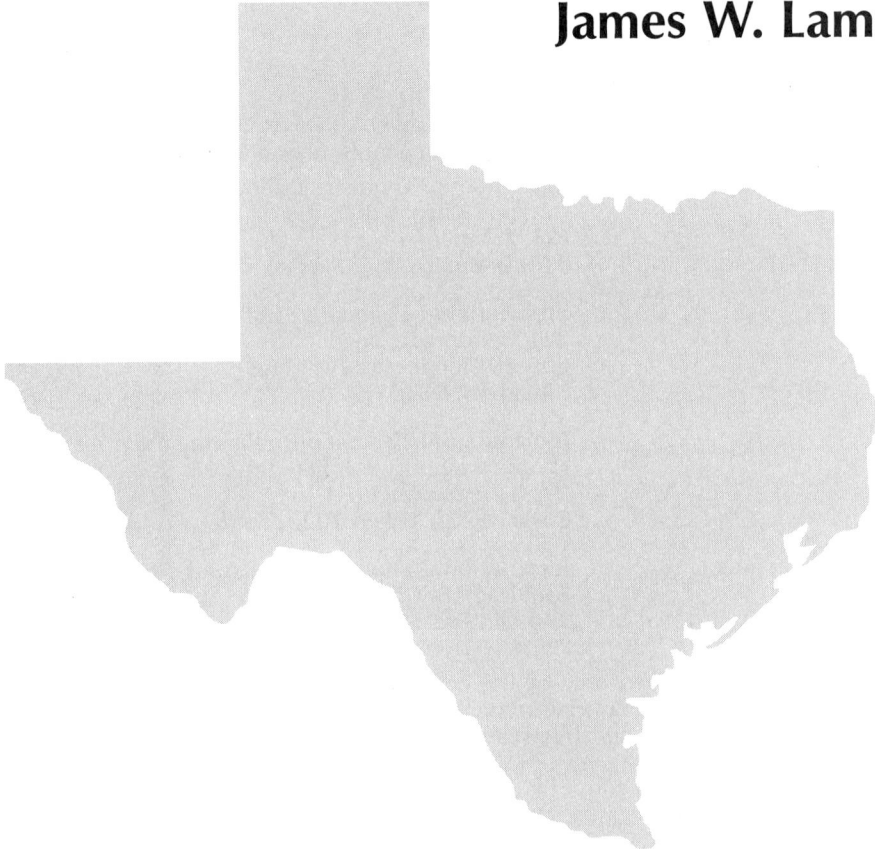

West / Wadsworth

I(T)P® An International Thomson Publishing Company

Belmont, CA • Albany, NY • Bonn • Boston • Cincinnati • Detroit • Johannesburg • London • Madrid
Melbourne • Mexico City • New York • Paris • Singapore • Tokyo • Toronto • Washington

Political Science Editor: Clark Baxter
Development Editor: Sharon Adams-Poore
Editorial Assistant: Amy Guastello
Production Service: Carol Carreon Lombardi
Print Buyer: Barbara Britton
Permissions Editor: Veronica Oliva
Composition: Parkwood Composition
    Service, Inc.

Marketing Manager: Jay Hu
Cover Design: John Odam
Cover Photographs: Cowboy/oil wells by
    Photo Disc; La Raza by Shel Hershon;
    capitol by Hulton-Deutsch
Printer: Malloy Lithographing, Inc.

Printed in the United States of America
1 2 3 4 5 6 7 8 9 10

For more information, contact Wadsworth Publishing Company at 10 Davis Drive,
Belmont, CA 94002, or electronically at http://www.thomson.com/wadsworth.html

International Thomson Publishing Europe
Berkshire House 168-173
High Holborn
London, WC1V 7AA, England

International Thomson Editores
Campos Eliseos 385, Piso 7
Col. Polanco
11560 México D.F. México

Thomas Nelson Australia
102 Dodds Street
South Melbourne 3205
Victoria, Australia

International Thomson Publishing Asia
221 Henderson Road
#05-10 Henderson Building
Singapore 0315

Nelson Canada
1120 Birchmount Road
Scarborough, Ontario
Canada M1K 5G4

International Thomson Publishing Japan
Hirakawacho Kyowa Building, 3F
2-2-1 Hirakawacho
Chiyoda-ku, Tokyo 102, Japan

International Thomson Publishing GmbH
Königswinterer Strasse 418
53227 Bonn, Germany

International Thomson Publishing Southern Africa
Building 18, Constantia Park
240 Old Pretoria Road
Halfway House, 1685 South Africa

This book is printed on acid-free recycled paper.

Library of Congress Cataloging-in-Publication data
Lamare, James.
    Texas politics : economics, power, and policy / James W. Lamare. –
– 6th ed.
        p.   cm.
    Includes bibliographical references and Index.
    ISBN 0-314-20481-4
    1. Texas—Politics and government—1951– 2. Texas—Economic conditions.
3. Elite (Social sciences)—Texas.   I. Title.
JK4816.L36 1997
320.9764—dc21   97-23747

To Mary

★★★★★ CONTENTS

★★★★★ PREFACE

The effort that has been undertaken to lift Texas out of the economic doldrums has affected the economics and politics of the state. Along the economic front, new institutions, especially in the banking and savings and loan communities, have emerged to take the place of the businesses that could not survive the recent recession. Regardless of this change of economic actors, previously documented patterns of economic domination continue in the state. That is, a relatively small number of major companies exercise a preponderant amount of influence over economic activities in Texas. Moreover, there are clear signs that these important firms are interconnected: An economic elite prevails.

What has changed are the geographic origins of these new dominating firms. In most cases, their headquarters are not in Texas. As a consequence, the state economy has become a more integral component of the national and global economy. Thus the economic elite that now prevails in Texas is not as well grounded in the state's history, culture, and society as was the former one.

Political institutions and leaders have been highly sensitive to the economic problems facing the state. Their proposals and policies have been written largely with the intent of righting the economic wrongs that have beset Texas. Hence, even though there has been some change in the cast of characters holding political office, the commitment to promote and protect the preferences of the state's dominant economic interests has remained constant among political decision makers. Individuals and groups not in synch with the political agenda of the dominant economic institutions still find it difficult to influence the policy-making process in the state.

This edition examines Texas in light of these features. In this revision, I have tried to thoroughly update the material without losing sight of the pro-business tilt of Texas's political system.

Acknowledgments

In preparing the manuscript I have greatly benefitted from the comments of the following reviewers: Layne Hoppe (Texas Lutheran College), Robert Locander (North Harris College), Mark Priewe (University of Texas at San Antonio), Gregory G. Rocha (University of Texas at El Paso), Allan Saxe (University of Texas at Arlington), and Carter Whatley (Texas A&M, Corpus Christi).

Texas Politics
Economics, Power, and Policy SIXTH EDITION

INTRODUCTION

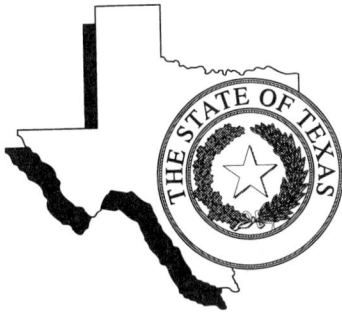

Political Power in Texas

In 1798, the Tenth Amendment was added to the United States Constitution. It specifically guarantees that "the powers not delegated to the United States by the Constitution, nor prohibited by it to the States, are reserved to the States respectively, or to the people." In effect, this amendment is part of the foundation of our political system, ensuring state governments a prominent role in exercising political power. Defined simply, *power* is the ability to achieve desired goals. *Political power*, a distinct type of power, refers to achieving goals that affect a substantial segment of the population. A person has political power if, when her or his goals are attained, the larger society is affected.

★★★★★ ABOUT POLITICAL POWER

The struggle for political power is most obvious in situations where individuals, groups, or institutions compete for scarce resources. For instance, over the last quarter century, a variety of people and interests have been entangled in a controversy involving the proper method of funding public education in the state of Texas. This dispute has affected, among others, members of the U.S. Supreme Court, state legislators, executives, administrators, and judges, local school districts, poor and rich Texans, and voters. The temperature of the debate rose sharply in 1989, when the Texas Supreme Court ruled that the existing method of financing public schools violated the state constitution. The boiling point was reached two years later, after a state district court judge ruled that unless Texas rectified the problem by June 1, 1993, all state funds allocated for public education would be frozen, in effect shutting down the public school system.[1] Since funds for education are scarce, a resolution

1

of this struggle meant that some individuals and groups would win, while others would lose. In other words, some actors would reach their goals, thus achieving political power. Others would not be so successful, and hence be less politically powerful.

Political power is displayed not only in situations where there is conflict over limited resources. It is possible that after achieving numerous successes, certain actors might reach positions of such superiority that they no longer faced any serious challenge. When this occurs, power has become highly structured. It is also possible that the powerful can, sometimes without exerting much effort, control the political agenda and, in so doing, minimize the materialization of threats to their positions.

Any person or organization whose activities have an impact on the public is politically powerful. In other words, it is possible to have political power independent of the government. However, in modern industrial societies, such as Texas, government is inextricably involved in the exercise of political power. People and groups often align themselves with, and rely on, the government because the public is much more likely to abide by policies if the government has sanctioned them. There are two principal reasons for this widespread acceptance.

First, most modern governments are considered by their constituent populations to be the highest authorities. So overwhelming is this supportive feeling that citizens often obey governmental requests simply out of respect for the government. Second, government can compel obedience through the threat or the actual use of force. The most distinguishable characteristic of a government, according to the eminent sociologist Max Weber, is that it "successfully upholds a claim to the monopoly of the legitimate use of physical force in the enforcement of its order."[2]

Since government in the United States has traditionally been accepted by its citizens as the legitimate source of rules and regulations, individuals and groups have understandably sought its blessing in their quest for political power. Requests for government assistance take two general forms. At times, the government is asked to adopt and implement programs and ideas that promote the interests of certain groups and individuals. On other occasions, private interests seek assurance that they can engage in certain activities without government intervention.

State governments are heavily engaged in formulating policies in the areas of education, welfare, transportation, taxation, public safety, and the regulation of business, labor, and social behavior. Overall, it has been concluded that states are growing in importance more than any other level of government in the United States.[3] At the local level, city, county, and special district governments have an immediate impact on citizens. Local governments are primarily responsible for providing public services such as education, water delivery, sanitation facilities, streets, and fire fighting and police protection.

This book investigates political power at the state and local levels in Texas. It examines who has political power in Texas, and why.

There are two prevailing theoretical approaches to studying the distribution of political power in the United States. One is *pluralism;* the other
is the *economic-elite* perspective.[4]

Pluralism and economic-elite theory are at odds in their interpretations
of almost every aspect of the political-power question. They do, however,
have one belief in common: Each school of thought agrees that government
at all levels in the United States is actually run by a relatively small
group—an elite. They disagree dramatically about the nature of the elite,
its composition, and its accountability to the public. An examination of
each theory follows.

★★★★★ PLURALISM (IDEA)

Pluralism contends that political power is widely dispersed in the United
States.[5] No one group or person has a monopoly on it. Political decisions
are made openly in government institutions by officeholders representative of, and accountable to, the public. The ties between leaders and ordinary citizens are many and both parties benefit from the relationship.

Several things keep political leaders close to the public:

1. *Political leaders are plentiful.* Thousands of Americans hold offices in
local, state, and federal government. Leadership positions tend to cluster
around specific policy issues. For example, those who make decisions in
the area of education—members of school boards, superintendents, and
so on—do not enter other areas, such as welfare or the building of prisons. Tax collectors do not plan city traffic-light patterns. Consequently,
numerous leadership groups exist in government. Each is autonomous
and each specializes in a given policy area. As the public increasingly
demands resolution of crucial issues, new leadership groups (boards,
commissions, agencies, legislative committees, etc.) are born. Thus, the
public does not lack government institutions to hear its complaints. The
more formidable problem often becomes finding the right officeholders to
redress grievances. In those rare instances in which one leader or a small
group of leaders dominates the decision-making process, these key officials are usually elected, and therefore accountable to the voting public.

2. *Diversity of the political elite, both in their social background and in their
issue orientation, is pronounced.* Leaders reflect the social and cultural
diversity found in the United States. Consequently, within each specialized leadership group, and across the broad spectrum of political leaders,
officials are drawn from all walks of life. No one social group—such as a
race, region, economic class, gender, or religion—controls all leadership
posts; each demographic group has representation in the elite. Moreover,
leaders vary in their issue perspectives: their outlooks are as distinct as
their social backgrounds.

3. *Political leaders are firmly committed to democratic values.* Although diversity characterizes the social origins and ideological viewpoints of office-holders, they are alike in their adherence to the democratic creed. That is, they share a common commitment to procedural fair play, tolerance for diverse, even deviating, points of view, and respect for individual freedom. They encourage nonviolent solutions to social problems, including highly volatile ones, and emphasize the importance of mass participation in the political process. They believe that all disagreements over policy matters should be handled by following democratic rules and procedures.

The masses also play a crucial role in pluralist thinking. Citizens communicate their preferences to leaders in several ways:

1. *It is not difficult for the average person to join the ranks of political decision makers.* Becoming a leader is largely a matter of ambition and desire. If a person wants to hold political office, opportunities are ample. Apathy is the major reason most people don't seek a position of leadership. Accordingly, a citizen who is interested in becoming more involved can easily act on those feelings and seek political office.

2. *Citizens control their leaders' behavior through the electoral process.* The ultimate route to becoming a leader is the winning of votes. Failure at the polling booth effectively prevents attainment of a leadership post. Even appointed officials are influenced by mass sentiment, since they are ordinarily selected by popularly elected leaders. The threat of electoral defeat is often enough to shape the behavior of officeholders. Hence, candidates—including incumbents—monitor opinion polls closely and frequently modify their behavior to accord with the mood of the majority.

3. *Citizens affect the political process through membership in diverse interest groups.* Group membership is established either by actually joining an organization or by simply being in an identifiable group, such as Texans, women, Generation X, Latinos, Southerners, or African Americans. Either type of group is bound to have representatives within the political elite. Indeed, many officeholders launch their political careers after being leaders of groups. Moreover, members can present their viewpoints to leaders through the active participation of their groups—ranging from having a hand in candidate selection to direct lobbying for specific policy proposals—in the political decision-making process.

The results of the close interaction of leaders and followers are as follows:

1. *Political leaders make decisions based on input from various groups and individuals.* The government listens to the proposals of all concerned parties and formulates its policy after a neutral weighing of each side.

2. *Final decisions reflect the interests of large and diverse segments of the population.* Because of the many voices reverberating in the government's ear, public policy is usually a compromise among many viewpoints. It is only through the delicate art of negotiation that the bargain among competing interests is struck and policy is formulated.

3. *A change in policy is often initiated by the masses, or by leaders in anticipation of demands coming from the public.* Since many perspectives enter into policy discussions, change is usually moderate and arrived at slowly. Over time, however, a series of incremental changes can result in major policy shifts.

In short, pluralism concludes that the United States political system is citizen-based. Political decisions reflect the interests of most of the public, and the beneficiaries of public policy are many people—usually more than a majority. Hence, most sectors of American society reach their goals through the political system: each group, to some extent, thus has political power.

★★★★★ ECONOMIC-ELITE THEORY

Fight between consumers & producers c producers winning.

Economic-elite theory asserts that political power in the United States is concentrated in the hands of a relatively small economic elite.[6] Put simply, those people and institutions that dominate the production and distribution of economic goods and services also collect most of the rewards to be gained from governmental decision making. The average citizen takes a back seat to the economic elite in influencing decision makers and benefiting from public policy.

The following points about the economic elite stand out:

—The average citizen is not represented

1. *Members of the economic elite command the operations of the major businesses in America.* They are the principal stockholders, managers, and members of the boards of directors of the country's largest corporations. These institutions exercise great influence over the economy. Since there are relatively few big businesses at this level of importance, the elite comprises an extremely small minority of Americans. By the very nature of their lofty status and their unique experiences, members of the economic elite are largely atypical of the general population.

2. *Basically, members of the elite see eye-to-eye on financial matters.* The goal of the economic world is to maximize profits. Given this orientation, there is little internal dissension within the business elite. Although there may be conflict over which firms should acquire the most profit and over the best means to obtain profit, it is rare that the giant corporations publicize these disagreements. In times of acute economic disequilibrium, such as during a deep recession, corporations may operate autonomously in order to survive. During more ordinary times, concerted attempts are made to resolve any major conflicts among elite members quickly and within the business community.

3. *The economic elite is united through many bonds.* First, purely economic connections link distinct corporate entities; companies are drawn together through interlocking directorates, shared stock ownership, and joint business ventures. Formal interest groups, such as the Business Council, the Business Roundtable, the Council on Foreign Relations, the Committee for Economic Development, the Texas Research League, and the Trilateral Commission, consolidate corporate viewpoints. Finally, there are social ties among members of the business community. Membership in private clubs (such as Houston's River Oaks), marriage, and common educational and social experiences are vital points of unity.

The interests of the economic elite are communicated to the government as follows:

1. *The field of candidates for electoral office is limited by the economic elite.* Care is taken to select candidates to ensure that the field of choices available to the voting public is composed of people not at odds with the priorities of economic leaders. The campaigns of favored candidates are assisted through generous financial contributions from members of this elite.

2. *The appointment of persons to government posts is also influenced by members of the economic elite.* Often, appointees come directly from the ranks of this elite. In this way, economic leaders hold positions in governmental offices that often benefit their business interests.

3. *Extensive lobbying of the government by big business is commonplace.* In attempts to influence the policy-making process, members of the economic elite provide research, experts, entertainment, financial inducements, and basic support to government officials. Organizations representing corporate interests are adept players at the game of lobbying political decision makers.

4. *The very structure of government institutions in the United States simplifies the corporate lobbying and campaign contribution process.* Government decisions are primarily made in decentralized quarters. The major work on policy proposals occurs in legislative committees, in specialized administrative agencies, and in obscure courtrooms. Consequently, to be effective, efforts to shape decisions usually need only be directed at the appropriate targets. It is not ordinarily necessary for dominant economic interests to be concerned with contacting or influencing all personnel in the government.

The relationship between the dominant economic elite and political officeholders yields several results:

1. *Public policy mostly reflects the interests of the economic elite.* Government decisions largely further the priorities of the business sector. To be sure, nonbusiness groups may benefit from the public policy-making process, but only if their preferences coincide with the goals of the economic elite or if the economic elite has no particular stake in the policy matter being decided.

2. *The masses exercise little direct control over the political process.* Citizens are reduced to voting for candidates who have been hand-picked

by members of the higher economic circles. In essence, voters are specta-
tors at an electoral game in which the key movers are members of the economic elite. Groups that emerge to represent the public's interest are usually understaffed, underfinanced, and relatively unsuccessful in affecting
the political decision-making process. Therefore, they are far less powerful than economic elite–sponsored groups in the lobbying process.

3. *Changes in public policy occur only if initiated by the economic elite.*
Political change is not mass-driven. Before change occurs, it is often necessary to show members of the elite that it is in their best interest to alter
the status quo. Failure to do so generally means no shift in public policy.

Neither pluralism nor economic elite theory concludes that the
American political process is fully democratic. In a pure democracy, all
people would not only be knowledgeable and interested in political matters, but would also be directly involved in political decision making. No
political system has ever attained this ideal. Consequently, pure democratic theory does not accurately describe the real world of politics,
although it may be an appropriate normative standard by which to evaluate the current American political system.

A major point of disagreement between these two theories is the question of whether the economic elite has political influence. Pluralists hold
that business is no more powerful than many other groups. Certainly,
leading economic actors have some valuable political resources (such as
wealth and status). However, noneconomic groups and other individuals
also possess important political tools (such as social standing, strength in
numbers, and the vote) that can offset the advantages held by business.
Furthermore, many pluralists discount the likelihood that an economic
elite even exists in the United States, claiming that competition—not
cohesion—characterizes business relations. Conversely, economic elite
theory not only argues that an economic elite is present in America, but
also contends that members of this elite prevail over the political system.
In short, it claims that politics is run by and for the people and institutions that control the economy.

The major thesis of this book is that an economic elite does dominate the
political system of Texas. The principal political questions brought before
state and local governments involve the allocation of economic resources.
The resolution of these economic matters usually benefits those who control these resources. Therefore, this book examines the distribution of political power in Texas along the lines suggested by economic-elite theory.

Many diverse observers of modern Texas have attested to the inordinate
importance of economic interests in the politics of the state. Writing a half
century ago, political scientist V. O. Key, Jr., a native of the West Texas
town of Lamesa, commented that "the Lone Star State is concerned about
money and how to make it, about oil and sulfur and gas, about cattle and
dust storms and irrigation, about cotton and banking and Mexicans."[7]
Speaking at the state Democratic Party convention in 1947, the chair of
that party proclaimed that "it may not be a wholesome thing to say, but

the oil industry today is in complete control of state politics and state government."[8] In the mid-1970s, a survey administered by Dun and Bradstreet to businessmen across the nation found that they regarded the state "as having the most favorable climate for business in the nation."[9] One of Texas's larger banks at the time concluded from this study "that Texas government, by its actions and inactions, has created a climate which is very appealing to employers."[10] More recently, politicians, academics, journalists, and business and community leaders have been quick to offer advice to the government about how to keep the state's economy on the right track. The ideas offered are usually designed to strengthen the most important economic actors in the state.

Although this book applies economic-elite theory to Texas politics, it is important to note what is *not* assumed in using this approach. First, the economic elite is not assumed to be sinister or conspiratorial in its actions. Rather, its members are presumed to be rational and forthright in their behavior. That is, they are seeking to optimize their interests in the business world and, when necessary, in the world of politics. Rarely do business leaders set out to deliberately harm the public through their political activities.

Second, dominant economic actors are not assumed to be fully immune from the effects of adverse pressures. Bad management, a poor business climate, an unforeseen downturn in the market, natural disasters, and an unexpected surge of unpopularity among, say, workers, consumers, or environmentalists are but a few of the factors that can make life difficult for even the most effective of businesses. Such calamities can, and do, ultimately lead to the demise of once-mighty firms.

Finally, it is not assumed that Texas politics is completely determined by an economic elite. Noneconomic groups and other individuals occasionally prevail over economic ones in the political arena. This is especially likely to occur when important economic players are experiencing disequilibrium in conducting business or when they are divided in their goals or their strategies.

Even with these assumptions taken into consideration, Texas's upper classes, as concluded in a recent study by sociologist Chandler Davidson, "in state politics . . . are a formidable force that wins more often than it loses in confrontations with . . . the largely depoliticized masses that party realignment has not succeeded in mobilizing."[11]

★ ★ ★ ★ ★ ## NOTES

1. For a comprehensive, yet concise, examination of the school financing controversy in Texas, see Gregory G. Rocha and Robert H. Webking, *Politics and Public Education: Edgewood v. Kirby and the Reform of Public School Financing in Texas* (St. Paul, MN: West Publishing Co., 1992).
2. Max Weber, *The Theory of Social and Economic Organization,* ed. Talcott Parsons (New York: The Free Press, 1964), p. 154.

3. Ira Sharkansky, *The Maligned States: Policy Accomplishments, Problems and Opportunities,* 2d ed. (New York: McGraw-Hill, 1978), p. 1.

4. In discussing these two theories, I have addressed only the core elements of each. Variations in each school, both subtle and more obvious, have been ignored.

5. The literature on pluralism is overwhelming. A comprehensive statement of the theory and its application to understanding the American political scene is given in Robert A. Dahl, *Pluralist Democracy in the United States: Conflict and Consensus* (Chicago: Rand McNally, 1967).

6. This profile of economic-elite theory is drawn from many sources. A fairly recent formulation of the perspective may be found in James W. Lamare, *What Rules America?* (St. Paul, MN: West Publishing Company, 1988) and in G. William Domhoff, *Who Rules America Now* (Englewood Cliffs, NJ: Prentice-Hall, 1984).

7. V. O. Key, Jr., *Southern Politics in State and Nation* (New York: Vintage, 1949), p. 254.

8. Quoted in Robert Engler, *The Politics of Oil: A Study of Private Power and Democratic Directions* (Chicago: University of Chicago Press, 1961), p. 354.

9. Robert Lockwood, "The Business Situation in Texas," *Texas Business Review* 50 (January 1976), p. 1.

10. Texas American Bancshares, *Annual Report,* 1977, p. 16.

11. Chandler Davidson, *Race and Class in Texas Politics* (Princeton, NJ: Princeton University Press, 1990), p. 84.

PART I

The Context of Contemporary Texas Politics

State governments do not function in a vacuum. They are surrounded by structural forces that give shape to their operations and decisions. History, culture, and social and economic relations are major elements that constrain the governing process. Chapter 1 discusses Texas history as it has influenced the development of social, cultural, economic, and basic political features of the state. Chapter 2 examines the contemporary economy of Texas with an eye toward identifying key economic players and how they have fared during the recent economic troubles afflicting the state.

CHAPTER 1

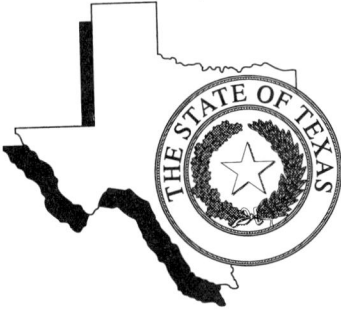

About Texas

Texas was created through conquest; it developed in a climate of violent confrontation and harsh physical struggle. From the very beginning, political power was often achieved in Texas only through the use of brute force. To win their independence, the predominantly Anglo Texans, who formed migrant settlements on land controlled by Mexico, fought the Mexicans, first losing at the Alamo on March 6, 1936, and then winning decisively at San Jacinto six weeks later. Once Texas was admitted as a state in 1845, it proudly joined ranks with the U.S. military to defeat Mexico in 1848. Thirteen years later, fearing the loss of their unique way of life, most Texans agreed to secede from the Union and fight on the side of the Confederacy in the Civil War. At various times throughout this period, citizens of the republic and of the state of Texas engaged in combat with Native Americans in an attempt to gain a stronger foothold in the territories occupied by the latter. During the latter part of the nineteenth century, violent skirmishes, unleashed by residual tensions arising from these earlier events, were fairly common. The state's rich yet tumultuous history has shaped its culture, society, and politics.[1]

★★★★★ SOCIETY AND CULTURE

Deeply embedded in the culture of Texas are beliefs, attitudes, and values that reflect the rough-and-ready historical development of the state. Self determination, self-defense, and self-confidence combined with a strong dose of individualism to produce a proud, perhaps even slightly arrogant, core population in Texas during its formative years. These Texans perceived the world around them as fraught with threat, yet filled with promise. Individuals who worked hard and persevered, they believed, could overcome all the surrounding dangers. Such endeavors resulted in struggle, which was often rewarded by success. Leaders who spearheaded these efforts—for example, Sam Houston—became cultural heroes, to be lauded, emulated, respected, and obeyed.

In its early years, a hierarchical social order, introduced by the numerous Southerners who came into the state, was instituted in Texas. The imported-slave system, and the rigid differences in social and racial status that were part of it, encouraged elitism and subordination. The merit of this type of social structure was widely publicized, at times accompanied by the threat of repressive violence.

A society based on rugged individualism and rigid hierarchy produced some disturbing practices in Texas. Former enemies were distrusted, denigrated, and victimized. Compassion, tolerance, and reconciliation were not traits valued in the dominant culture. Since many of the foes of the early inhabitants had been Hispanics, African Americans, and Native Americans, racism became an accepted component of the prevailing order. Moreover, the overwhelming majority of the early settlers were men, most of whom were schooled in the masculine norms of aggression, assertiveness, and independence that characterized frontier societies. The relatively few women inhabiting Texas in the nineteenth century were expected to be virtuous and obedient homemakers. Finally, Texans also viewed their natural surroundings as hostile, but tamable. To the victor went the spoils, even if that meant the ravaging of natural resources, including soil, animals, and timber.

It is likely that a less hierarchical and more tolerant and community-oriented set of beliefs formed among a minority of the Texan population during this early period, leaving in its wake a strong desire to create a free, open, and liberal society in the Lone Star State.[2] However, the more powerful Texans were firmly committed to the values of individualism and deference to power (and their derivative aspects). Moreover, they were in a strong position to restrain the spread of liberal thinking and ensure that their conservative point of view was handed down to succeeding generations. Consequently, Texas culture is steeped in beliefs supporting both individualism and respect for traditional patterns of authority.[3] Each individual is considered responsible for his or her successes or failures in life. Those who reach the top, embody achievement, and manifest its trappings, are to be respected and revered. Conversely, people at the bottom of society have only themselves to blame for their lack of advancement and should, at best, be ignored. Challenges to established authority are treated suspiciously or contemptuously. Individual solutions are preferred to organizational or group efforts in solving Texas's problems. Predictably, although pockets of liberalism are present in the state, Texans today are still mostly conservative in their beliefs. We shall explore these patterns more fully by examining the racial, religious, and economic backgrounds of the state's residents as well as their general orientations.

Population, Race, and Ethnicity

Texas society, of course, has not stood still since its early days. Among other things, the size of the state's population has increased dramatically. In 1850—the year that the U.S. Census was first taken in Texas—the state contained 212,000 people, approximately 30 percent of whom were slaves. Sixty years later, nearly four million Texans were counted.[4] Throughout the twentieth century, the U. S. population steadily increased, reaching a high of almost 19 million in the mid-1990s, surpassing New York as the second most populated state (California took first place). Texas should reach 20 million just after the turn of the twenty-first century; one projection estimates that the Lone Star State will be home to 33.8 million people in 2030.[5] Between 1990 and 1996, Texas gained 2.14 million people, the highest numerical increase recorded by any state. About half of that growth resulted from new births, 23 percent was from migration from other countries, and 17 percent came from interstate migration.[6]

Ethnic and racial diversity characterizes the state's population. About 11.5 percent of the population is African American and 28.7 percent is Hispanic, preponderantly of Mexican origin. Nearly 2 percent of Texas's residents are Asian Americans, most of them Vietnamese or Chinese. Members of minority groups constitute about 42 percent of Texas's population, up 7 percent from 1980. Moreover, the state's minority population is growing. About half the population growth recorded in Texas recently can be attributed to expansion of the state's Hispanic population; 10 percent came from increases in the number of African Americans; and 7 percent was accounted for by the arrival of Asian Americans. If these rates continue, Texans from minority groups will constitute the majority of the state's population in 2008.[7] In some locales, this pattern is already evident. Hispanics and African Americans make up 56 percent of Houston and 50 percent of Dallas. Hispanics account for 56 percent of San Antonio and 69 percent of El Paso. They constitute the majority in 35 of Texas's 254 counties, most of which either border on Mexico or are located in the south central part of the state.[8]

As noted above, racism was a main component of Texas culture during the state's formative period. African Americans and Hispanics have borne the brunt of discriminatory attitudes and behavior. Some of these negative attitudes were revealed in a 1963 poll showing that only 8 percent of whites would approve of their children's having an African American roommate at college; just 23 percent would attend a social event with blacks outside their homes, and only 13 percent would invite an African American into their homes; 23 percent would accept a black's living next door.

While some change in these views was evident by 1968, the prevailing pattern was still one of racial separation: only 26 percent of white Texans would accept their children sharing a college dorm room with an African American; 36 percent would allow an African American to attend a social gathering at their homes; 37 percent would use the same public swimming pools with African Americans; 43 percent would accept an African American as a neighbor; 49 percent would socialize with blacks outside of their homes; 63 percent would permit an African American to teach their children at school; and 69 percent would permit their children to attend a racially integrated school.

A 1986 poll found a much greater acceptance of African Americans as college roommates (68 percent), neighbors (86 percent), and teachers (84 percent), in social gatherings at home (77 percent), in public swimming pools (78 percent), and in racially integrated schools (81 percent). Moreover, there is very little resistance among white Texans to having an African American as a boss or a fellow worker, although 46 percent of whites reject the notion of becoming related to African Americans through marriage. Nearly 70 percent would accept an African American as president.

A similar pattern of opinion toward Hispanics is currently found in Texas. Non-Hispanic whites are willing to accept Latinos in diverse social, economic, and political settings. The number objecting to such encounters rarely exceeds 10 percent of the Anglo population. Members of Texas's major minority groups express an almost total acceptance of Anglos in a variety of situations. Indeed, "blacks and Mexican Americans are more accepting of Anglos than they are of each other."[9]

Religion

Religion is important in Texas.[10] More than six of every ten Texans profess a preference for a Protestant religion. Nearly one third are Baptists. Twenty-five percent belong to the Roman Catholic church. Only about 4 percent have no religious affiliation. Regardless of their specific denomination, about 70 percent note that religion is "very important" to their lives.

A majority of Texans profess a traditional commitment to their religion. An additional 19 percent characterize their faith as fundamentalist, evangelical, or charismatic; only 4 percent consider themselves "New Age." Almost 80 percent say they attend religious services at least twice a month. Most (54 percent) are God-fearing Christians who "say that [they] have been born again or have had a born-again experience." When asked if they had "ever tried to encourage someone to believe in Jesus Christ or accept Him as . . . [his or her] Savior," almost two thirds answer yes, a response given by only 45 percent of a national sample of Americans. Most Texans think religion belongs in the public schools. Religious beliefs also affect opinions about the sale of liquor, legalized gambling, the lottery, and abortion in Texas.

Economic Status

From the beginning, economic inequality has been the norm in Texas. In 1850, for example, less than 10 percent of the population possessed all the real and personal property (including slaves) and wealth in the state. Things improved slightly over the succeeding decade, because "on the eve of the Civil War, 7.1 percent of the population owned 56 percent of Texas wealth; 92.9 percent of the population owned the rest."[11]

These patterns of economic concentration continued throughout the nineteenth and twentieth centuries. Even during the boom times of the late 1970s, a period when riches abounded and Texas ranked among the top three states in total wealth, economic inequity was obvious. As one observer summarized the situation, "Income growth in Texas during the 1970s was not an equalizing force among income classes. If anything, more of the gains went to higher income groups, and income distribution became slightly less equal than it had been."[12]

More recent figures have shown that 250,600 Texans, less than 2 percent of the population, possessed nearly 40 percent of the state's assets. On the average, each member of this group was worth about $1 million; ninety-nine of them had fortunes valued at more than $50 million.[13] In contrast, nearly half of the state's adult population had an annual income below $25,000 in 1990.[14]

About 17.5 percent of Texans (3.2 million people) live below the poverty line, which is defined by a family of four living on $14,800 or less per year. Moreover, "poor people are the fastest growing segment of Texas's population."[15] In terms of sheer numbers, Texas ranks fourth among all states in poverty. The poor in the state are distinguishable along several dimensions.

Age   More than half of Texas's impoverished are either over 65 or under 18. Twenty-one percent of Texans between 65 and 74 are poor; 38 percent of the 75-plus group are impoverished, as are 24 percent of the state's children.[16]

Race and Ethnicity   In 1993, 35 percent of African Americans and 33 percent of Hispanics living in Texas were impoverished.[17] About four out of every ten minority children were living below the poverty line. All told, while 11.5 percent of the state's population is African American, some 28 percent of Texas's poor are black. Similarly, Hispanics constitute 28 percent of all Texans, but account for more than 40 percent of the state's poor.[18]

Residency   Some 85 percent of the poor live in the large cities.[19] But poverty is not confined to urban areas, because 61 of the state's 254 counties have a poverty rate greater than 26 percent. Most of these counties lie in the Panhandle or along the Mexican border: 40 percent of the population living in ten of the state's border counties are below the poverty line. Starr County has a poverty rate of 60 percent, the second highest in the United States.[20]

Texans have traditionally supported economic inequity. One of the major tenets of the state's culture is that economic success is difficult to achieve and that therefore the minority who reach the top are deserving of respect and praise. Not surprisingly, the public accords a great deal of legitimacy to business institutions and their chief executives. The opinions, beliefs, and perceptions that Texans have about economic matters are "a form of traditional attachment to a familiar set of practices to which one responds without much reflection."[21] Economic views are largely shaped through the socialization process, a kind of learning that begins in childhood. The educational system and the mass media play a significant role in this process.

Educational System   Schools in Texas are adept at inculcating positive attitudes toward capitalism. A study conducted in the Dallas area suggests that children start school holding rather naive notions about economic matters. At an early age, they believe in economic equality and support government-sponsored efforts to redistribute economic resources in society. As they progress through school, they come to value private property, private enterprise, and private possessions and become suspicious of labor unions and government. Moreover, they believe that poor children, if they so desired, could improve their economic status and climb out of poverty without any government assistance. One observer concluded that Texas's schools serve "primarily as a mechanism not only to legitimate the corporate order, but also the general structure of social inequality in American life."[22]

Mass Media   Texans, like most Americans, depend largely on the mass media, especially television and newspapers, for news about society and politics. Before television became an important media source, newspapers in Texas played a critical role in disseminating information, shaping the political agenda, and affecting the electoral chances of candidates. Although there were more newspapers at that time than there are today, the press operated, in the words of sociologist Chandler Davidson, as a "conservative monolith."[23]

Today, most of Texas's leading newspapers are part of media chains. More than 75 percent of the state's daily papers are members of multi-member groups; collectively, these chains account for 84 percent of newspaper circulation in Texas. Independent newspapers are confined principally to rural areas and have relatively few readers. Likewise, nearly 60 percent of Texas's television stations are chain-owned. Fewer than a dozen companies control the state's cable systems.[24]

Corporations are the principal owners of mass media chains. It is not unusual to find one company holding an interest in several types of media. The Belo Corporation of Dallas, for instance, owns that city's *Morning News,* eight Texas regional newspapers, Dallas's WFAA-TV, and KHOU-TV (which serves the Houston metropolitan area), as well as television stations in Sacramento, Tulsa, Norfolk, New Orleans, and Seattle. Belo's board of directors includes several of Dallas's most prominent corporate leaders, including individuals with links to PepsiCo, Prudential Insurance, Lomas Financial Corporation, Texas Utilities, Guaranty Federal Savings Bank, NCH Corporation, SYSCO, Central and South West, and Trammell Crow.[25]

Corporate control of the media, according to critics of this practice in Texas, "means that most news and information is filtered through a probusiness perspective. The result has been a kinder, gentler treatment of corporate America by the media—and an increasing emphasis on making money over informing the public."[26] Indeed, one study questions whether the Texas media provide their audiences with any political news whatsoever.[27]

The media also rarely give space to much criticism of the economic or political leaders of the state. On the other hand, there have been times when members of the economic elite, usually through the public relations divisions of corporations, have used the media to transmit messages directly to the public. As noted by one observer, "Corporate PR had a hand in converting Texas newspapers into something of a plaything for the propertied class, beginning around 1945. Indeed public relations and the press became intertwined."[28]

★★★★★ POLITICS

The frontier spirit that is so ingrained in Texas culture is also evident in the structure of the state's political institutions, the general feelings Texans have toward the political system and politicians, and political participation in Texas. We shall address each of these topics in turn.

The Texas Constitution

The framers of the United States Constitution established a federal political system in which the national government would share power with state governments. Article VI of the U.S. Constitution clearly states that "this Constitution, and the laws of the United States which shall be made in Pursuance thereof . . . shall be the supreme Law of the Land." The Supremacy Clause notwithstanding, states were allowed to write their own constitutions and create their own governments, investing them with powers that did not contravene the U.S. Constitution.

Since it gained its independence from Mexico, Texas has had six constitutions. The present-day constitution, which went into effect in 1876, is basically a product of the political and economic discontent that swept across Texas in the aftermath of the Civil War.[29] At that time, an intense struggle took place over who was to rule the state. The battle pitted Radical Republicans against secessionist Democrats. The Radicals were committed to political equality for African Americans and the punishment of

Texans who had aligned themselves with the Confederacy. The Democrats were reluctant to improve the status of freed slaves and adamantly opposed any penalties for Texas's participation on the losing side of the Civil War.

By 1870, through the electoral process, Radical Republicans had secured the reins of state government. Republican Edmund J. Davis was governor. A majority of state legislators were Republicans, and Governor Davis, with the consent of the Texas Senate, appointed Radicals to fill most of the state's judicial posts. While in office, Radicals enacted a series of laws that profoundly affected the lives of most Texans. Radical government attempted to promote racial equality through inclusion of former slaves in the political system. In the name of preserving law and order, a state militia and police force were established and placed under the direct command of Governor Davis. All male citizens between the ages of 18 and 45 were ordered to serve in the militia, although military duty could be avoided by paying the state $15. The governor had the power to send the militia or the police to any place in the state. Furthermore, he could declare martial law in cases of emergency and, in so doing, could suspend individual rights. The governor was also authorized to fill vacancies that opened for any political office in the state, even at the local level of government, through appointment. During his tenure as governor, Davis appointed 8,500 local officials.

In order to vote, Texans had to register in person before judges appointed by the governor. These judges could deny the right to vote as they saw fit. Voting was permitted only at the county seat, and it usually took place under the watchful eyes of armed militiamen. The government promoted economic growth by using tax money to subsidize corporations, especially railroad companies. Personal taxes rose dramatically during Republican rule; indeed, one historian estimates that about 20 percent of all personal income in the state went to the government in the form of taxes.[30] It is indicative of the unpopularity of many of these laws that Texans dubbed them the "obnoxious acts."

The list of complaints against Republican rule was long. Texans with Southern sympathies were angry at the efforts to assist African Americans. Charges of tyranny, fiscal irresponsibility, and outright corruption were leveled at the "obnoxious acts" of the Radicals. Many Texans were dismayed that several of these laws were passed only after ten legislators, who opposed them, were placed under house arrest and prevented from casting votes against them. Civil liberties were frequently denied by the governor, the police, and the militia.[31] Taxes were biting into the already financially strapped citizenry. Even with high taxes, the state was on the verge of bankruptcy because of its generous outlays of cash to political officials and corporations. A few legislators who supported giving financial aid to railroad companies were accused of accepting bribes: "Some of the Democratic papers expressed wonder at the fact that certain members of the . . . Legislature, whose only visible income was their per diem [$8], should be able at the end of the [legislative] session to invest in fine horses and expensive furniture and make long trips north on vacation."[32] Although Governor Davis appears not to have been corrupt, his adjutant general, James Davidson, "absconded with $37,000 in state funds in 1872."[33]

By 1872, a plurality of Texans had had enough of Radical Republican rule. In legislative elections held that year, Democrats scored a decisive victory. The new legislature—over the objections of holdover Radical Governor Davis—repealed most of the "obnoxious acts" and called for a general statewide election in 1873. In that election, Democrats again won most state offices, including the governor's chair. But the defeated Republicans refused to abide by the electoral results, charging that the Texas election code was faulty. The Radical-controlled Texas Supreme Court agreed and denied Democrats their apparent success. When elected Democrats came to Austin anyway to claim the fruits of victory, they were met by the state militia. The troops, under orders from Governor Davis, had sealed the doors of the capitol building and stood guard inside. Unfortunately for the Radicals, the militia let its guard slip and the Democrats gained entrance to the building. An eminent Texas historian describes the scene as follows:

> While the Negro troops were asleep early one morning, Democrats used a ladder to secure admission to the legislative halls on the second floor, organized the legislature for work, counted the votes and declared Coke [the Democrat] elected governor. Governor Davis appealed to President Grant for aid and additional troops as soon as the Democratic plans were apparent, but the president telegraphed his refusal to interfere; the governor then withdrew from his office and from Texas public life.[34]

The 1875 Constitutional Convention Once secure in office, the Democrats undertook a concerted effort to stamp out all remnants of Republican rule. The most glaring reminder of Radical control was the Texas Constitution of 1869. Many felt that this document had directly authorized, or indirectly aided, the "obnoxious acts." Mainly, however, the 1869 constitution symbolized all that was wrong with Radical government. To rid the state of unpleasant memories—and to avoid a possible return of Radical rule—the Democrat-controlled state government called for a new constitutional convention.

Three delegates from each of thirty geographically distinct districts were elected to write a new state constitution. These ninety delegates began their work in Austin on September 6, 1875, and completed their task in sixty-eight days. About 80 percent of the delegates were Democrats. By occupation, most were farmers and lawyers. Only four had been born in Texas, although the vast majority were from Southern states. The delegates' average age was 45. No women were present. Of the ninety, five (all Republicans) were African Americans.[35]

Delegates to the Constitutional Convention of 1875

Photo courtesy of Archives Division, Texas State Library.

The one formal interest group that was well represented at the constitutional convention was the Grange. The Grange movement, composed mostly of farmers, began in 1867 and spread quickly across the agricultural sections of the United States, reaching Texas in 1873. Within a year, hundreds of local Granges had cropped up in the state, and the organization counted 50,000 Texans as members. The Grange was greatly disturbed about the decline in the economic standing of farmers throughout the United States. Farm prices had plummeted after the Civil War, and the Grange placed the blame squarely on the shoulders of railroad companies and banks, accusing state governments of complicity in the banks' misdeeds. Railroads were singled out for arbitrarily overcharging farmers to transport agricultural products. During this time, major banks were failing, thus making money very difficult to obtain. Loans to many farmers were being called and numerous farms and ranches were foreclosed. State governments resisted controlling the banks and railroads; indeed, they seemed more intent on protecting them, at great expense to farmers. Thirty-eight delegates at the Texas constitutional convention were Grangers, and their views were reflected in the new state constitution.

Contents of the Texas Constitution   From the moment when the gavel first called the delegates to order, the watchwords of the convention were "retrenchment and reform." *Retrenchment* was mostly understood to mean fiscal constraints on the government. As a direct response to the excessive expenditures of the Radical government, the new constitution limited the spending and tax-raising authority of state and local government. For instance, salaries for officeholders were cut and codified. The borrowing capacity of the state government was limited to a maximum of $200,000 unless it was facing imminent danger of attack. Revenue for the public school system was greatly restricted. Taxes were also lowered and capped.

Reform meant a comprehensive weakening of the authority of state government and a strengthening of the rights of individuals. The duties, procedures, and power of government institutions in Texas were delineated and restricted by the constitution. Following the principles of separation of powers and checks and balances embedded in the U.S. Constitution, the Texas Constitution created three major political institutions to govern the state: the legislature, the executive, and the judiciary. Each institution was to have limited power and its members were to be directly accountable to the voters.

The legislature was composed of two chambers, the House and the Senate. For a bill to become law, it would have to be approved by at least a majority in each of the two chambers. Legislative sessions were restricted to once every two years. When it did meet, the legislature was allowed only 140 days in which to conduct its business. Salaries were set low. Senatorial terms were reduced from six to four years. Constraints were placed on the spending power of the legislators. Moreover, major changes in the operation of the legislature could be written into law only by amending the constitution. There is no doubt that in establishing the Texas Legislature, the framers of the constitution were guided by the overarching principle that "the government that governs least governs best." Indeed, about one half of the original fifty provisions about the legislature contained in the constitution were designed to control the activities of that institution.

The framers of the Texas Constitution believed that the executive branch of government had the greatest potential for abuse. To counter this possibility, they fragmented the executive branch into several different offices. In addition to the governor's chair, the constitution established the offices of lieutenant governor, comptroller, treasurer, attorney general, and commissioner of the general land office. Each of these positions was designed to be independent of the others and, more important, of the governor. These executive officials were to be elected. The governor was deprived not only of the opportunity to centralize the executive; he or she also lost the authority to appoint many members of this branch. As a contemporary critic of the Texas Constitution stated, "the executive branch is divided into fiefdoms run by independently elected officials, who may or may not see their way to cooperate with the governor. The result is that the government works as single horses, each carrying one rider in whatever direction the rider wants, rather than as a team pulling the same load in the same direction."[36]

The judiciary was overhauled as well. A complicated, multilayered court system was instituted. Texas is one of the only two states (Oklahoma is the other) that have a judicial branch with two courts at its head: the Supreme Court and the Court of Criminal Appeals. The Supreme Court was created primarily to hear cases involving civil law on appeal from lower courts. The Court of Criminal Appeals was established to consider criminal cases appealed from lower courts. To ensure popular control over judicial behavior, the constitution requires that persons seeking a position in the state court system, even at the highest level, must be elected.

In addition to creating the basic governing structure of the state, the Texas Constitution also incorporated some substantive policy preferences of the framers, who were determined to implement proposals that would promote and protect their economic interests through the fundamental legal system of Texas. One of those interests was the creation of a comprehensive transportation system that would link Texas farmers with consumers both inside and outside the state. To accomplish this, expansion of the railroad was urged. Texas had only about 1,500 miles of track at the time of the constitutional convention; most of these rails were laid in the central and eastern sections of the state. Yet however much the delegates wanted growth of the railroads, many still had a basic distrust of, and hostility toward, the railroad companies. This ambivalence was reflected in the constitution. On the one hand, it gave the state the right to regulate rail operations (especially rates charged to customers) and, on the other, it distributed large tracts of land to companies for the laying of track across the state.

Other big businesses did not fare as well as railroad companies in the Texas Constitution. For instance, the antipathy that the Grangers felt toward banks was patently manifested in the document: the delegates simply prohibited banks from ever incorporating in the state.

The principal legacy of the 1875 constitutional convention was the creation of fragmented and weak political institutions in Texas. It was, in the eyes of one observer, "clearly an attempt to create the least powerful government possible that could still govern."[37]

Recent efforts to revise the state constitution have not been successful. In 1972, for instance, Texas voters authorized the state legislature to totally rewrite the constitution. The legislature created a constitutional revision committee, which was to study the document and offer recommendations for change. In 1974, the legislature acted as a constitutional convention and deliberated the fate of the 1876 constitution. After more than half a year (and $5 million in tax revenues), the convention fell three votes short of approving a new constitution. In its next regular session, however, the legislature approved eight amendments to the constitution, which, if approved, would have fundamentally revamped and updated the document. In 1975, voters overwhelmingly rejected these proposals.

Major opposition to constitutional revision came from the heights of the Texas business community. Efforts to block constitutional reform were led by George Brown, at the time considered to be among the most influential economic leaders in the state. When Brown was asked why he favored retaining the old constitution, he candidly replied, "I never argue with success and we have been pretty successful doing it the way we have been doing it."[38] Obviously, in the time since it had been written, members of the corporate community had come to value the Texas Constitution.

Corporate Benefits   Although the Texas Constitution was intended to make state government directly accountable to the voters, most citizens, for one reason or another, were slow to take up this challenge. Quicker in their response were members of the business community, who soon learned that through active political participation, they could promote and preserve their interests through government action, or, in some cases, inaction. The weak structures of the state institutions were conducive to making these groups powerful. Hence, subsequent attempts to strengthen the government have been resisted by these interests. Among other things, many business leaders have opposed raising the low salaries of Texas's legislators, because, according to one observer, "It is much easier to pressure poorly-paid legislators than well-paid ones."[39]

Corporations also discovered that they could use the constitution's amendment procedures to their advantage. It has been relatively easy to amend the Texas Constitution. Altering the document is accomplished if two thirds of the state legislature recommends a change and a majority of voters approve this recommendation. Between 1876 and 1996, only one legislative session has ended without any attempt to amend the constitution. The voters have been busy with about 500 proposals during this period, and in two thirds of the cases they have approved the amendments. Some examples of amendments that have benefited business and wealthy interests are the following:

In the early years of the twentieth century, a major discovery of oil was made in Texas and a great deal of money came into the state. Without state-chartered banks (originally prohibited by the Texas Constitution), financial transactions were hampered. Economic interests affected by this burden successfully amended the constitution in 1904 to allow establishment of banks, thus facilitating the smooth flow of money. However, banks were still prohibited from opening branches across the state. In 1986, with major banks in tatters, the constitution was amended again to permit branch banking. Hence Texas has gone from a state in which suspicion of banks originally led to the constitutional prohibition of chartered banks to one that accepted banking activities with certain restrictions, and, most recently, to one that fully encourages increasing the concentration of capital among a few large banks.

Automobile companies and petroleum firms have a common economic stake in the sale of cars propelled by gas combustion engines. The construction of roads for travel, however, is too costly a project for these corporations to fund. Yet without paved surfaces on which to drive, consumers would probably not find cars an attractive means of transportation. The problem has been resolved in Texas by the state government's use of taxpayers' dollars to build highways. The highway lobby successfully passed an amendment to the state constitution in 1946 that permanently dedicates tax revenue for the building and maintenance of roads and highways.

Finally, in 1978 voters were presented with a package of propositions designed to bring tax relief to Texans through constitutional amendment. This omnibus measure offered at least some modicum of savings for most taxpayers and was, not unexpectedly, approved by an overwhelming majority. But the major beneficiaries of the amendment are the wealthy property holders in Texas. The owners of large tracts of farm, ranch, and timberland, for instance, gained significant reductions in their property taxes, because agricultural land is now taxed on the basis of its revenue-generating capacity and not, as was formerly the case, on the basis of its fair market value. In other words, if the land, or any piece of it, is not producing a salable item, it is not subject to full property taxes. As one county tax appraiser has quipped, "The joke is all you need to get an ag exemption is one cow and two blades of grass."[40]

Because of this exemption, in the early 1990s Exxon paid only $22.68 per year on property valued at $65,300 that it owns in the Tomball Independent School District. A subsidiary of Exxon sent $228.38 to the Aldine

Independent School District for 250 acres located in the district's tax catchment area. If the agricultural exemption had not been in place, Exxon would have owed $21,742 in property taxes to Aldine. Likewise, Ross Perot's company, the Perot Group, was required to pay a tax of $21,300 on 15,420 acres it owns near Denton. If it had had to pay taxes based on the market value of this property, the Perot Group would have had to fork over $750,000 to the tax collector. Altogether, it is estimated that some $64 billion in agricultural land—about two thirds of all open land in the state—has been removed from the tax rolls, owing to the 1978

constitutional amendment. This exemption costs schools some $800 million in annual revenue and forces the property tax burden onto others, such as homeowners.[41]

In sum, the Texas Constitution was written in reaction to political and economic events that befell the state's population more than a century ago. The framers were mostly of an agrarian cast of mind and drafted a document designed to remedy the misfortunes that had been their lot. The constitution reflected and enshrined the Texas frontier spirit. At its core, it established a very weak state government. According to the prevailing Texas creed, private individuals were in a better position than politicians to cope with the problems confronting Texans; moreover, common people were considered more honest. The constitution was originally ambivalent toward big business. The framers were leery of some corporate practices, but also recognized the need for corporate involvement in Texas in order to promote economic development. Nevertheless, corporate privilege soon found its way into Texas politics through the ability of business interests to take advantage of the state's weak government and through the practice of amending the constitution.

Feelings about Government

Texans, especially natives, describe themselves as friendly, honest, cowboys, bigger than life, proud, independent, down to earth, confident, outspoken, haughty about their state, and brash—in that order. In this individualistic milieu, it is not surprising that most Texans are unmoved by the idea that government should be much involved in promoting the general welfare of society or that it has a responsibility to provide each individual with a decent standard of living. Rather, a strong majority believe that each individual is responsible for his or her own well-being. Texans also support, overwhelmingly, the individual's right to privacy.

The antigovernment spirit that guided the writing of the Texas Constitution is also evident in the state's political culture. When Texans were asked in the early 1980s to name the most important problem facing the state, they were more likely to say "elected officials" than anything else. Only a small number express great trust in their state's political institutions and politicians, including the governor's office, the state legislature and its members, and courts and judges. Only 3 percent believe that the ethical standards of state and local officeholders are "very high," and a majority believe that laws regulating the ethical behavior of officeholders should be strengthened.

Conversely, nearly two thirds praise the work of the police and almost 75 percent feel that the regulatory powers of the state government are effective. A majority of Texans say that state agencies serve the public well, although only a minority think that these agencies deliver high-quality performances, free of errors.[42] Some deference to administrative authority, perhaps indicative of the traditional strain that runs through the state's culture, seems evident.

The Texas public is not very well informed about political matters in the state. For instance, even though he had just been indicted for violating state ethics laws in 1991, nearly 60 percent of Texans did not know the name of Gib Lewis, then the Speaker of the Texas House of Representatives. Four out of every five Texans identify George W. Bush as the state's governor, but very few Texans can correctly name the lieutenant governor (15 percent), the comptroller (12 percent), the commissioners of agriculture (6 percent) and the general land office (13 percent), and the attorney general (21 percent).[43] As noted by University of Texas political scientist Bruce Buchanan, "this suggests that much of [Texas] government remains submerged and unrecognized by the majority of people."[44]

Surveys that take an ideological sounding of the public reveal that Texans are twice as likely to call themselves conservatives as liberals. When they are asked about their ideological stance on specific policy matters, they tend to judge abortion, the death penalty, the prison system, government spending, and public education more from a conservative perspective than from either a liberal or a moderate one.[45] Nearly 60 percent hold that "political groups should be able to demonstrate only after a committee says it's safe and won't violate community values."[46]

Hence there is ample evidence suggesting the existence of an individualistic, traditional, conservative culture in Texas. These cultural patterns, however, have not been fully endorsed by all Texans, since the state's history is replete with examples of people banding together to defy and confront the existing power structures. At times, both African Americans and Hispanics have fought collectively against the injustices and discriminatory practices of traditional elites.[47] During the 1970s, for example, Latinos living in Crystal City came together to oppose the dominant political and economic system in their city.[48] For a while, this challenge proved successful. However, the Crystal City example is the exception that proves the rule, for most Hispanics in Texas are well immersed in the state's traditional political culture—individualism and deference to authority are prominent features of their belief system.[49]

There are some signs of a cultural "generation gap" in Texas. Many Texans over 62 express traditional conservative views; for instance, 40 percent think that women should be in the home and not in politics, 53 percent hold that men are emotionally more suited to politics than are women, only 27 percent favor increased controls on handgun sales, less than one third think racial discrimination is a serious problem in Texas, and 55 percent think government restrictions on abortion contravene the rights of individuals. Texans of 30 or younger are significantly more liberal on each of these issues. Relatively few of the younger Texans consider women unfit for active political life. Nearly a majority want tighter controls on the purchase of handguns. Fifty-one percent think racial discrimination is a major problem in the state. Fully 71 percent see government restrictions on abortion as an infringement on individual rights.

Although these findings suggest that Texas culture may be somewhat different in the future, the generation gap goes only so far. For instance, older and younger Texans are similar in their ideological leanings: equal numbers say they are conservative, and only a minority (about 13 percent) in each age bracket call themselves liberal.[50]

Political Participation

The hierarchical past of Texas featured the exclusion of various groups from active involvement in the economic, social, and political life of the state. In particular, African Americans, Hispanics, the poor, and women were denied, through both law and custom, the right to participate politically. In the relatively few places that allowed political involvement for African Americans, Hispanics, and impoverished Texans, participation was often highly restricted: members of these minority groups were told how to act and for whom to vote. It was only well into the twentieth century (see Chapter 3) that many of these restrictions were lifted.

In addition to legal prohibitions on political participation, women, the poor, and minorities faced other exclusionary obstacles. Social tradition at

Inscription on wall of the State Library Building in Austin, Texas.

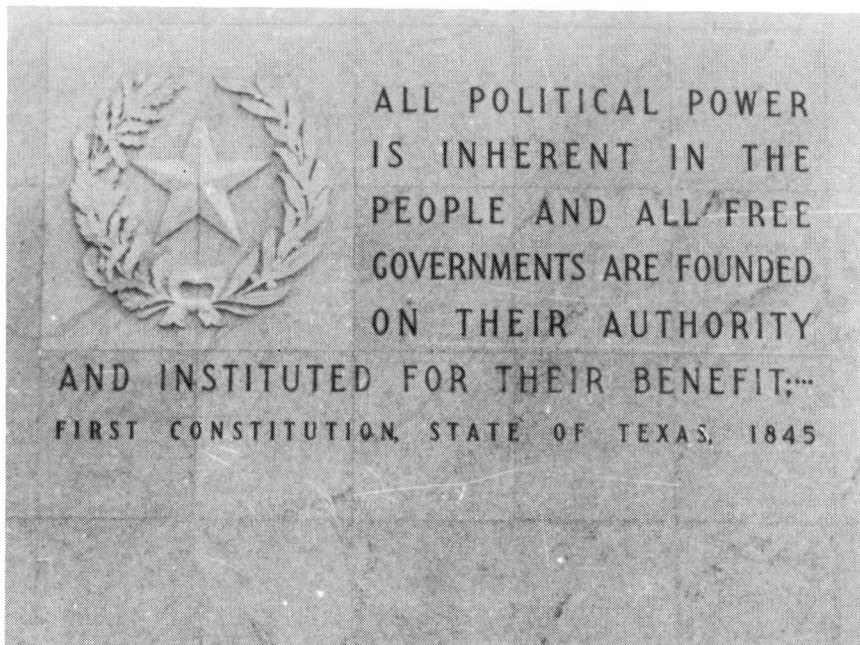

ALL POLITICAL POWER IS INHERENT IN THE PEOPLE AND ALL FREE GOVERNMENTS ARE FOUNDED ON THEIR AUTHORITY AND INSTITUTED FOR THEIR BENEFIT;···
FIRST CONSTITUTION, STATE OF TEXAS, 1845

times operated to deter political activity. Vigilantism, including lynching and other forms of mob violence, was directed at African Americans and Hispanics who publicly expressed discontent at their inferior status. The education system was not geared to teach these powerless people the skills necessary to become informed, concerned, and empowered citizens. Residential segregation, which was usually the result of deliberate business and political policy, kept members of different minority groups clustered together in impoverished geographic locales, isolated from each other and from other sectors of society. Political parties and important interest groups refused to mobilize the politically dispossessed. Consequently, elites traditionally had little to fear politically from Texans located at or near the bottom of the social and economic order.

Moreover, as we will discuss in detail in Chapter 3, lack of a participatory tradition in Texas hampers to this day the active involvement of many citizens in the state's political life. Voting rates, for instance, remain relatively low in Texas, leaving the electoral and lobbying process mostly in the hands of the more affluent, non-Hispanic white, conservative-minded Texans.

★ ★ ★ ★ ★ CONCLUSION

The historical development of Texas spawned the conditions that promote economic elitism. A traditional social order permeated social relations throughout the state. Individualism flourished in an environment of struggle and conflict, and became the rationale for defending people who made it to the top, especially economically, and for rejecting collective and governmental solutions to social problems.

This culture has been transmitted to succeeding generations of Texans through the socialization process, which is greatly influenced by individuals and institutions sympathetic to elitist notions. Although some of the more virulent strains of the culture, such as extreme racial prejudice and segregation, have diminished, the emphasis on individualism and respect for traditional order remains largely intact. It is reflected in conservative religious, economic, social, and political views.

This culture is also embodied in the basic governing document of the state—the Texas Constitution. Weak political institutions were created so that government would not or could not interfere very much with the social and economic order and the individual rights and freedoms of most citizens. Political organizations have largely shied away from appealing to, and mobilizing, powerless people. Therefore, there has been little sustained mass political action to counteract the political influence of the economic elite. The door to control of state government is mostly open to individuals and groups that are favored by the political structure and culture of the state; mainly, this means interests with an abundance of economic resources.

★★★★★ NOTES

1. A concise but informative review of Texas's violent past is found in Robert A. Calvert and Arnoldo De Leon, *The History of Texas* (Arlington Heights, IL: Harlan Davidson, 1990), especially Chapters 3 through 7.

2. This is the case made by Chandler Davidson, *Race and Class in Texas Politics* (Princeton, NJ: Princeton University Press, 1990), Chapter 2. Chandler's thesis is mostly developed by debunking the evidential base of the pervasiveness of conservatism in Texas culture. The presentation of solid evidence pointing to a liberal culture is not very convincing, however.

3. Daniel J. Elazar, *American Federalism: A View from the States,* 2d ed. (New York: Crowell, 1972), pp. 93–114, and T. R. Fehrenbach, *Lone Star: A History of Texas and Texans* (New York: Macmillan, 1968).

4. Robert A. Calvert and Arnoldo De Leon, *The History of Texas,* pp. 99 and 215. The figure for the number of slaves in Texas at this time comes from Chandler Davidson, *Race and Class in Texas Politics,* p. 18.

5. Chris Kelley, "Data Suggest Troubling Trends," *Dallas Morning News,* July 28, 1996, p. 20A.

6. Michelle E. Koidin, "Texas Gained More Residents Since 1990 Than Any Other State," *The Monitor,* January 1, 1997, p. 6D.

7. Chris Kelley, "Data Suggest Troubling Trends."

8. Bureau of the Census, U.S. Department of Commerce, *General Population Characteristics: Texas* (Washington, DC: Government Printing Office, 1992).

9. James Dyer, Arnold Vedlitz, and Stephen Worchel, "Social Distance among Racial and Ethnic Groups in Texas: Some Demographic Correlates," *Social Science Quarterly* 70 (September 1989), p. 611; *Texas Poll,* Fall 1986; and *Belden Poll Report,* October 4, 1970.

10. The information presented in this section on religion is from the *Texas Poll,* Spring 1990, and the Texas Poll, April 1985.

11. Calvert and De Leon, *A History of Texas,* p. 105.

12. Caldwell Ray, "Income Distribution and Economic Growth in Texas," *Texas Business Review* 57 (May–June 1983), p. 108.

13. This figure is calculated on the basis of information provided by two sources. The number of the wealthy comes from the U.S. Department of Commerce, Bureau of the Census, *Statistical Abstract of the United States: 1991* (Washington, DC: Government Printing Office, 1991), p. 469; the portion of all assets owned by this group is found in Davidson, *Race and Class in Texas Politics,* p. 65.

14. Kelley, "Data Suggest Troubling Trends."

15. Ibid.

16. Ibid., and Department of Human Services, *1994 Annual Report* (Austin: Department of Human Services, 1995).

17. James C. Harrington, "Deep in the Heart of America's Third World," *Dallas Morning News,* February 28, 1993, p. 12J.

18. Bureau of the Census, *General Social and Economic Characteristics: Texas,* p. 138, and House Research Organization, *The Welfare Debate: State Policy on AFDC* (Austin: House Research Organization, 1992), p. 5.

19. Bureau of the Census, *General Social and Economic Characteristics.*

20. Victoria Lee, "Beyond City Limits: Rural Texas Is Home to Highest Percentage of People in Poverty," *Dallas Morning News,* February 28, 1993, pp. 1A and 23A.

21. Herbert McClosky and John Zaller, *The American Ethos: Public Attitudes Toward Capitalism and Democracy* (Cambridge, MA: Harvard University Press, 1984), p. 138.

22. Scott Cummings and Del Taebel, "The Economic Socialization of Children: A NeoMarxist Analysis," *Social Problems* 26 (December 1978), p. 205.

23. Davidson, *Race and Class,* p. 27.

24. Based on Jim Lee and Eric Bates, "Who Owns the Media?" *Texas Observer,* January 29, 1993, pp. 12–15, and Ronan G. Lynch, "Newspapers in Chains," *Texas Observer,* March 13, 1992, pp. 17 and 21.

25. Information found in *1996–97 Texas Almanac* (Dallas: Dallas Morning News, 1995), pp. 341–345. The *Texas Almanac* is published by the Belo Corporation.

26. Lee and Bates, "Who Owns the Media?" p. 12.

27. Discussed in the June 1974 issue of the *Texas Monthly.*

28. George Norris Green, *The Establishment in Texas Politics* (Norman: University of Oklahoma Press, 1979), p. 10.

29. Much of the material presented in this section on the background of the Texas Constitution is drawn from Seth McKay, *Seven Decades of the Texas Constitution of 1876* (Lubbock: Texas Tech University Press, 1943).

30. T. R. Fehrenbach, *Lone Star: A History of Texas and Texans,* p. 422.

31. Some of the violations of civil liberties are reported in A. J. Thomas and Ann Van Wynen Thomas, "The Texas Constitution of 1876," *Texas Law Review* 35 (October 1957):907–18.

32. Seth McKay, *Seven Decades of the Texas Constitution,* p. 34.

33. Mike Kingston, "A Concise History of Texas," in the *1986–87 Texas Almanac and State Industrial Guide* (Dallas: Belo Corporation, 1986), p. 209.

34. Seth McKay, *Seven Decades,* p. 46. Reprinted by permission.

35. At first, six African-American Republicans were present. A few days after the convention began, one resigned and was replaced by a white Democrat. There is some difference of opinion about the social background of the ninety delegates. I have followed the description by J. E. Ericson, "The Delegates to the Convention of 1875: A Reappraisal," *Southwestern Historical Quarterly* 67 (July 1963):22–27.

36. Gregory Curtis, "A New Foundation," *Texas Monthly,* February 1992, p. 10.

37. Ibid., p. 12.

38. Quoted in Kaye Northcott, "New Charter Foundering," *Texas Observer,* October 31, 1975.

39. Hart Stillwell, "Texas: Owned by Oil and Interlocking Directorates," in *Our Sovereign State,* ed. Robert S. Allen (New York: Vanguard Press, 1949), p. 330.

40. Harris County chief tax appraiser Jim Robinson, quoted in the *Lubbock Avalanche-Journal,* February 15, 1993, p. A9.

41. This information was gathered by the *Houston Chronicle* and reported in "Schools Lose Tax Dollars in Legal Loophole," *Lubbock Avalanche-Journal,* February 15, 1993, p. A-9, and the *Texas Observer,* February 26, 1993, p. 23.

42. This portrait is based on several sources, including James Dyer and Don Haynes, *Social, Economic and Political Change According to the Texas Poll* (Austin: College of Communication, University of Texas at Austin, 1987); Institute for Constructive Capitalism, *Concerns, Issues and Attitudes: A Texas Survey* (Austin: University of Texas at Austin, Graduate School of Business Administration, 1981); Dennis Gamino, "Most Texans Upbeat about State Government, Poll Finds," *Austin American-Statesman,* September 30, 1996; and several reports of the *Texas Poll,* including those issued in October 1985, Fall 1987, Winter 1988, Spring 1989, Spring 1990, March 1991, May 1991, May 1992, August 1992, and March 1993.

43. Based on the Texas Poll, March 1991, and Ken Herman, "Gov. Who? Texans Fail Politician Test," *Austin American-Statesman,* March 17, 1996.

44. Quoted in the *Texas Poll,* May 1992, p. 8.

45. *Texas Poll,* Spring 1990.

46. *Texas Poll,* August 1992.

47. For examples, see Calvert and De Leon, *The History of Texas,* pp. 156–159 and 234, and David Montejano, *Anglos and Mexicans in the Making of Texas: 1836–1986* (Austin: University of Texas Press, 1987), pp. 32–33.

48. See John Shockley, *Chicano Revolt in a Texas Town* (Notre Dame, IN: University of Notre Dame Press, 1974), and Armando Gutierrez and Herbert Hirsch, "The Militant Challenge to the American Ethos: 'Chicanos' and 'Mexican Americans,'" *Social Science Quarterly* 53 (February 1973):830–845.

49. See James W. Lamare, "Language Environment and Political Socialization of Mexican American Children," in *The Politics of Future Citizens,* ed. Richard G. Niemi (San Francisco: Jossey-Bass, 1974), Chapter 4; "The Political World of the Rural Chicano Child," *American Politics Quarterly* 5 (January 1977):83–108; and "The Political Integration of Mexican American Children: A Generational Analysis," *International Migration Review* 16 (Spring 1982):169–88.

50. Evidence from the *Texas Poll,* November 1990.

CHAPTER 2

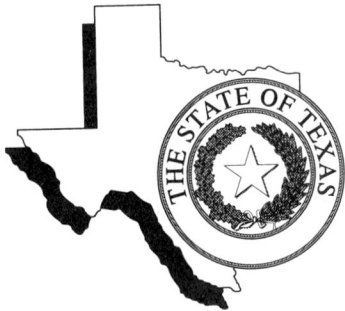

The Texas Economy

The Texas economy has been unsettled in recent years. Boom, bust, and recovery have characterized the business cycle. This chapter examines the Texas economy with an eye to discussing its core components and the leading economic actors in the state. Its main purpose is to identify the state's economic elite.

★ ★ ★ ★ ★ RECENT ECONOMIC TIMES

The late 1970s and early 1980s were times of great economic growth in Texas. The state's economy was buoyant and robust, the envy of the nation. Texas ranked at or near the top in total personal income, employment opportunities, retail and agricultural sales, bank deposits, construction contracts, manufacturing output, and petroleum and mineral production. But as the supply of oil became much greater than the demand for petroleum products, the boom turned to gloom. Every one-dollar drop in the price per barrel of oil resulted in a loss of 25,000 jobs. When the cost of a barrel of oil plummeted from $27 in December 1985 to $10 three months later, the effect was economically devastating. By mid-1986, unemployment had risen to a post-Depression high of 10.5 percent. Fully 846,000 Texans were without jobs.[1] With the petroleum industry in tatters, real estate markets in major cities approached the brink of collapse. Bankruptcies were rampant (see Highlight 2–1 for one example) and many of the state's leading financial institutions collapsed under the economic strain.

Most Texans felt the impact of the economic slide. By 1988, 86 percent of the public reported that they had been hurt by the economic downturn; nearly one third said that the recession had caused the unemployment of a member of their household; 44 percent experienced a reduction of income;

★ ★ ★

Highlight 2–1: The Bankruptcy of John Connally

The saga of the late John Connally embodied the nature of the collapse well. In the course of Connally's political career, he held several key offices. He was first elected governor of Texas in 1962 and served in that position until 1968. Prior to being elected governor, he was Secretary of the Navy. In 1963, he was wounded during the assassination of President John F. Kennedy in Dallas. During the 1960s, he switched political parties, defecting from the Democrats to the Republicans. He was chosen to be Secretary of the Treasury during the Nixon Administration, and made an unsuccessful attempt to run for President in 1980. By 1988, Connally had accumulated debts totaling $48 million and had joined the ranks of the bankrupt. To help pay his bills, the Connallys sold their personal belongings in a widely publicized auction. Within days of this event, Connally appeared in television ads for University Savings, urging Texans to invest their money wisely and avoid the mistakes that he himself had made. Within a year, University Savings itself declared insolvency and was eventually absorbed by NationsBank, a North Carolina–based bank that first gained a strong foothold in Texas through its acquisition, in late 1988, of the bankrupt First Republic Bank of Texas (once the largest financial institution in the state). Connally died in 1993.

---

and 51 percent dipped into their savings to make ends meet. A majority expressed a lack of confidence in the state's economic prospects.[2]

During the 1990s, economic conditions have been improving in Texas. More jobs have been generated in Texas than in any other industrial state in the nation. By late 1996, the state's unemployment rate hovered around 6 percent, significantly lower than a decade earlier. Both retail sales and the construction and sales of new homes flourished. The petroleum industry was still in neutral, but the state's economy was becoming more diversified. Services, particularly in the health care area, state government, consulting, engineering, private education, and manufacturing, especially the making of durable goods, expanded. Continued steady economic growth was forecast for the remainder of the century.[3]

The driving force in the Texas economy is its corporate sector. Large companies provide most of the jobs, invest most of the capital necessary for growth, and produce the lion's share of goods and services available in the state. The remainder of this chapter investigates the most important economic arenas of the state, detailing the extent to which these economic sectors are dominated by a relatively few companies, which are connected with each other.

★★★★★ ENERGY

Texas and energy are practically synonymous. Much of the twentieth-century economic history of the state is written in the oil that was first discovered in large quantities at Spindletop in 1901. Although oil is still important, natural gas, coal, uranium, electricity, and chemicals have become components of the state's energy complex—an industrial matrix unmatched in size, assets, or volume of business anywhere in the country.

Oil and Gas

At the core of this energy complex are the recovery, refining, and distribution of crude oil and natural gas. For the greater part of this century, Texas has met most of the petroleum needs of the United States. Although the gap is closing, it continues to lead all states in the production of crude oil and natural gas.[4]

In 1975, 1.2 billion barrels of oil came from the state's fields. Twenty years later, that figure had been cut by more than half, to 512 million barrels. Throughout the 1970s, about one third of the nation's petroleum came from Texas; in 1995, Texas provided about 23 percent of the total, the lowest percentage recorded during this century. Likewise, the production of natural gas fell from 7 million cubic feet in 1980 to 4.45 million cubic feet in 1995, 23 percent of the national total.[5] The value added to the state's economy by crude oil and natural gas production declined from $48 billion in the mid-1980s to $22.5 billion ten years later.[6] During this period, the contribution of the petroleum business to the state's economy decreased from 27 percent to about 11 percent.[7]

Who controls the petroleum industry in Texas? At first glance, given that there are approximately 6,000 oil and natural gas producers registered to conduct business in Texas and 33 companies engaged in refining the state's petroleum products, the petroleum business environment appears to be strikingly pluralistic. However, on closer inspection (see Table 2–1), patterns of concentration become evident. In 1994, twelve firms accounted for 47 percent of Texas's crude oil production (Table 2–1, column A) and 51 percent of the recovery of its natural gas (Table 2–1, column B); only seven companies were responsible for 58 percent of the refinery runs (Table 2–1, column C).[8] Six major companies—Exxon, Mobil, Chevron, Shell, Texaco, and ARCO—are among the leaders in all three areas of the petroleum business. These oil giants are responsible for more than one fourth of the production of the state's crude oil and natural gas, as well as nearly half of its refining. Moreover, five other companies—Amoco, Pennzoil, Phillips, Union Pacific, and USX-Marathon—appear in two of the columns of Table 2–1. With very few exceptions, the companies listed in Table 2–1 rank among the largest corporations in the United States.

Petrochemicals

Raw crude oil and natural gas contain a multitude of chemicals that can be converted into commercial products. Xylene, toluene, ethylene, ammonia, and benzene are among the many valuable chemicals extracted from oil and gas. Products made with these compounds include insecticides, fertilizers, dyes, drugs, plastics, nylons, solvents, glue, rubber, and clothing. Not unexpectedly, many of the major oil companies operate petrochemical plants in Texas. They are joined in this practice by several other large-scale companies, the most important of which (as measured by the number of Texans employed) are Dow Chemical, DuPont, Goodyear Tire and Rubber, and Union Carbide, in that order.[9]

Pipelines

Crude oil and natural gas are conveyed from their sources to refineries, factories, and homes through an extensive pipeline system that crisscrosses Texas and connects the state to many outlets throughout the country. About 2.3 million cubic feet of gas was shipped from the state in 1994. Five pipeline companies—Natural Gas Pipeline Company of America (a subsidiary of Occidental Petroleum), Tenneco, El Paso Natural Gas, PanEnergy (formerly Panhandle Eastern), and Transco (which is now owned by the Williams Companies), ranked in that order—transmitted 77 percent of Texas's gas to other areas of the United States.[10]

More natural gas is consumed in Texas than in any other state. About 300 large companies receive most of this gas, followed by 281,600 small businesses and 3.3 million residential customers.[11] The transmission of

★ **TABLE 2–1**
Top Oil and Natural Gas Companies in Texas (1994)

A. Crude Oil Production Company	B. Natural Gas Amount Produced (%)	Production Company	Amount Produced (%)
1. Amoco	7.5	1. Exxon	8.0
2. Exxon	6.3	2. Union Pacific	5.2
3. Shell	5.3	3. Shell	5.0
4. Texaco	4.7	4. TransTexas	4.5
5. Mobil	4.2	5. Texaco	4.3
6. USX-Marathon	3.9	6. Mobil	4.3
7. Chevron	3.6	7. Chevron	3.8
8. Amerada Hess	3.1	8. Amoco	3.8
9. Union Pacific	2.6	9. ARCO[1]	3.7
10. ARCO	2.0	10. Pennzoil	2.9
11. Pennzoil	1.8	11. USX-Marathon	2.8
12. Unocal	1.7	12. Phillips	2.7
Total %	46.7	Total %	51.0
Total Amount	542 million barrels	Total Amount	4.46 MCF

C. Refining Company	Amount (%)
1. Exxon	11.2
2. Mobil	8.5
3. Phillips	8.3
4. Chevron	8.0
5. Lyondell[2]	7.7
6. Star[3]	7.5
7. Shell	6.9
Total %	58.1
Total amount	3.55 million barrels per day

SOURCES: *Oil Directory of Texas* (Austin: R. W. Byram, 1995) and Texas Railroad Commission, *1994 Oil and Gas Annual Report,* vol. 1 (Austin: Oil and Gas Division, 1995), pp. A86–87.
[1]Includes ARCO's holdings in Vastar Resources.
[2]Formerly, Lyondell was a fully owned subsidiary of ARCO. ARCO now owns 49.9 percent of Lyondell.
[3]Star Enterprises is a joint venture between Texaco and the Saudi Arabian government.

gas within Texas is mostly the work of a few corporations: five operators—Lone Star Gas (a division of ENSERCH), Texas Utilities, Entex (now owned by Houston Industries), Enron, and MidCon (also owned by Occidental Petroleum), in that order—accounted for two thirds of all sales of natural gas in the domestic Texas market in 1994.[12]

Electric Companies

Texas leads the nation in both the generation and the consumption of electricity. In 1993, more than 6 million industrial, residential, and com-

★ ★ ★

Highlight 2–2: Exxon and Texas

Exxon is a direct descendant of the Standard Oil empire. Standard Oil was founded in the nineteenth century by John D. Rockefeller. By the turn of the century, it had achieved control of America's petroleum business. The U.S. Supreme Court ruled in 1911 that Standard had reached its position through deliberate acts designed to create a monopoly and, therefore, that it violated the country's antitrust laws. The court ruled that Standard must be divided into several different companies. Although they were allowed to own controlling stock in all of the newly established firms, each member of the Rockefeller family could manage the day-to-day operations of only one company. John D. Rockefeller chose to run Standard Oil of New Jersey.

Standard Oil did not participate in the initial discoveries of large quantities of oil in Texas. Indeed, there was strong opposition among Texas oilmen—some of it violent—to allowing Standard any access to the state. Standard of New Jersey circumvented this resistance by forming a partnership with Humble Oil of Texas. For nearly fifty years, Humble dominated the oil business in the state. Any distinction between Standard Oil of New Jersey and Humble was dissolved in 1972, when they officially merged into the Exxon Corporation. In 1990, Exxon moved its corporate headquarters from New York City to Irving, Texas.

Currently, Exxon is Texas's foremost refiner and natural gas producer. It ranks second in crude oil production to Amoco, which, as Standard of Indiana, was also carved out of the original Standard Oil empire. With an asset value of about $88 billion, Exxon is one of the world's largest industrial corporations. In 1994, its revenues totaled $114 billion, more than three times the amount of money that the Texas state government collected in its general fund that year. Exxon's profit on yearly sales is usually over $5 billion.

mercial customers bought electricity in the state. About 75 percent of this market is serviced by three power companies: Texas Utilities, Houston Industries (Houston Lighting and Power), and Central and South West (Central Power and Light, West Texas Utilities, Southwestern Public Service of Louisiana, and Public Service of Oklahoma).[13]

Alternative Sources of Energy

Since the energy crisis of the 1970s, there has been a movement toward the discovery, recovery, and use of sources of energy other than crude oil and natural gas. In Texas, this search has mostly centered on lignite and uranium. Lignite, a soft, brown, porous type of coal, is plentiful in Texas. Currently, the state has 23 billion short tons of lignite in its reserves. It is estimated that less than half of this lignite has commercial value. Texas ranks sixth among all states in the production of coal/lignite, most of which is used to generate electricity.[14] Some 620 million pounds of uranium—the third largest quantity among the states—lie beneath south and west Texas. In 1993, 56.5 million tons of uranium were mined in Texas.[15]

The corporate hand is clearly visible in the development of alternate energy sources. Texas Utilities, the state's foremost electric company, extracted more than half of all the lignite strip-mined in 1993. The leading uranium miners in Texas have been three oil companies: Chevron, Conoco (owned by DuPont), and Exxon.[16]

The importance of alternative fuels is reflected by the fact that currently 46 percent of the electricity generated in Texas comes from lignite/coal, 45 percent from natural gas, and 9 percent from uranium.[17] Most of the state's major electric companies have invested heavily in the construction of nuclear power plants. Texas Utilities has built two nuclear reactors at its Comanche Peak site, near Glen Rose. Houston Lighting and Power (Houston Industries) is the lead partner in a consortium of companies (which originally included Central and South West and the municipally owned electric companies of San Antonio and Austin) that built the South Texas Nuclear Project on Matagorda Island. Gulf States Utilities invested heavily in the River Bend nuclear reactor, located in Louisiana. Likewise, El Paso Electric became a major player in the Palo Verde nuclear power project in Arizona. In each case, as detailed in Highlight 2–3, the decision to develop nuclear-powered electricity led to problems.

Service Firms

Another component of Texas's energy complex is the group of firms that provide the equipment, tools, machinery, and plants for the producers, refiners, and generators of energy in the state. The leading service firms in Texas are Halliburton, Schlumberger, Cooper Industries, Dresser Industries, and Baker Hughes. Each of these firms has an asset value and annual sales amounting to billions of dollars. Halliburton is one of the world's largest and most diversified oil field services and heavy construction companies. Its Brown and Root subsidiary built Texas Utilities' Glen Rose nuclear power reactors and was the original contractor for the South Texas Nuclear Power project. Schlumberger is a Dutch-based company that secured a strong presence in Texas through the 1984 acquisition of SEDCO, a company founded by former state governor Bill Clements.

In addition to its service operations, Cooper Industries also owns Champion Spark Plugs. Dresser Industries provides work for nearly 10,000 people statewide, and Baker Hughes employs 6,540 Texans.

In sum, the discovery of oil in Texas led to the development of an extensive energy empire in the state. The important actors in that empire are a relatively few large corporations.

Table 2–2 lists the major firms in each of the key sectors of the energy complex. In sum, thirty-five corporations are dominant forces. The cornerstone of Texas's energy business lies among the nation's largest oil companies. Several of these petroleum giants dominate more than one economic arena. Exxon, for instance, is a leading refiner and producer of crude oil, natural gas, petrochemicals, and uranium.

★ ★ ★ ★ ★   # AGRICULTURE

The land in Texas has also been generous to farmers, ranchers, and woodcutters, since its fertile soil is suitable for grazing and for cultivating

★ ★ ★

Highlight 2–3: Nuclear Problems

The decision to build nuclear reactors created three formidable problems for some utilities and their ratepayers.

First, construction was rarely accomplished either on time or at the originally estimated price. For instance, by 1993 Texas Utilities' Comanche Peak was behind schedule and its costs had escalated from $800 million to more than $11 billion. The completion of Houston Lighting and Power's South Texas Nuclear Project was delayed by ten years and its price tag was substantially above its originally estimated cost.[1]

Second, safety questions have dogged these nuclear power projects. Citizens' groups, employees of the construction firms building the reactors, and government inspections and officials have raised substantial doubts as to the safety of some of these reactors. After an investigation of the South Texas Nuclear Project, the Nuclear Regulatory Commission of the federal government stated that "the basic problem at [the project] can be summarized as inadequate licensee control of the construction process, leading to serious deficiencies in the quality assurance program."[2] Houston Lighting and Power was fined $100,000, the maximum allowable under law, for not adequately overseeing the safe construction of the plant. Texas Utilities paid $10 million to a citizen intervention group to quiet public opposition to the government's issuing operating licenses to its plants.[3]

Third, the profit from generating electricity from uranium was sometimes less than anticipated. For example, once El Paso Electric and Gulf States Utilities were able to deliver electricity from their nuclear power plants, each discovered that it could not find enough consumers to purchase the power it had available. Caught in the squeeze between the need to pay the huge debts they had incurred to build their reactors and the low demand for their product, each of these firms faced severe financial difficulty in the early 1990s. El Paso Electric filed for bankruptcy in 1992 and its situation remained uncertain in 1995, after Central and South West reneged on a proposed merger between the two utilities. Unable to recover financially, Gulf States Utilities was taken over by Entergy Corporation, located in Louisiana.

Notes

1. See Anne Marie Kilday, "Comanche Peak Gets Unit 2 OK," *Dallas Morning News*, April 7, 1993, p. A–33, and Patricia Kilday Hart, "Power Play," *Texas Monthly*, November 1988, p. 135.
2. John F. Ahearne, *Regulation and Construction of Nuclear Power Plants—South Texas Nuclear Power Project* (Hearing Before the Subcommittee on Oversight and Investigations of the committee on Interstate and Foreign Commerce, House of Representatives, 96th Congress, 2d session, 1981), p. 3.
3. Marshall Surratt, "Critical Compromises," *Texas Observer*, June 30, 1989, p. 1.

---

fibers, foodstuffs, and timber. Cash receipts from the sale of agricultural products in Texas were nearly $13 billion in 1994, second only to California's. The total asset value of land, machinery, livestock, buildings, crops, and farming households and investments is around $76 billion, more than that of any other state. Agriculture contributes about $42 billion to the Texas economy each year.[18]

The abundance of relatively inexpensive land in Texas in the past gave many people more than just a means to make a living. It also afforded them the opportunity to own property and provided a strong reason to believe in the virtues of rugged individualism, self-reliance, and personal

★ **TABLE 2–2**
The Dominant Energy Companies in Texas

Crude Oil Production	Natural Gas Production	Refining
Amoco	Exxon	Exxon
Exxon	Union Pacific	Mobil
Shell	Shell	Phillips
Texaco	TransTexas	Chevron
Mobil	Texaco	Lyondell (ARCO owns 49.9 percent)
USX-Marathon	Mobil	Star (Texaco is a major partner)
Chevron	Chevron	Shell
Amerada Hess	Amoco	
Union Pacific	ARCO	
ARCO	Pennzoil	
Pennzoil	USX-Marathon	
Unocal	Phillips	

Pipelines (interstate)	Pipelines (in-state)	Electric Utilities
Tenneco	ENSERCH (Lone Star Gas)	Texas Utilities
Panhandle Eastern (PanEnergy)	Texas Utilities	Houston Industries
Occidental (Natural Gas Pipeline)	Houston Industries (Entex)	Central and South West
El Paso Natural Gas	Enron	
Transco (Williams Companies)	Occidental (Midcon)	

Natural Gas Delivery	Alternative Energy	Service Firms
ENSERCH (Lone Star Gas)	Texas Utilities (coal/lignite)	Halliburton
Houston Industries (Entex)	Exxon (uranium)	Dresser Industries
	Chevron (uranium)	Cooper Industries
	DuPont (uranium)	Baker Hughes
		Schlumberger

Petrochemicals*
Dow Chemical
DuPont
Goodyear Tire and Rubber
Union Carbide

* Does not include the names of oil companies already listed in this table.

freedom. Recently, however, the number of people who own agricultural land in Texas has been declining.[19]

Between 1940 and 1992, the number of farms and ranches in Texas fell from 418,000 to 180,644. At the same time, the number of Texans classified as farmers and ranchers decreased from 20 percent of the workforce to less than 2 percent. Indeed, these days a majority of the operators of the state's agricultural units declare their principal occupations to be something other than farming or ranching.

The average size of agricultural units has increased from 439 acres in 1950 to 725 acres in 1992. That year, on the average, each agricultural unit had sales of $66,453, but recorded a profit of only $8,224. Moreover, there are great disparities among the economic standings of Texas's farmers and ranchers.

At the low end of the scale, in 1992, 29 percent of farmers and ranchers had gross sales of $2,500 or less. Six out of every ten farmers and ranchers received no more than $10,000 in revenues; altogether, they accounted for a mere 3 percent of all agricultural sales. Fully 93 percent of these low-earning units are owned by individuals and families. These growers face a number of dangers, including the rising cost of supplies, poor prices for their products, and, in recent years, drought.

The costs of supplies continue to rise. Between 1987 and 1992, for instance, Texas's agricultural operators confronted escalating costs for chemical fertilizers, electricity, petroleum products, seed bulbs, mixed-formula feed, livestock, hired labor, and machinery. Overall, it has been difficult for many of these individual farmers and ranchers to make ends meet. In 1985, for example, earnings exceeded costs in only six of Texas's twenty-two farming regions and for only seven of its ninety-one marketed crops. As one Wharton County farmer noted at that time, "We are selling our crops for the same price as we did 10 years ago, where everything we buy has as much as tripled in price."[20] At about the same time, more than $14 billion in farm debt had accumulated in Texas and many small farmers and ranchers, facing strong pressure to repay their loans, either sold their holdings, usually at a depressed price, or lost their land to their creditors.[21] Adding to their problems, between 1994 and late 1996 a lack of rain affected farmers and ranchers across the state. The drought mostly endangered cattle ranchers and growers of cotton, rice, corn, and sorghum, forcing many of these operators to seek emergency loans and some of them to sell their land.[22] The federal government subsidizes farmers and ranchers, but most of the $1.4 billion sent to Texas does not go to economically marginal operators (those whose annual sales are less than $10,000).

The largest portion of income from Texas's agricultural sales is earned by a very small minority of farms and ranches. In 1992, 163 agricultural units (out of 180,644) recorded a total of $4.3 billion in sales, 36 percent of all agricultural sales in the state. Only 12 percent of these top earners are owned by individuals or families. Although only 2.7 percent of Texas's farms and ranches are owned by corporations, 69 percent of these high-earning units are corporate entities. Half of these corporate entities are public companies or family corporations with more than ten stockholders. All told, corporate farms and ranches earn about $4 billion a year, about one third of the total agricultural yield in Texas.

The most obvious case of corporate ownership of Texas's agricultural land occurs in the timber business. Timber sales are worth about $1 billion annually to the state's economy. Most of the commercial harvesting is

★ ★ ★

Highlight 2–4: The King Ranch

The King Ranch corporation owns 825,000 acres of land, scattered across seven counties located between Brownsville and Corpus Christi. The King Ranch is almost 200,000 acres larger than the state of Rhode Island. Although the principal economic activity on the ranch is raising 60,000 head of cattle, breeding racehorses, and growing crops (cotton, sugarcane, and grain sorghum), the land also produces oil and natural gas revenue. In recent years, the ranch has experienced some economic difficulties, most revolving around the decline in the petroleum market and various lawsuits involving some of the 100 descendants of the ranch's founder, Captain Richard King. The King Ranch has met these challenges by diversifying its operations and by naming outsiders from major corporations to its board of directors. The current chief operating officer of the company is neither a King family descendant nor a farmer/rancher. He rose from the oil and natural gas division of the company and manages the company's business from Houston, not Kingsville.[1]

Notes

1. Joanne Harrison, "Change on the Range," *Texas Monthly*, July 1988, pp. 38–45, and *Hoover's Guide to the Top Texas Companies* (Austin: Reference Press, 1994), pp. 116–117.

---

done on the nearly 12 million acres of forest land located in East Texas. Major corporations with interests in wood, paper, and pulp own the most productive units.[23] The Temple Inland company, which owns about a million acres of timberland, and Champion International head the list.

The largest single owner of Texas's agricultural land is the Texas Pacific Land Trust, which holds 1.14 million acres of grazing land spread across 21 counties in West Texas. Most of this acreage was accumulated by the Texas and Pacific Railroad during the nineteenth century (see Chapter 1). After the Texas and Pacific Railroad went bankrupt, the trust was instituted. Most of its land is leased to ranchers for grazing, but many oil wells are also located on the land.

Corporations dominate the processing and distribution of agricultural products. Processors and distribution centers are necessary to bring raw materials to the buying public. The foremost food processors are giant corporations such as Philip Morris and RJR Nabisco. In the words of former Texas Commissioner of Agriculture Jim Hightower, "while there are 32,000 food processing firms in America, . . . 50 of them now make more than 90 percent of the profits in the industry."[24] In any one line of food, only a relatively small number of these giants are responsible for what is processed. For instance, only three companies—Kellogg, General Mills, and Post (owned by Philip Morris), in that order—control over 80 percent of the breakfast cereal market. All the way down the shopping list, one finds oligopoly (control by the few) widespread in the food processing industry.

Texas is home to some large food processors and distributors. Based on the number of Texans employed, the following agribusiness companies stand out: Frito-Lay (owned by PepsiCo), makers of snack food; Pilgrim's

Pride, chicken processing; Decker Food, owned by agricultural giant ConAgra; Yoplait yogurt, a subsidiary of General Mills; two breweries, Miller's (owned by Philip Morris) and Anheuser Busch; the Texas Coca-Cola Bottlers; Dr. Pepper/Seven Up, makers of the third-largest-selling soft drinks; the Associated Milk Producers, the country's leading dairy farmers' cooperative; Tyson Foods, poultry and meat processing; and Blue Bell Creameries' ice cream products.

Corporations also play an important role in getting agricultural products directly to the consumer. Food is mostly bought in corporate-owned grocery stores and restaurants. In Texas, the leading supermarkets (measured in terms of number of employees) are San Antonio's H.E.B. (which has more than 200 stores in Texas), Kroger, Randalls Food Markets (based in Houston), and Albertsons. When people dine out, they are most likely to eat at a corporate-owned fast food outlet, the foremost of which (in terms of sales) are McDonald's, Kentucky Fried Chicken, Pizza Hut, and Taco Bell (all owned by PepsiCo), and Burger King (owned by the Grand Metropolitan insurance company of England). The Sysco corporation of Houston has become prominent in agribusiness by becoming the nation's largest distributor of food products to stores and restaurants.

In short, although agriculture generates a substantial amount of income in Texas, the proceeds are unevenly distributed. The typical farmer or rancher does not fare well. Large firms, family corporations, and owners of large tracts of land, as well as major food processors and retailers, are the principal beneficiaries of the bounty derived from agriculture.

★★★★★ FINANCIAL INSTITUTIONS

During the boom times in Texas's economy, the state's financial institutions—principally commercial banks, savings and loan firms, and insurance companies—helped finance the state's economic expansion. When the crash came in the 1980s, many of these institutions were caught short; this precipitated a crisis in the financial community. Between 1985 and 1993, 516 banks closed in Texas, reducing the number of banks doing business in the state from about 1,400 to about 935. Nine of the state's top ten banks either failed or were saved only through the intervention of out-of-state buyers. The leading banks operating in Texas today are listed in Table 2–3.

NationsBank, whose headquarters are in Charlotte, North Carolina, is Number One in the state. In 1995, it held $43 billion in assets: 22.1 percent of all bank assets in Texas. With 1995 assets of $21 billion (or 10.8 percent of the Texas total), Texas Commerce ranked second in the state. In 1986, Texas Commerce was purchased by Chemical of New York. Texas Commerce/Chemical subsequently acquired the most important components of the First City Bancorporation, once among Texas's elite handful

★ **TABLE 2–3**
The Top Five Banks in Texas

	1995 Total Assets*	% Total Assets	Cumulative Percent	1996 National Rank
1. NationsBank	$43.0 billion	22.1%	22.1%	4
2. Texas Commerce**	$21.0 billion	10.8%	32.9%	1
3. Bank One	$18.2 billion	9.4%	42.3%	10
4. BankAmerica	$ 7.9 billion	4.1%	46.4%	3
5. Wells Fargo (First Interstate)	$ 6.3 billion	3.2%	49.6%	9

SOURCE: *San Antonio Express News,* August 11, 1995, p. 8H.
*The total amount of banking assets in Texas on June 30, 1995, was $194.2 billion.
**Texas Commerce is owned by the Chase Manhattan Corporation of New York.

of banks. Adding another chapter to the story, Chemical Bank absorbed the Chase Manhattan Bank of New York in 1995. The new company, the Chase Manhattan Corporation, is now the largest banking institution in the United States.

Third among banks in Texas is Bank One, located in Columbus, Ohio. In 1995, Bank One controlled 9.4 percent of the state's bank assets, worth $18.2 billion. The fourth largest bank operating in Texas is the San Francisco-based BankAmerica, the nation's third largest banking institution. In 1995, BankAmerica had $7.9 billion in assets, 4.1 percent of the Texas total. First Interstate, another California bank, was fifth in bank assets in 1995. It held $6.3 billion of the state's assets, 3.2 percent of the total. First Interstate is now owned by Wells Fargo of California.

Briefly, in 1995 the top five banks in Texas held half of the state's bank assets. None of these key banks is Texan-owned. Rather, each is owned by a financial institution that ranks among the top ten banks in the nation. Hence, much of the control over the state's banking community has gone to out-of-state institutions.

The savings and loan business in Texas has been devastated in recent years. Freed from tight federal and state government regulation in the early 1980s, savings and loan firms embarked on an extensive and ambitious spending binge. They invested their depositors' money heavily in real estate, both commercial and residential. Wild speculative deals, illegal business practices, and the overall decline of the Texas economy combined to produce a near-collapse in the state's savings and loan industry. Between 1987 and 1993, 237 savings and loan companies failed in Texas; by 1996, only 58 remained. The top three, First Nationwide, Bank United, and Guaranty Federal (owned by timber giant Temple Inland), controlled 59 percent of all savings and loan assets and held 60 percent of the state's

★ ★ ★

Highlight 2–5: The Saga of First Nationwide in Texas

The story behind First Nationwide's move into the Texas savings and loan market is intriguing. It arose from the rubble left after this industry's collapse in the 1980s. During that time, two major firms—Gibraltar Savings and Loan and First Texas—went bankrupt and were taken over by the federal government. The government was eager to sell these institutions and in 1984 found a ready buyer in Texan J. Livingston Kosberg. Kosberg's financial empire deteriorated three years later, when First Texas was declared insolvent and Gibraltar Savings had a net worth barely above the minimum required by the government for continued operation. At the end of 1988, by order of the federal government, Gibraltar went into bankruptcy.[1] The government then arranged for the sale of both Gibraltar and First Texas to Ronald Perelman, a New York investor with extensive holdings in the Revlon cosmetics company, for $315 million. The purchase of what became First Gibraltar was sweetened by a government subsidy of $5 billion and a tax relief guarantee worth $900 million to the new owner. One critic of this deal claims that taxpayers would have saved money if the federal government had simply closed Gibraltar Savings and First Texas and paid off their depositors, many of whom were eligible for the maximum government-insured guarantee of $100,000.[2]

First Gibraltar grew rapidly, and by 1989 it was turning a profit. In 1992, Perelman's investment firm, MacAndrews and Ford, sold part of First Gibraltar to BankAmerica. The remainder of First Gibraltar was renamed First Madison. First Madison expanded its position in the Texas savings and loan sector by purchasing First Nationwide Financial from its parent, the Ford Motor Company, for $1.1 billion in 1994. The First Madison name was dropped and First Nationwide became the state's foremost savings and loan firm in 1996, with an asset worth of $14.7 billion (24.7 percent of all savings and loan assets in the state). Blurring the lines between companies, the chair of First Nationwide is Gerald Ford (not to be confused with the former president of the United States), who also happens to be the chair of First Gibraltar, a wholly owned subsidiary of BankAmerica, Texas's fourth largest bank.

Notes

1. Peter Elkind, "Rock Bottom," *Texas Montly*, June 1989, p. 84.
2. The analyst is Jeff Porter of the Federal Home Loan Bank of Dallas. Reported in Robert Rosenblatt, "Subsidized Sale of Failing Thrift Is Under Attack," *Los Angeles Times*, May 2, 1990, p. 1.

deposits.[25] First Nationwide (see Highlight 2–5) possesses 25 percent of these assets and nearly 28 percent of the deposits.

More than $35 billion in insurance premiums are paid each year in Texas; almost half of this amount is for property and casualty insurance, including automobile, workers' compensation, fire, and product liability coverage. By and large, the most important insurers in Texas are major national companies. For example, in 1993, two companies—Allstate and State Farm, both of which have their headquarters in Illinois—collected about one third of all property and casualty insurance premiums in Texas.[26]

The largest insurance company to emerge in Texas is Houston's American General. In 1994, this company had an asset worth of $46 billion, placing it among the top ten public insurance companies. Its subsidiary, the Variable Annuity Life Insurance Company (VALIC), held $22 billion in assets and is ranked among the top 1 percent of the nation's life insurance firms.[27]

★ ★ ★ ★ ★   ## NEW HORIZONS

Energy, agriculture, and financial dealings have constituted the backbone of the Texas economy for most of this century. Indeed, it could easily be argued that the state's overall economic well-being has largely been based on the value of its petroleum products. The fragility of such a one-dimensional economic foundation was fully revealed when the recession hit in the 1980s. Falling prices for oil and natural gas, as we have discussed previously, jeopardized its economic health. Diversification became the battle cry for many forward-looking Texans. The state's leadership has been especially active in promoting high technology and free trade as tonics to cure Texas's economic ills.

High Tech

An electronics industry was in place in Texas long before the current emphasis on developing high tech. Fort Worth's Tandy (owners of Radio Shack), IBM, Texas Instruments, and Electronic Data Systems (which was founded by H. Ross Perot and is now owned by General Motors) are four examples of indigenous electronics firms with a strong foothold in the state.

Moreover, a Texas-based defense industry, which is deeply involved in the manufacturing and testing of advanced electronic technology, has been well nourished by generous federal government subsidies since World War II. In 1989, for instance, $29 billion in defense money came to Texas. At that time, defense work accounted for 322,000 jobs in the state. Although there were about 1,300 defense contractors in the state, most of this money went to relatively few major companies, such as Lockheed Martin.[28] In recent years, major cuts in defense spending have forced most defense contractors to scale back production and reduce their labor forces.

Conversely, the recent development of the high-tech industry has resulted in additional factories, businesses, and jobs. Compaq, Dell, Motorola, Westinghouse, and Rockwell International have all either opened new facilities or expanded old ones in Texas. Between 1978 and 1984, the number of electronics firms doing business in Texas increased from 1,638 to 7,541.[29] The largest new arrivals are Microelectronics and Computer Technology Corporation (MCC) and Semiconductor Manufacturing Technology Institute (Sematech), both of which chose to locate in Austin after it outbid several other cities.

After its 1983 arrival in Austin, MCC grew until it employed 500 people and had a budget of more than $75 million, although in 1993 it showed some signs of floundering. Sematech's 1988 decision to locate in Austin promised an infusion of $1.6 billion into the local economy and employment for 700 people.[30] Half of its $200 million annual research budget comes from the U.S. Department of Defense. Overall, some 100,000 Texans now work in the electronics industry, and continued job growth is forecast for the immediate future.[31]

Free Trade

Texas business hopes to reap a handsome profit from better, and more open, relations with its southern neighbor, Mexico. The North American Free Trade Agreement (NAFTA), which became effective on January 1, 1994, is designed to establish a large regional market, in which Canada, Mexico, and the United States cooperate in the production and distribution of goods and services across the continent. In the regional economy created by NAFTA, the primary location for production and manufacturing will be Mexico. Already, according to one analysis, "the strip of land that runs for 1,500 miles from California to Texas has become a highway of Fortune 500 companies."[32] About 700,000 Mexicans are currently employed by the 2,000-plus factories, known as maquiladoras, that cluster on the Mexican side of the border. What mainly attracts companies to move to Mexico is the prospect of paying employees lower wages. A Mexican working at the Zenith factory in Reynosa (across the Rio Grande River from McAllen) makes television sets for between 50 cents and $1.60 per hour; her counterpart, when TV sets were still made in America, would have earned, on the average, $7.00 per hour.[33]

The recent devaluation of the Mexican peso has further eroded the earning power of that country's workers. At the same time, since the products made at these factories are bought mostly with U.S. dollars, the profit margins of corporations and the salaries of their key executives have increased. For example, the CEO of Allied Signal was paid $12.4 million in 1994, while the 3,800 workers at his company's plant in Mexico collectively earned an estimated $4.6 million less![34]

The supporters of NAFTA argued that the treaty would generate many jobs in Texas, largely in service areas (such as retail sales, wholesale trade, and eating and drinking establishments), the financial world, and the electronics industry.[35] However, preliminary employment figures show mixed results. While El Paso appears to have added jobs within the first year after NAFTA's enactment,[36] the first major study of employment patterns indicates that very few jobs have been generated by the treaty.[37]

★★★★★ OTHER ECONOMIC LEADERS

Joining the ranks of Texas's leading businesses in energy, agriculture, finance, and technology are companies that, although they do not do business in these arenas, nonetheless make important contributions to Texas's economy. General Motors, for example, owns a major electronics firm, EDS, and operates a substantial auto assembly plant in Arlington. With 47,000 Texans on its payroll, General Motors is Texas's largest private-sector employer. SBC (Southwestern Bell) and GTE provide both phone service to the state's residents and employment for 16,000 and 14,000 Texans, respectively. Three major airlines—American, Continental, and Southwest—have extensive operations in the state. Burlington Northern, whose main offices are in Texas, has greatly expanded its rail transportation holdings through the purchase of the Santa Fe–Southern Pacific railroad. Finally, the corporate headquarters of J. C. Penney and Kimberly-Clark are located in the Dallas area.

★ ★ ★ ★ ★ # COHESION IN THE TEXAS ECONOMY

Texas's economy is dominated by relatively few corporations. Domination alone, however, would not make them an economic elite. For an elite to exist, there must be cohesion among its members. Business leaders in Texas are bound together through several social and economic ties.

Social Ties

The individuals who command the highest positions in Texas's leading corporations share a great deal of social space. A survey of many top managers of Texas-based companies finds that the state's executive class is composed largely of men raised in upper-status families. Most are Protestant, usually Presbyterian and Episcopalian (not Southern Baptist). They are highly educated, with degrees mostly from prestigious Ivy League universities or from the University of Texas at Austin. During childhood, they "are taught early that they are different from common people and have special entitlements."[38] Many receive their primary and secondary education at exclusive private schools. Often they spend their vacations together at camps located in the rural parts of the state. Social interaction is maintained during their adulthood through membership in exclusive private clubs, such as Houston's River Oaks, Bayou, Coronado, University, Tejas, Ramada, and Petroleum. While elite women are usually excluded from membership in these clubs, they generally congregate in parallel social organizations, such as the Junior League. The result of these social experiences is that, as sociologist Chandler Davidson has pointed out, "the Texas rich are bound together in complex ways. Instead of a band of pecuniary cowboys seeking their individual fortunes, they are an upper class in the precise meaning of the term: a social group whose common background and effective control of wealth bring them together politically."[39]

Economic Ties

There are several economic ways to unify the dominant businesses in Texas. This section will explore shared ownership, joint ventures, mergers, and interlocking directorates as means to link the state's leading firms.

Shared Ownership   Shared ownership exists when companies have the same investors. A pattern of common ownership has prevailed among the state's foremost petroleum producers. In 1981, for example, only a few stockholders controlled enough stock (1 percent or more of the total shares) to exercise influence over nine of the state's top oil companies.[40] Most of the major stockholders in these corporations were institutional investors, especially banks, insurance companies, and investment houses, and not families or individuals. For example, in the 1980s the J. P. Morgan bank of New York City possessed a major stake in eight major energy firms operating in Texas: Exxon, Mobil, Chevron, Tenneco, El Paso Natural Gas, Panhandle Eastern (now PanEnergy), Transco (now the Williams Companies), and Halliburton.[41] Similarly, Pennzoil currently

owns 9 percent of Chevron. Common ownership tends to reduce competition between nominally rival companies and promotes economic cohesion.

Mergers   Mergers occur when one company acquires another. The effect of these acquisitions is to reduce the number of companies that operate in the economy. In recent years, mergers have been commonplace in the United States, transforming the landscape of the corporate world. Texas has not escaped this restructuring.

In the energy sector, between 1980 and 1996, DuPont took over Conoco, Texaco captured Getty Oil, Chevron acquired Gulf Oil and the oil division of Tenneco, Royal Dutch Shell fully absorbed Houston's Shell Oil, Mobil purchased Superior Oil, U.S. Steel (now USX) purchased Marathon Oil and Texas Oil and Gas (TXO), Houston Natural Gas merged with Inter-North of Omaha to form the Enron company, Occidental bought Mid-Con and Natural Gas Pipeline, Entergy gained control of Gulf States Utilities, Panhandle Eastern (now called PanEnergy) secured Texas Eastern, the Williams Companies of Oklahoma consumed Transco, Schlumberger gained control of SEDCO, Brown and Root became a subsidiary of Halliburton, and Houston Industries bought NorAm Energy (Entex).

Financial institutions, as we discussed earlier in this chapter, have been revamped through mergers. As a result, the number of firms dominating banking and the savings and loan business in the state has been dramatically reduced. SBC (Southwestern Bell) has greatly enhanced is telecommunications operations through the purchase of California-based Pacific Telesis.

Joint Ventures   Joint ventures are formal arrangements between companies to engage in a business activity together. They are very common among oil producers; one study finds thousands of joint ventures in the petroleum business.[42] Chevron and Texaco formed Caltex (headquartered in Dallas) to market petroleum products globally. Recent advances in high technology in Texas have been led by consortiums of companies.

Microelectronics and Computer Technology Corporation (MCC) began as a joint venture of ten companies and by 1986 had expanded its membership to include twenty-one firms, including RCA (owned by General Electric), Boeing, Rockwell International, NCR (owned by AT&T), National Semiconductor, Motorola, and Advanced Micro Devices. Likewise, Sematech is composed of eleven firms, including IBM, NCR (AT&T), Texas Instruments, Rockwell International, Intel, Hewlett Packard, National Semiconductor, and Advanced Micro Devices.

Interlocking Directorates   Interlocking directorates exist when a member of the board of directors of one company also sits on the board of another. Federal law (the Clayton Act of 1914) forbids interlocking directorates for firms that are direct rivals. A member of the board of directors of Exxon is legally prohibited from serving on Amoco's board. It is not illegal, however, for directors of competing companies to sit on a third, non-rival board. A representative from Exxon and one from Amoco could sit on a board of the Chase Manhattan Corporation of New York. According to one study, 90 percent of the boards of the country's 250 largest corporations are interlocked.[43] As summarized by sociologist William G. Roy, "virtually all studies of contemporary American interlocking directorates have found a single, unified network."[44] Banks are at the center of this network.

An interlock network exists among major firms doing business in Texas. Its core is the board of directors of the Chase Manhattan Corporation. Recall that in 1995 Chemical Bank of New York, the owner of the Texas Commerce Bancorporation, acquired Chase Manhattan, also of New York. The newly merged companies now operate as Chase Manhattan. Table 2–4 details the board connections that emerge from the Chase Manhattan/Texas Commerce nucleus.

Many of Texas's leading companies are represented on the Chase Manhattan/Texas Commerce boards. More specifically, serving as board members are directors from four of the state's leading petroleum firms (Mobil, Unocal, Amoco, and Union Pacific), two of its pipeline giants (PanEnergy and Enron), a principal service firm (Cooper Industries), two large agribusiness firms (Champion International and the King Ranch), a premier transportation company (Burlington Northern), the state's foremost home-grown insurance company (American General), two of its largest private-sector employers (General Motors and J. C. Penney), and several electronics firms (Westinghouse, General Electric, Rockwell International, and Motorola), all doing business in Texas.

Second, the companies that have directors on the Chase Manhattan/Texas Chemical board are linked with many other corporations that dominate the state's economy. Through these secondary and tertiary connections, the Texas interlock network expands beyond the companies we have already mentioned, to include other leading energy and petrochemical companies (Halliburton, Central and South West, DuPont, Goodyear Tire and Rubber, ARCO, Tenneco, Exxon, USX, Phillips Petroleum, Texaco, El Paso Natural Gas, Baker Hughes, Williams Companies, Union Carbide, Dow Chemical, Chevron, Dresser, Texas Utilities, and Royal Dutch Shell), the remaining dominant banks (Wells Fargo, Bank One, BankAmerica, and NationsBank), several agribusiness firms and food and beverage enterprises (Coca-Cola, General Mills, Kroger, Temple Inland, Anheuser Busch, PepsiCo, Philip Morris, Sysco, and ConAgra), a large portion of its principal aerospace and electronics manufacturers (Compaq, IBM, Texas Instruments, Lockheed Martin, and Dell), a major insurance firm (Allstate), and leading employers and other Texas-based corporations (Kimberly-Clark, American Airlines, Southwestern Bell, and GTE).

Finally, the Texas Commerce/Chase Manhattan network is part of a much wider and denser corporate network that reaches into many of

★ **TABLE 2–4**
Texas in the National Interlock Network

Chase Manhattan/ Texas Commerce:*	Links to Other Boards	Links to More Boards
Mobil		
Unocal ——————————— Halliburton		
Amoco		
Union Pacific ——————— American Express ——————— Dow Chemical		
PanEnergy ———————— Coca Cola		
General Mills		
Enron ———————— Central and South West ——————— Sysco		
Compaq		
Wells Fargo ———————— Chevron		
ConAgra (Decker Foods)		
Cooper Industries ———— DuPont		
Kroger		
Temple Inland ——————— Dell		
Champion International——— Anheuser Busch		
King Ranch		
Westinghouse		
General Electric ———— PepsiCo ———————— NationsBank		
Dresser		
Kimberly-Clark ——————— Allstate		
Philip Morris		
Goodyear Tire and Rubber		
Rockwell International		
Motorola		
General Motors ———————— American Airlines		
Ameritech ———————— ARCO ———————— Texas Utilities		
Bank One		
Tenneco		
NYNEX ———————————— Exxon		
Squibb Bristol Myers ———— IBM ———————— Shell		
Procter and Gamble ———— USX		
Phillips Petroleum		
Texas Instruments		
Lockheed Martin		
Southwestern Bell		
GTE		
American Home Products —— Texaco		
Burlington Northern ———— BankAmerica		
El Paso Natural Gas		
Baker Hughes		
American General		
Prudential Insurance ———— Williams Companies		
J.C. Penney ———————— Union Carbide		

*Includes members of the 1996 boards of directors of Chase Manhattan and Texas Commerce–Houston.
Note: An interlock is shown by a line connecting the companies.

the nation's other leading financial institutions (such as Citicorp, J. P. Morgan, American Express, Prudential, and Metropolitan), major manufacturers (for example, the Ford Motor Company, Boeing, Unisys, United Technologies, and Allied Signal), giant entertainment and telecommunications firms (Time Warner, U.S. Sprint, AT&T, Ameritech, and NYNEX), and several leading home-care companies and pharmaceuticals (such as Squibb Bristol Myers, Procter and Gamble, Warner Lambert, American Home Products, Pfizer, and Eli Lilly).

In short, there is an important interlocking network that clusters around the Chase Manhattan/Texas Commerce boards of directors. This network incorporates many of Texas's and the nation's leading firms. Indeed, about 75 percent of the state's major companies, as identified in this chapter, are interlocked through board ties that fan out from Chase Manhattan/Texas Commerce. The importance of these connections is underscored in a report issued by a committee of the U.S. Senate:

> Interlocking directorates provide a special opportunity for intercompany communication and consensus. The linkages at the boardroom table are personal connections by which key information can be passed, arrangements can be made and policies formed. Board meetings are corporate proceedings where management policies are specifically reviewed and approved or corrected. Thus, to the extent that a board contains members who are also directors of actual or potential competitors, suppliers, customers of financial organizations, there is a potential for anti-competitive abuse.[45]

★ ★ ★ ★ ★   ## CONCLUSION

Texas has traditionally had three principal economic arenas: petroleum, agriculture, and finance. Other important business activities have emerged in the state, especially in technology. Expanded trade relations with Mexico offer hope for more economic growth. Some heavy manufacturing (of automobiles and military hardware, for instance) also occurs.

A few large corporations dominate economic activities in each of these sectors. In the past, many of these leading businesses were Texas-based. However, the great economic difficulties experienced in Texas during the 1980s precipitated a major economic restructuring, which included the collapse of many well-established Texas companies. As a result, national institutions entered the state in force, especially in the financial world, through takeovers and other acquisitions.

Cohesion exists among Texas's leading businesses. Social ties, through education, social clubs, and common experiences, link members of the Texas elite. Economic connections are also common. Nominally distinct companies share owners. Joint ventures contractually bind companies. Mergers have reduced the number of dominant firms. The interlocking-directorate network is tight, is national in scope, and brings together many leading companies.

★★★★★   ## NOTES

1. *Texas Observer,* July 31, 1986.

2. *The Texas Poll Report,* vol. 4, no. 4, Fall 1987.

3. *1996–97 Texas Almanac and State Industrial Guide* (Dallas: Dallas Morning News, 1995), pp. 551–552.

4. Ibid., pp. 589–590.

5. Phone conversation with the Library of the Texas Railroad Commission.

6. *1992–93 Texas Almanac and Industrial Guide* (Dallas: Belo Corporation, 1991), pp. 502, 609.

7. Ibid., p. 517.

8. *Oil and Gas Directory of Texas and Production Survey* (Austin: R. W. Byram and Co., 1995), *passim,* and the Texas Railroad Commission, *1994 Oil and Gas Annual Report,* vol. 1 (Austin: Oil and Gas Division, 1995).

9. *The Texas 500* (Austin: The Reference Press, 1994), pp. 32–33.

10. Texas Railroad Commission, *1994 Oil and Gas Report,* pp. A86–87.

11. Figures calculated from the *1996–97 Texas Almanac and State Industrial Guide,* p. 568.

12. Gas Services Division, *Annual Report, Fiscal Year 1995* (Austin: Railroad Commission of Texas, 1995), pp. 194–201.

13. Information from the Texas Public Utility Commission, *1993 Texas Electric Utility Company Profile* (Austin: Public Utility Commission, 1994).

14. 1996–97 Texas Almanac, p. 586.

15. *Austin American-Statesman,* April 19, 1994, p. E-1, the Public Utility Commission, *1993 Texas Electric Utility Company Profile,* and the Texas Railroad Commission, *Information and Statistical Facts on Coal and Uranium Mining in Texas* (Austin: Surface Mining and Reclamation Division, 1985), p. 31.

16. Ibid. In response to a softening in the uranium market in the 1980s, DuPont eventually closed its uranium mining operation.

17. Public Utility Commission, *1993 Texas Electric Utility Company Profile.*

18. *1996–97 Texas Almanac,* p. 597.

19. Unless otherwise noted, figures presented in this section come from the U.S. Department of Commerce, Bureau of the Census, *1992 Census of Agriculture: Texas State and County* (Washington, DC: Government Printing Office, 1994).

20. Texas Department of Agriculture, *Crisis in Texas Agriculture* (Austin: Texas Department of Agriculture, 1986), pp. iv–v.

21. Ibid., pp. iii and v.

22. "Beyond the Drought," *Fiscal Notes,* July 1996, pp. 1 and 6–10.

23. *1996–97 Texas Almanac,* p. 85, and Bruce Cory, "Taxing Timberland in East Texas," *Texas Observer,* July 21, 1978, p. 8.

24. Interview with Jim Hightower in the *Texas Observer,* March 23, 1983, p. 11, and Michael Parenti, *Democracy for the Few* (New York: St. Martin's, 6th ed., 1995), p. 12.

25. *Texas Savings and Loan Directory* (Austin: Texas Bank Store, 1996), pp. 16 and 18.

26. Texas Department of Insurance, *State of Texas Property and Casualty Insurance Experience by Coverage and Carriers* (Austin: Department of Insurance, 1994), pp. 1–15.

27. *Moody's Bank and Finance Manual* (New York: Moody's Investors Services, 1995), p. 3355.

28. Lawrence Wright, "The Price of Peace," *Texas Monthly,* February 1990, pp. 94–97 and 132–134. *Dallas Morning News,* April 27, 1993, p. A-12.

29. *1986–87 Texas Almanac and Industrial Guide* (Dallas: Belo Corporation, 1985), p. 572.

30. Paul Sweeney, "Bobby Ray Inman and the High-Tech Sweepstakes," *Texas Observer,* January 29, 1988, p. 7.

31. *1996–97 Texas Almanac,* p. 556.

32. Donald L. Barlett and James B. Steele, *America: What Went Wrong?* (Kansas City: Andrew and McMeel, 1992), p. 35, and Karen Olsson, "With His Lawbook in His Hand," *Texas Observer,* October 25, 1996, pp. 8–12.

33. Donald L. Barlett and James B. Steele, *America: What Went Wrong?,* p. 37.

34. Sarah Anderson and John Cavanagh, "U.S. Executives Live Well at Expense of Workers," *Los Angeles Times,* August 15, 1995, p. B-2.

35. Richard Alm, "Dallas' Top Rank in NAFTA Study Surprises Rivals," *Dallas Morning News,* February 28, 1993, p. H-3.

36. *1996–97 Texas Almanac,* pp. 553–554.

37. Sara Silver, "NAFTA Job Impact 'Near Zero,'" *The Monitor,* December 20, 1996, p. 1C.

38. This portrait is drawn from Chandler Davidson, *Race and Class in Texas Politics* (Princeton, NJ: Princeton University Press, 1990), pp. 70–71 and 88–89. The quotation is taken from p. 89.

39. Ibid, p. 64.

40. The nine companies were Exxon, Amoco, Chevron, Mobil, Gulf, Phillips, ARCO, Shell, and Texaco.

41. The data used in this investigation come from Corporate Data Exchange, *CDE Stock Ownership Directory: Energy* (New York: Corporate Data Exchange, 1980).

42. Edward S. Herman, *Corporate Control, Corporate Power* (Cambridge, MA: Cambridge University Press, 1981), pp. 205–208.

43. Harold Salzman and G. William Domhoff, "The Corporate Community and Government: Do They Interlock?" *Power Structure Research,* G. William Domhoff, ed. (Beverly Hills, CA: Sage Publications, 1980), p. 233.

44. William G. Roy, "The Unfolding of the Interlocking Directorate Structure of the United States," *American Sociological Review* 48 (1983):257.

45. Committee on Governmental Affairs, United States Senate, *Structure of Corporate Concentration: Institutional Shareholders and Interlocking Directorates Among Major U.S. Corporations* (Washington, DC: Government Printing Office, vol. 1, 1980), pp. 5–6.

PART II

Access to Political Decision Makers in Texas: Elections and Lobbying

Business interests shape public policy by first gaining access to political officials who make decisions in the name of the state. Obtaining political access is the key step toward becoming politically powerful. The quest for political access is facilitated if government officials are sympathetic to one's preferences, desires, interests, and concerns. There are two principal means of achieving such a state of affairs: to play a predominant role in the selection of political officials and to effectively pressure decision makers to act in accordance with one's views. Chapter 3 of this book discusses elections in Texas. Chapter 4 explores the techniques used by various individuals and groups, especially those in business, to lobby officials of the state government.

CHAPTER **3**

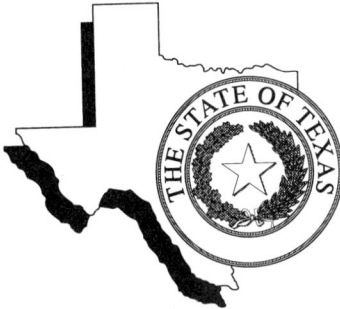

Elections and Political Parties in Texas

In democratic societies, elections are the major means by which the public selects government officeholders. Ideally, democratic elections make it difficult or impossible for a few persons or organizations to dominate the lives of the many through control of the political system. Approaching this ideal requires elections that are open to most of the public and that provide a meaningful choice to voters. Open and competitive elections should produce political leaders who are responsible and accountable to, as well as representative of, the general public. This chapter assesses how well Texas's elections conform to the democratic ideal. Here the mechanics of the state's electoral system and the nature of its party system will be addressed.

★ ★ ★ ★ ★ TEXAS ELECTIONS

For the democratic ideal to be fulfilled, elections should be the principal way to fill government offices and it should be relatively easy for people to vote. As we will discuss in this section, most of the key offices in state government are filled through a variety of types of elections that are reasonably open to voter participation.

Elected Officials in Texas

A large number of state officials are selected through public elections in Texas. Every two years, the 150 positions in the state House of Representatives and, at staggered four-year intervals, the thirty-one Texas Senate seats are filled through election. Texas also elects numerous executive and administrative officials. The governor is chosen every four years. In addition, the state ballot contains, at various times, candidates for the jobs of lieutenant governor, attorney general, comptroller of public accounts, treasurer, and the commissioners of agriculture and of the General Land Office, as well as candidates for the fifteen slots on the State Board of Education and the three positions on the Railroad Commission. The vast majority of state judges are also chosen by the voters. Election of members of the judiciary extends from Texas's lower courts (e.g., the Justice of the Peace and judges in the county and district courts) to its higher ones (e.g., the Supreme Court and the Court of Criminal Appeals). In sum, about 2,900 judicial posts are filled through election. The statewide ballot also frequently contains amendments to the Texas Constitution and other propositions, such as bond issues. Add to this already long list the electoral contests conducted at the city and county level and it is easy to conclude that there are plenty of people and policy matters that Texas voters decide on.

Types of Elections

There are three types of elections in Texas: primaries, special elections, and general elections.

Primaries have been used by political parties since 1905 to determine each party's candidates for offices contested in the general election. If a political party in Texas has received 20 percent of the total vote cast in a previous general election for governor, it must hold a primary. Parties receiving fewer votes in the gubernatorial race may select their candidates either through a primary election or at a convention. In effect, currently only the Republican party and the Democratic party are legally bound to hold primaries.

Primaries occur in even-numbered years on the second Tuesday of March. Each party conducts and administers its own primary in Texas—a practice found in only a few other states. Texas has an open *primary*, which means that on the day of the primary, voters may go to the polling place of the party of their choice, regardless of the party with which they identify. It is not legal to vote in the primaries of both parties, although incidents of voting in both have been recorded in the state. Historically, it was fairly common for Republicans to vote only in the Democratic primary—usually for conservative candidates—and then to return to the G.O.P. in the general election.

To win the primary election outright, a candidate must receive a majority of the votes cast. If no one candidate does so, a runoff primary must be conducted within thirty days of the first primary. Runoffs, which are very common in Texas, pit the two candidates who received the most votes in the first primary against each other.

General elections occur in even-numbered years on the Tuesday following the first Monday in November. The candidate receiving a plurality of votes wins this election. General elections for statewide races are not conducted at the same time as presidential elections. Instead, they are scheduled in the even-numbered years that fall between presidential elections.

[handwritten margin notes: happens 30 days p election]

[handwritten notes at bottom: Don't want people thinking Republican — Governor in different years then president (ie. 1994, 2000   1994, 1998)]

The Office of the Secretary of State oversees general elections in Texas. Among other duties, the Secretary of State determines whether a person's name may appear on the ballot. County officials carry out the mechanical tasks involved in conducting general elections. The commissioners' court of each county appoints election judges and selects the means to be used to vote (voting machine or paper ballot) and to count ballots (by hand or by computer). The counties and the state share the expense of administering general elections.

Special elections are called to fill unexpected vacancies in offices, to decide the fate of constitutional amendments and bond issues, and to select the governing bodies of most cities in Texas, as well as the members of local school boards. If a state- or federally elected position becomes vacant because of the resignation or death of its occupant, the governor appoints an interim officeholder and sets a date for a special election. These elections are administered by the same officials who oversee general elections. Special elections are open to all candidates. That is, it is not necessary for a candidate first to win a party's primary in order to run in a special election. Party labels do not appear next to the names of candidates in these elections. Inevitably, special elections attract a large field of office seekers. With widespread competition the norm, it is difficult for a candidate to receive a majority of the vote. Hence, runoffs between the two leading candidates are commonplace. In 1993, a special election was called to fill the U.S. Senate seat vacated when Lloyd Bentsen was appointed Secretary of the Treasury in the Clinton administration. The special election ballot, held in May of that year, contained the names of 24 candidates, including Democrat Bob Krueger, who had been appointed by Governor Ann Richards to replace Bentsen. Krueger was eventually beaten in a runoff by Republican Kay Bailey Hutchison.

Voter Eligibility

Texas has had a checkered past where voter eligibility is concerned. Until the 1970s, certain segments of society, especially the poor, African Americans, and Hispanics, were systematically excluded from voting in the state. Between 1902 and 1966, for example, Texans had to pay a poll tax, ranging from $1.50 to $2.05 depending upon the geographical area, to vote. The tax was collected between October 1 and January 31 during an election year. In 1967, the poll tax was replaced by a formidable registration law: "one of the most, if not the most, restrictive among the fifty states in terms of voter convenience."[1] Before 1972, Texans had to register between October 1 and January 31 of each election year. Severe limitations were imposed on actual registration, such as requiring personal appearances at the county courthouse during business hours. Finally, the "white primary" allowed a political party to exclude nonwhites from voting in its primary. Until 1944, the Democratic party, then the dominant party in the state, permitted only whites to vote in its primary. Obviously, this practice denied African Americans and members of other minority groups the right to meaningful participation in the Texas electoral system.

The good news is that all these restrictions have been eliminated. The bad news is that in every case we have mentioned, the impetus for change came from outside the state. The poll tax began to fade after the Twenty-fourth Amendment to the U.S. Constitution was passed by Congress and ratified by three fourths of the states. Even though this amendment legally eliminated the poll tax entirely, Texas continued to require it for state and local elections. A federal court eventually ordered a ban on the poll tax in all elections.[2] Texans finally approved an amendment to the state constitution prohibiting the tax in 1966. The "white primary" was held unconstitutional by the U.S. Supreme Court in the case of *Smith v. Allwright.*

The push to liberalize Texas's voter registration law also came from a federal court.[3] Under the close watch of this court, the Texas Legislature, in 1973, enacted a more relaxed registration law. These changes expanded the period of time during which potential voters could register and eliminated annual registration and the restrictions on the places where they could register. Assuming that other legal standards are met (i.e., a person is age 18 or older, a citizen of the U.S., and a resident of the state), any person can register, as long as this occurs at least thirty days before an election. Registration through the mail or at convenient neighborhood locations is permissible. Immediate relatives may register for a person. Motor-voter laws are also in place, allowing Texans to register when they obtain or renew their driver's licenses. Reregistration has also been made much easier.

★★★★★ VOTER TURNOUT

Despite the easing of restrictions on voting, turnout for elections in Texas is low. It has consistently lagged behind national turnout rates in presidential elections, for instance. In the 1996 contest among Bill Clinton, Bob Dole, and Texan H. Ross Perot, less than a majority (some 43 percent) of eligible Texans voted, about 6 percent below the national average. Texas consistently ranks low among all states in presidential vote turnout.

More troublesome, the presidential election is usually the high-water mark for voting turnout. Statewide races rarely attract more than one third of the eligible voters. For instance, only 34 percent of the voting-age population turned out for the 1994 gubernatorial contest between Ann Richards and George W. Bush. Local elections fare much worse. Commonly less than 10 percent of voters participate in school board, city council, and even mayoral elections in Texas.

Voting figures tallied in the 1994 Republican and Democratic party primaries typify the pattern of low turnout in Texas. There were 72 contests for state or federal offices to be decided by the voters in that year's primaries. Fully 188 candidates ran for these positions. Nonetheless, no more than 11.2 percent of voting-age Texans went to the polling booths in the first primary; only about 7 percent voted in the runoffs. This lack of participation affects, among other things, the operations of party organizations in Texas, a topic to which we shall now turn.

★ ★ ★ ★ ★   PARTY ORGANIZATION

The formal structure of Texas's two major political parties, the Democrats and the Republicans, is designed to promote close contact with voters. As outlined in Figure 3–1, party organization forms around voters who participate in the selection of the party leadership. A citizen becomes a member of a political party in Texas simply by voting in that party's primary. This act entitles the voter to attend the party's precinct convention, which is held the night of the primary (the first Tuesday of March in even-numbered years).

Precinct Conventions

Texas's 254 counties are divided into about 8,700 precincts, each containing between 50 and 3,500 registered voters. A very small number of people attend precinct conventions. One statewide study found that 10 percent of Texans who voted in the primary also participated in precinct conventions held that night. Slightly more Republicans than Democrats (5 percent) went to precinct meetings.[4] The main task of the precinct meeting is to choose representatives to attend the party's county convention. A precinct is allowed one delegate at the county convention for every twenty-five votes received by the party's candidate in the precinct at the last general election for governor.

County Conventions

The county convention is held on the second Saturday after the second Tuesday in March of even-numbered years. The larger counties of Texas, such as Tarrant, Harris, Dallas, and Bexar, contain so many people that, for organizational purposes, they are divided into districts. These districts coincide with the geographical boundaries of the state senatorial lines located in the county. Each of these districts holds the equivalent of a county convention. The major function of the district or county convention is the selection of delegates to the party's state convention. The number of delegates allocated to each county or district is again determined by the number of votes received in the last governor's race by the party's candidate. A county or district is allowed one delegate to the state convention for every 300 to 660 votes cast for the party's gubernatorial candidate within its boundaries.

✪ **FIGURE 3–1**
Party Structure in Texas

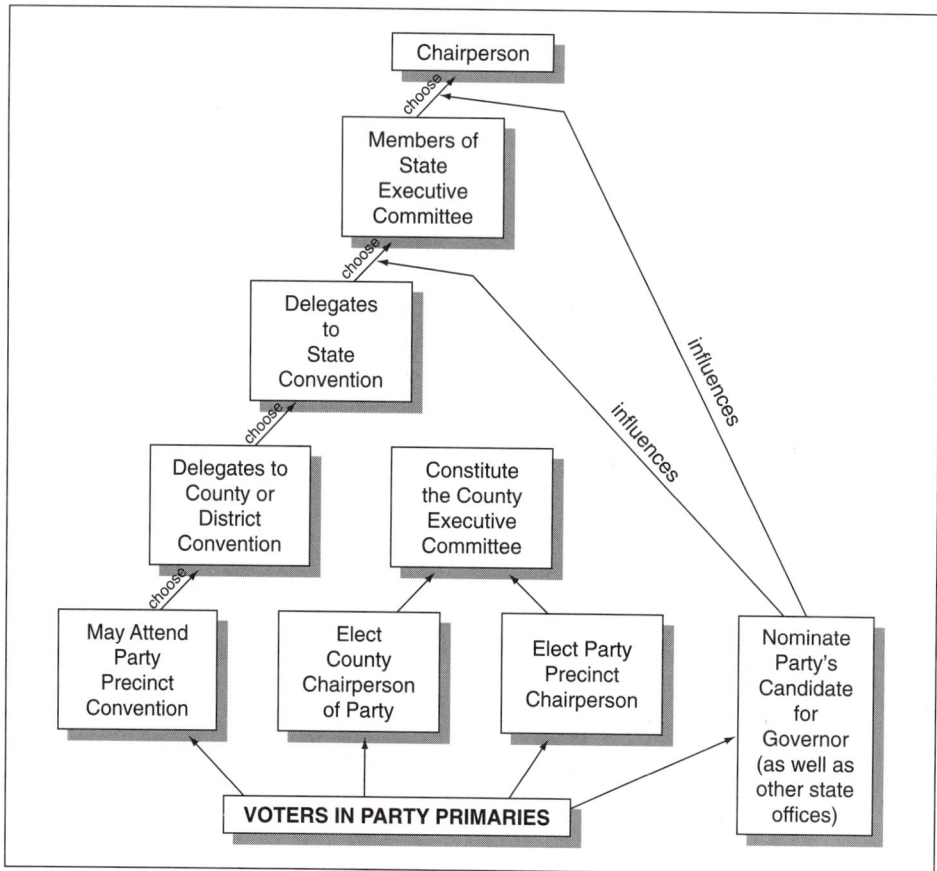

State Convention

The state convention of each major party, which meets every June in even-numbered years, performs the following tasks. In presidential years, the convention selects delegates to attend the party's national nominating convention—electors pledged to vote for the party's presidential candidate if he or she wins the presidential race in Texas—and a committeeman and a committeewoman to serve on the party's national committee. Delegates at the state convention also validate the names of the party's victorious candidates for statewide offices decided in its March primary, and forward this list to the Office of the Secretary of State for inclusion on the general election ballot. Finally, the state convention formulates the party's platform (a document stating the party's stands on issues) and chooses its state leadership, including the party chair, the vice-chair, and members of its state executive committee.

Party Leadership

Low turnout for primaries and, especially, for the precinct conventions seriously weakens the links between party leaders and the general public. Not unexpectedly, a small minority of leaders actually run and control party activities in Texas.

At the lowest level, the precinct chairs, who are elected by the few Texans voting in the primaries, become the leaders. Elected for two years, each precinct chair is expected to conduct party business, such as raising money, recruiting candidates, getting out the vote, and promoting the party, at the precinct level. The effectiveness of the precinct chair depends on personal motivation and local pressure. For instance, these leaders are generally more energetic in competitive party precincts.

The next level in the party hierarchy is the county executive committee, which is composed of all precinct chairs in the area and the county chair. This group conducts the party's county convention and oversees its primary. The single most important leader at the local level in the party organization is the county chair, who is elected for a two-year term by voters in the party's primary. Recruiting candidates, mobilizing the vote, and collecting campaign donations, as well as presiding over the county executive committee, are among the more important jobs of these leaders.

The state executive committee, which is chosen at the state convention, is the highest organizational unit in the party. The committee is composed of sixty-two people, two from each of the state's thirty-one senatorial districts. The caucus from each of these districts elects its two representatives—a man and a woman—to the state executive committee. The foremost official in the party is the chair of the state executive committee. The party's chair and vice-chair, one of whom must be a woman, are officially selected by the delegates at the state convention.

All members of the state executive committee, including the chair and vice-chair, serve two-year terms. The party's candidate for governor, especially if he or she is the incumbent, has a considerable amount of influence, if not full control, over the composition of the state executive committee and, especially, the naming of the party's chair and vice-chair.

It is the responsibility of the state executive committee to lead the party through the performance of all its major functions: raising funds, recruiting candidates, receiving the applications of candidates who want to run in the party's primary, getting out the vote, formulating the party's stands on issues, and coordinating the layers of the party organization, from the federal to the local level, including organizing the party's state convention.

In short, party organization in Texas is formally structured along democratic lines. The voters have ample opportunity to influence party operations and activities. However, because of low rates of voter participation, the party organization and the actual performance of the party's functions are largely left in the hands of a small cadre, thus lending a strong elitist cast to electoral and party process in Texas.

★★★★★ THE CHALLENGES OF LOW TURNOUT

The ranks of the nonvoters are swelled by the impoverished and the members of Texas's minority populations, especially Hispanics. As indicated in Table 3–1, non-Hispanic whites are overrepresented among the registered and actual voters. Anglos comprise two thirds of the state's voting-age population, 74 percent of its registered voters, and 76.4 percent of its voters. Hispanics make up 23 percent of Texas's eligible voters, but only 15 percent of its registered voters and 13.6 percent of its actual voters. Moreover, only about 40 percent of the poor, as measured by low educational levels, anticipated voting in the 1992 presidential election, as compared with the 84 percent of college graduates who said they would be voting.

Poverty often breeds a preoccupation with one's own well-being and a lack of interest in the political world, which is perceived by most of the poor as distant and alien. In the case of racial and ethnic minorities, this indifference is often reinforced by the painful reminder that the state once, and not very long ago, legally excluded most of them from participation in the political process. A legacy of discrimination does not die quickly in people's minds. Ignorance, lack of interest, and apathy were cited by 46 percent of a sample of nonvoters in the 1982 state primaries as reasons for their lack of participation. The minority of Texans who voted in the primaries did so out of a sense of civic duty.[5]

Concerted attempts have been made to improve voting turnout in Texas. Several organizations, such as the Southwest Voter Registration Educa-

★ **TABLE 3–1**
Voting Participation, Ethnicity, and Education*

Ethnic Background	Percent Eligible	Percent Registered	Percent Voting
Anglo	66	74	76.4
Hispanic	23	15	13.6
African American	11	11	10

Said Would Vote in 1992 Presidential Race Education Level:	Yes	No	
Little or No High School	40%	60%	
College Graduate	84%	16%	

SOURCES: Southwest Voter Research Institute, *Dallas Morning News,* April 26, 1993, p. A-13, and *Texas Poll,* May 1992, p. 2.
*Actual participation in the 1992 presidential contest.

tion Project, have spearheaded successful drives to register a greater number of eligible citizens to vote. Currently, 71 percent of Texas's voting-age population is registered, a figure 11 percent higher than that recorded in the late 1970s. Texas has also liberalized its absentee voting procedures. Starting in 1988, any Texan could cast an absentee ballot at any time during the three weeks preceding an election without actually being absent from his or her place of residence on election day. As a consequence, *early voting* has been greatly facilitated in Texas. Since 1991, early voting may take place at several different locations, including county offices, shopping malls, grocery stores, or mobile units that move around Texas. In the state election held in November 1994, it is estimated that one third of the total votes were cast through early voting.[6]

Even given these efforts and innovations, voting in Texas lags behind that in most of the nation. Part of the reason might be the lack of meaningful choices offered in Texas's elections. People with little interest in politics and historically scarred by systematic exclusion may need a jolt to join the ranks of electoral participants. The presence of substantial ballot alternatives might galvanize the apathetic, erase memories of the past, and encourage registration and actual voting.

★ ★ ★ ★ ★ PARTY COMPETITION

There are signs of growth in electoral competition in Texas, principally as a result of the development of a two-party system in the state. After Reconstruction ended in the 1870s, Texas was firmly in the grip of the Democratic party. Republican rule after the Civil War, as we have discussed in Chapter 1, had been characterized by an unpleasant combination of corruption, tyranny, ineffectiveness, and violence. Most white Texans were quick to reject it. With the imposition of state laws barring nonwhites from meaningful political participation in Texas, Republicans were denied a natural constituency among black Texans to build a lasting power base for the "party of Abraham Lincoln."

Loyalty to the Democratic party soon became deeply embedded in Texas's political culture. Identification with the Democrats was transmitted from generation to generation; this practice made one-party dominance a prominent feature of the state's political landscape and produced the ever-reliable "yellow-dog Democrats," who would rather vote for a yellow dog than for any Republican candidate. However, this is no longer the case. The Republican party has emerged in the last two decades as a formidable force in Texas politics. Indicators of this change abound.

There was a time when very few Texans voted in the Republican primaries. In 1972, for example, only 114,000 voters cast ballots in the G.O.P. presidential primary; fully 2.2 million people voted in the Democratic primary that year. Fast-forward to 1996: with 921,256 Texans voting in the Democratic presidential primary and 1 million in the Republican presidential primary, party parity is obvious.[7] Likewise, psychological identification with a party has undergone a dramatic transformation in Texas. In 1964, only 8 percent of the state's voting-age public called themselves Republicans, as compared with the 65 percent who said they were Democrats. Thirty years later, 30 percent identified themselves as Democrats and 29 percent as Republicans.[8] Even more to the point, Republicans have begun to win far more elections in Texas.

At the federal level, Texas has supported the Republican candidate for president in every election since 1976. Since 1961, one of the two U.S. Senators from Texas has been a Republican; since 1993, both Senators have been from the Republican party. Of the 30 members of the U.S. House of Representatives elected in Texas in 1996, fourteen are Republicans, including the highly influential majority leader of the House, Dick Armey (Lewisville).

At the state level, in 1978 Bill Clements became the first Republican to be elected governor since Reconstruction, a feat he repeated in 1986. George W. Bush continued the Republican presence by defeating Ann Richards in the 1994 gubernatorial race. That election also resulted in a Republican sweep of the three seats on the Texas Railroad Commission and a G.O.P. majority on the State Board of Education. Although the leader of the Texas Senate, Lieutenant Governor Bob Bullock, is a Democrat, the voters in 1996 elected a Republican majority in the Texas upper house, something that had not happened in 125 years. The G.O.P. also made a strong showing in races for Texas's House of Representatives: 68 of the 151 members elected in 1996 were Republicans. Following the 1996 election, six of the nine members of the state's Court of Criminal Appeals are Republicans and the G.O.P. has a seven-to-two edge over the Democrats in Texas's Supreme Court. By 1991, 159 of the seats on the state's 380 district courts were occupied by Republicans, and since that time the number of G.O.P. members holding these judicial positions has increased.[9]

The future for the Republican party looks equally bright. The party is drawing its followers disproportionately from prosperous younger, urban, white (non-Hispanic) segments of the Texas population. A large share of the state's growing number of "yuppies" is Republican. The G.O.P. is also more attractive to people who have moved into the state within the last decade and to Texans flocking to the suburbs that are growing rapidly in the Houston, Dallas–Fort Worth, and Austin areas.

Meanwhile, the strength of the Democratic party lies increasingly in the state's minority population, especially among African Americans and Hispanics.[10] As noted by one commentator, "Mexican Americans are now the dominant faction in the Democratic party."[11] To be sure, the party still retains support among older Texans, in particular those living in rural settings. However, this is not a particularly strong population base on which to build the party's future. Among other things (such as mortality), there is every indication that the traditional rural constituency of the Democrats is eroding as the party aligns itself with the interests of minority groups.[12] Finally, the largest group of Texans to become Republicans in the 1980s were people who had previously called themselves conservative Democrats.[13]

The Republican party has put a great deal of effort into expanding its support base. Both nationally and in Texas, the G.O.P. has raised and spent substantial sums on public opinion polls, media advertisements, and canvassing of citizens using phone interviews.[14] In Texas, the party has developed an extensive computer data bank containing names of all of the state's 10 million registered voters.[15] With this information readily at hand, the party can easily contact potential voters to collect more data and is well positioned to assist its candidates in their campaigns. The state's Republicans are also more effective than its Democrats in contacting their party faithful, in soliciting campaign contributions, in persuading voters to work for the party organization, in getting their followers to write letters to officeholders, and in turning out the vote on Election Day.[16]

★★★★★ # LIMITS ON COMPETITION

The transformation of the party system in the Texas electorate has resulted in two-party competition. Republicans and Democrats now appear to be more evenly matched in electoral contests than they have been in the state's recent past. However, the extent to which electoral competition actually exists can still be questioned. Reapportionment and gerrymandering, at-large elections, ideological similarity among candidates, a lack of minor-party alternatives, and the influence of business elites in candidate selection combine to limit electoral choice in Texas. Each of these points requires elaboration.

Reapportionment and Gerrymandering

Many officeholders in Texas are elected from geographically defined districts. All 181 members of the state legislature come from such districts, for example. The lines drawn to form these districts are the work of the Texas Legislature, subject to approval by courts and by the U.S. Department of Justice. Redistricting, or *reapportionment,* which is the drawing of district lines to accommodate any population shifts that may have occurred, is done every ten years, immediately after the national census is taken.

The findings of the last census, completed in 1990, were provided to the Texas Legislature in April 1991. The legislature completed its reapportionment exercise by the end of its 1991 regular session. In the past, reapportionment at the state level often resulted in the creation of great disparities between the numbers of people living in different districts and of districts that were able to elect more than one representative for each. Today, after many years of legal controversy, districts must be roughly equal in terms of population size and each district is to be represented by only one legislator. There are 150 districts for the House, one for every representative; each contains about 117,000 people. There are 31 separate senatorial districts; each elects one senator and encompasses approximately 566,000 constituents.

A bigger problem that must be addressed by reapportionment is *gerrymandering* (see Highlight 3–1), which is the practice of drawing districts to improve or harm the electoral chances of certain groups. The most likely types of groups affected by gerrymandering are racial, ethnic, and party groups. Almost inevitably, reapportionment plans are challenged on the basis of bias, either for or against a group. The 1991 reapportionment plan developed by the Texas Legislature was no exception.

First, Hispanic organizations claimed that the 1991 redistricting scheme curtailed the representational opportunities of Mexican Americans in Texas. A revised redistricting plan was subsequently denounced by Republicans who believed their party's electoral chances were being thwarted. Yet another revised redistricting scheme was attacked by Democrats who argued that now *their* party's electoral opportunities were being unfairly limited. A plan drawn by a panel of three federal judges was used in the 1992 state legislative races. A final plan, heavily influenced by Democrats, was used in the 1994 Texas Senate races.

Regardless of their genesis, reapportionment plans rarely create fairly proportioned districts. As a consequence, voters participate in legislative elections in which the deck has, in many cases, already been stacked. In 1996, for instance, of the twenty-five races conducted in Harris County for a seat in the Texas House or Senate, only one contest was competitive. In sixteen of these elections, the incumbents faced no opposition in the general election. In the remaining eight, incumbents outdistanced their opponents by a wide margin. According to political scientist Richard Murray, because of redistricting, Harris County has "virtually no competitive districts—they're wired to be safe for the incumbents."[17] It is little wonder that some eligible voters might refuse to become involved in such a one-sided affair. If districts were drawn to maximize competition, voter turnout might improve.

At-Large Elections

Many officeholders in Texas are not elected from geographic districts. Rather, they are elected *at large;* that is, from a general area, such as a county or a city. In at-large elections, several officials running for a governing body, such as a city council, are elected by all of the voters in the area. At-large elections are commonly held in Texas to elect candidates to school boards, local governing units, and courts. Most officials elected at-large are from white, non-Hispanic, middle-class backgrounds, even when their areas contain sizable low-income, minority populations. Consequently, at-large elections blunt the competitive edge of elections.

★ ★ ★

Highlight 3–1: Gerrymandering
The term *gerrymandering* comes from the 1812 Massachusetts reapportionment scheme, which, when drawn on paper, resembled a salamander. The odd shape prompted a newspaper editor to christen the plan a "gerrymander," after the governor of the state at that time, Elbridge Gerry. The name has stuck because of the continuing practice of creating outlandish-looking geographical districts.

Ideological Similarity

Parties and voters often differ in their political commitments, principles, and beliefs. A frequently used way of characterizing groups and individuals separates them into conservatives and liberals. These ideological groups differ along economic, social, personal, and political lines.

Economically, a conservative opposes direct government intervention in economic matters (especially pricing, profits, and wages), labor unions, most government regulations affecting business and the environment, and tax increases. A liberal envisions the government as playing a more active role in stimulating and regulating the economy, even if its actions mean higher taxes (preferably imposed on the wealthy).

A conservative shows little enthusiasm for government programs—for instance, affirmative action schemes—designed to alleviate the suffering of certain groups, such as the impoverished, women, and members of minorities. Liberals, on the other hand, view such programs as the best ways to overcome barriers that have denied social and economic opportunity to many members of these groups. Conservatives endorse government involvement in some personal activities, such as protecting unborn children and preserving public morality. They oppose laws designed to prevent discrimination against gays and lesbians. Liberals object to laws that restrict most personal behavior.

Politically, conservatives support a strong military. They also approve of government expenditures to increase a police presence and to incarcerate criminals. Liberals oppose a large defense budget, preferring instead that government spend its revenue on improving public services in areas such as education, transportation, and health. They also see law and order as a social and economic problem, solvable more by improving the societal conditions that lead to crime than by hiring additional police or building more prisons.

By and large, Texans are more conservative than liberal. A 1994 poll found that 38 percent of Texans considered themselves conservative, while only 17 percent identified themselves as liberal. Thirty-eight percent called themselves moderate.[18] A survey completed in 1982 gave Texans more ideological choices and found that 70 percent could be classified as at least "somewhat conservative." Almost all Republicans and nearly 62 percent of Democrats were in the conservative camp.[19] Consequently, for candidates running for office, "victory is gained by trying to convince the electorate that a candidate is more conservative than his opponent."[20] The two major political parties in Texas certainly use this strategy.

Within the Democratic party, the conservative wing has traditionally been dominant. Overwhelmingly, Democratic candidates elected to state offices have been identified with the conservative wing of their party. The rise of the Republican party to electoral prominence in Texas has not meant a deviation from conservative thinking. Rather, "the Republican party can best be described as having a conservative wing and a more conservative wing."[21]

Hence the similar conservative ideologies found among most successful candidates, whether they are Democrats or Republicans, limit choice for the voters. On the other hand, this conservative tilt is very advantageous for business interests in Texas. Conservatives virtually never challenge the privileged position granted to the business community by government. Moreover, conservatives raise few objections to specific policies such as the absence of a corporate income tax and the presence of "right-to-work" (anti-union) labor laws, both of which directly benefit business. Candidates may differ over which business interest (say, petroleum versus high tech) should be given the highest priority by state government, but a challenge to the preeminence accorded to business overall is rarely disputed in an election.

A large number of the leading candidates for important political positions are from the conservative business community. This is particularly evident among the top contenders for the position of governor. With a background deeply rooted in the rancher/business community of Texas, Democrat Dolph Briscoe, governor from 1972 until 1978, held impeccable conservative credentials. Briscoe's successor, William P. Clements, Jr. (governor from 1978 until 1982 and again from 1986 to 1990), came into politics directly from the corporate world. In 1947, he had founded SEDCO, which became one of the world's largest oil services companies. In 1986, he negotiated the sale of his company (for some $1.1 billion) to Schlumberger, a major oil services firm located in the Netherlands. At various times he was on the board of directors of one of Texas's leading banks, InterFirst (now NationsBank). His wife, Rita Crocker Clements, is on the board of directors of Bank One and serves on the University of Texas Board of Regents. Clayton Williams, the Republican candidate for governor in the 1990 election, has substantial business holdings in land, cattle breeding (the eleventh largest such operation in America), commercial cow production (seventh largest in the U.S.), petroleum, and telecommunications.[22] Governor George W. Bush comes from a prosperous background. His father, former President George Bush, created and developed Zapata Oil, once a major oil service company in Texas. The younger Bush, a graduate of Yale University, has been involved in many business ventures, including exploration for oil and ownership of the Texas Rangers baseball team.

To be sure, there is a liberal coalition in Texas and, at times, it has effectively mobilized some candidates.[23] The usual scenario has been success at the primary level for liberal Democrats, followed by defeat in primary runoffs. The process, as noted by historian George Norris Green, has been as follows:

> Several conservative candidates split the conservative vote in the first Democratic primary, allowing the lone liberal to get into the runoff with the leading conservative. The conservative vote and money and newspapers then coalesce behind the conservative candidate in the second primary, defeating the liberal, who invariably runs out of money and who never had any press support.[24]

On the rare occasions when liberals win in Texas, they are pressured by the Texan conservative establishment once they are in office. Some, such as former governor Ann Richards, remain on good terms with this establishment by not antagonizing conservative and business interests. Others, such as former governor Pappy O'Daniel (see Highlight 3–2), make disingenuous appeals to the liberal coalition while running for office, only to neglect their promises after election. When a liberal candidate confronts business directly, wins, and once in office abides by his or her electoral promises, there is usually a price to be paid. The rise and fall of Jim Hightower illustrates this situation.

Jim Hightower cut his eyeteeth in liberal politics. His earliest forays into electoral politics were made as an activist in the campaigns of Ralph Yarborough (Texas's foremost liberal U.S. senator in this century) and of progressive Fred Harris, who unsuccessfully contested the presidency in 1976. Hightower devoted much of his time revealing corporate malfeasance, especially in agriculture.[25] As editor of the state's leading progressive newspaper, *The Texas Observer,* he continued his assault on corporations. Noting in his farewell editorial that "there comes a time when writing about the bastards isn't enough,"[26] Hightower resigned his position at the *Observer* to become director of the Texas Consumers Union.

Hightower formally entered politics in 1980, when he announced his candidacy for the Democratic party nomination for the Texas Railroad Commission. He barely lost in the primary to Jim Nugent. His 1982 campaign against the incumbent commissioner of agriculture, Reagan Brown, fared much better. Hightower beat Brown by a comfortable majority in the primary and was elected commissioner of agriculture in the general election.

After election, one of Hightower's first actions was to reassure agribusiness and chemical firms that he would operate the Department of Agriculture in a sound, reasonable, nonthreatening manner. For instance, he sent this message to Harry Whitmore, Director of the Texas Chemical Council: "Look, I want to get along with you. I want agriculture in Texas to be improved, and I realize that you fellas have a big stake in it. You

━━━━━━━━━━━━━━━━━━━━━ ★ ★ ★ ━━━━━━━━━━━━━━━━━━━━━

Highlight 3–2: The Case of Wilbert Lee "Pappy" O'Daniel

Pappy O'Daniel was a man of many talents. Before entering politics, he managed a flour mill and led a country-and-western band, the Light Crust Doughboys, which included among its members the legendary Bob Wills. He also had a weekly radio show, during which he offered advice and counsel to his listeners. In 1938, as the Democratic primary approached, he asked his listeners if he should run for governor. Overwhelmingly, they said yes. O'Daniel's platform ostensibly attacked business privilege. Among other things, he campaigned against the poll tax, "saying that no politician was worth $1.75."[1] Indeed, he never paid the poll tax and thus was not eligible to vote in his own election. He also spoke in favor of the Ten Commandments and pensions for the elderly, and against imposing a sales tax on Texas consumers. Without a campaign manager or headquarters, he easily won the Democratic primary and, given the lack of much Republican competition, the general election. He was reelected governor in 1940.

O'Daniel deliberately cultivated his image as a "good ol' boy," a man of the people, a friend of the farmer, the downtrodden, and the elderly. Beneath that image, however, there was another side to O'Daniel. His financial backing came mostly from wealthy sources in Texas. For example, his major benefactor in his initial race for governor was the chairman of the board of the Fidelity Union Life Insurance Company, at the time one of the state's largest. When the river of money ran dry, O'Daniel's political career came to an abrupt halt. Moreover, once in office, he did little to ease the plight of less fortunate Texans. While he was governor, his old-age pension plan was never pushed very hard. His campaign promise not to impose a sales tax was quickly broken when he introduced just such a measure to the Texas Legislature, calling it a "transaction tax."

Listening to O'Daniel, voters might have thought he was challenging the rich on behalf of the poor. Certainly his listeners were captivated by his words. V. O. Key, Jr., says of O'Daniel, "Backed by a few wealthy men, he won the votes of many poor men [and women]. He talked the language of the lesser people, but on the whole he acted and voted [like] a *Chicago Tribune* Republican."[2] Equally important, the 1938 election of Pappy O'Daniel to the governor's office marked the time when "corporate interests took over the state, once and for all, perhaps permanently."[3]

Notes

1. William Earl Maxwell and Ernest Crain, *Texas Politics Today* (St. Paul, MN: West Publishing Co., 1978), p. 26.
2. V.O. Key, Jr., *Southern Politics* (New York, NY: Vintage, 1949), p. 271.
3. George Norris Green, *The Establishment in Texas Politics* (Norman, OK: University of Oklahoma Press, 1979), pp. 16–17.

───

don't need to worry about me doing anything crazy."[27] At least for a while, Whitmore seemed placated, commenting, "I don't see him [Hightower] as carried away with liberalism. He wants to do a good job. I don't think he'd let beliefs get in the way."[28]

Once in office, Hightower did institute some changes. He attempted to aid family farmers by establishing markets through which they could sell their produce directly to the public. He expanded the workforce at the agriculture department and increased the percentage of minority members hired.[29] His most far-reaching action was the imposition of new rules on the spraying of Texas farmland with pesticides, rules that require warnings before pesticides are used, intervals between sprayings, and the labeling of chemicals found in pesticides. These new rules angered many agribusiness and chemical interests. Hightower faced some fairly stiff opposition in his 1986 reelection bid, but won nonetheless.

In the late 1980s, the Texas Legislature became noticeably hostile toward the Department of Agriculture. An unsuccessful effort was made to replace the commissioner of agriculture (Jim Hightower) with a fifteen-member board. In 1990, both the FBI and a specially convened grand jury investigated the activities of the Department of Agriculture. Defenders of Hightower claimed that these investigations were part of a concerted effort, led by the Texas Farm Bureau and various political officials in the administration of President George Bush, to discredit the commissioner. Hightower commented, "they're doing this because we're nicking them where it hurts."[30] Opponents of Hightower rallied to support the Republican challenger, Rick Perry, in the 1990 contest for commissioner of agriculture. Perry beat Hightower, much to the delight of many, including Texas Farm Bureau President S. M. True, who stated, "we feel that our job ended when we got Rick Perry elected."[31]

In short, conservative ideology has a tight grip on Texas's electoral politics. Many Texans hold conservative values, and the electoral chances of candidates improve if they embrace conservatism. As a result, leading candidates do not offer a great deal of ideological choice to the voters. For members of the public holding nonconservative political perspectives, elections are frequently perceived as noncompetitive.

Minor Parties

Minor parties, or "third parties," tend to be issue-oriented. They usually arise to offer voters alternatives to the policies and ideas advanced by established, major parties and candidates. Although Texas history has been rich in third-party activity, such as that of the Greenbackers, Populists, Prohibitionists, States' Righters, Communists, Socialist Workers, members of George Wallace's American Independent Party, and *La Raza Unida* (discussed in Highlight 3–3), the life span of minor parties has generally been brief. There are four main reasons for this state of affairs.

First, it is fairly difficult to get—and stay—on the ballot in Texas. Ballot access for a minor party or an independent candidate requires the completion of several steps. Initially, voters must sign a petition supporting the inclusion of the names of third-party or independent candidates on the ballot. The number of signatures required for a third-party candidate to get on the state ballot equals one percent of the total vote count in the last gubernatorial race. In 1994, for instance, 4.4 million votes were cast in the gubernatorial election. A petition drive conducted between 1994 and 1998 for ballot access would require nearly 44,000 signatures. (See Highlight 3–4, on Ross Perot's efforts to get his name on the Texas ballot.) Only registered voters are eligible to sign the petition. Moreover, individuals voting in either the Republican or the Democratic primary are not eligible. The petition is sent to the Secretary of State's office for the signatures to be ver-

━━━━━━━━━━━━━━━━━━━━━ ★ ★ ★ ━━━━━━━━━━━━━━━━━━━━━

Highlight 3–3: *La Raza Unida*

The most successful minor party in Texas in recent years was *La Raza Unida*. This party was formed in the late 1960s and lasted about a decade. It was principally organized to represent the interests of Hispanics living in South Texas, and managed to win several local offices in Zavala County. *La Raza Unida* also fielded candidates at the state level. Although it failed to capture any statewide offices, the party did affect some state electoral outcomes. For instance, in the 1972 and 1974 gubernatorial races, its candidate, Ramsey Muniz, collected 6.3 percent and 5.4 percent, respectively, of the total votes cast, almost enough to keep the Democrats from winning. Its 1978 candidate received less than 1 percent of the vote, but this margin probably hurt the Democrats and helped Bill Clements become the state's first Republican governor in more than 100 years.

Throughout its brief history, *La Raza Unida* was plagued with problems. State officials blocked some of its key plans, such as the establishment of a collective farm in Zavala County. Internal discord fractured the party. Ramsey Muniz was sentenced to prison after pleading guilty to a drug offense. Charges of political corruption were leveled at some of its other leaders. Electoral defeats mounted, and by the early 1980s, the party was only a fading memory.

Notes

1. John Shockley, *Chicano Revolt in a Texas Town* (Notre Dame, IN: University of Notre Dame Press, 1974).
2. Tom Curtis, "Raza Disunida," reprinted in the *Texas Monthly's Political Reader* (Austin, TX: Texas Monthly Press and Sterling Swift Press, 1978).

---

ified. To facilitate the petition process, third-party and independent candidates turn to firms that gather signatures—at a cost of $2.25 per signature. To remain on the ballot, minor parties must receive at least 2 percent of the total vote. Failure to reach this figure means that the third party must start from scratch to get on the ballot for the next election.

Second, Texas elections are based upon the "winner take all" principle. That is, the victor is the candidate who amasses the greatest number of votes in the general election. Losers receive no rewards for their efforts. Since third parties rarely win when they initially appear on the ballot, it becomes very discouraging for their supporters to stick with them. Many people are reluctant to waste their votes and soon abandon (or never join) a new party. In electoral systems with *proportional representation*, whereby offices are allotted on the basis of the percentage of votes won in the general election, the life span of third parties is ordinarily longer.

Third, if a minor party gains a place on the ballot, attracts voters, and has a good chance of winning office, the established parties frequently will adopt its issue stands. This process, often referred to as *co-optation*, frequently spells defeat for the third party. Not surprisingly, when an established party co-opts the positions of a third party, it usually dilutes the issue stands of the latter.

Fourth, successful third parties that resist co-optation may find themselves being repressed by entrenched authorities. *Political repression* is the

★ ★ ★

Highlight 3–4: Ross Perot and Ballot Access

A petition placing the name of an independent candidate on the presidential ballot requires a number of signatures equal to 1 percent of the total vote in the last presidential race conducted in Texas. Ross Perot's supporters needed 54,200 signatures to qualify him for inclusion on the 1992 ballot. All told, they secured 228,219 signatures, less than half of which were certified by the Office of the Secretary of State as valid. In 1996, 61,540 valid signatures were needed to get on the ballot. It was required that those signing the petition be registered to vote and not have voted in the March presidential primaries of either the Democrats or the Republicans. In 1996, Perot's Reform Party abandoned efforts to put its name on the 1996 ballot, mainly because party members were reluctant to conduct conventions and hold primaries — activities that are required if the party gains ballot access. Perot's supporters instead chose to list their candidate as an independent on the Texas ballot. At least 48,000 of the signatures collected in this effort were obtained through the work of paid professionals.

In 1992, Perot received 22 percent of the presidential votes in Texas; four years later, his share of the vote dropped to 6 percent.

actual or threatened use of physical force, harassment, intimidation, or ideological manipulation by those in government. It is designed to eliminate the opposition from the political arena.

Business Influences and Candidate Recruitment

The direct recruitment of candidates by members of the business community focuses on screening those who aspire to elected office. Recruiting usually occurs far in advance of party primaries, in informal, private settings. One observer of this screening process notes, "The acceptable candidate must be born or educated into the middle or upper classes, displaying the linguistic and social styles of bourgeois personage. This requirement effectively limits the selection to business and professional people."[32]

Throughout much of this century, an informal cadre of economic notables, known as the "Suite 8F Crowd," routinely conducted screening tests in Texas to recruit candidates. Members of this group met for more than forty years in a suite of rooms numbered 8F in Houston's Lamar Hotel. George Brown, founder of Brown and Root (now owned by Halliburton), was the leader of the Suite 8F Crowd. Other members included founders of many of Texas's leading firms, including Texas Commerce Bank (now owned by the Chase Manhattan Corporation of New York), Tenneco, and American General Insurance. Collectively, they "called the shots on the most major business and political developments in Texas during the Thirties, Forties, Fifties and much of the Sixties."[33] They also groomed a distinguished stable of political warhorses, including former president Lyndon B. Johnson, former Texas governor John Connally, and Sam Rayburn (former Speaker of both the Texas and the U.S. House of Representatives).

Although the Suite 8F Crowd has now vanished, other business-oriented groups continue to screen candidates. The state's leading law firms, for example, help recruit candidates whose views are compatible with those of their corporate clients. The Big Three law firms of Houston—Vinson and Elkins, Fulbright and Jaworski, and Baker and Botts—are active in the screening process. According to a former state legislator,

> All the state officials go down and see them hat in hand. . . . You have to go through the firm before you can get to the client. . . . If the firm approves, you got access to the client. Unless you . . . get their blessings, you couldn't get the money from the client.[34]

This type of recruiting is commonplace throughout Texas, although it is usually hidden from public view.[35] As we will discuss in greater detail in Chapter 10, the Chamber of Commerce in Houston and the Dallas Citizens Council have been deeply involved in the candidate selection process. Failure to be invited to, or to pass, the screening test restricts the opportunities of potential candidates in Texas, primarily their ability to raise campaign contributions—a topic we will explore in detail in Chapter 4.

★ ★ ★ ★ ★   ## CONCLUSION

Widespread voter participation is not characteristic of Texas elections. Although past restrictions on voting in the state have been eased in recent years, most eligible voters, especially the poor and members of minority groups, still do not cast ballots or engage in party activity. Full-scale competition between the Democratic and Republican parties now exists, after a long period in the state's history during which the Democrats dominated state politics. However, voter choice is limited through reapportionment and gerrymandering, at-large elections, ideological similarity between the candidates of the two major political parties, a lack of minor parties, and the impact of candidate screening by business leaders.

Overall, a conservative ideology permeates electoral politics in the state. Candidate selection has traditionally been the province of a conservative bloc, "a loosely knit plutocracy comprised mostly of Anglo businessmen, oilmen, bankers, and lawyers."[36] Indeed, an elitist pattern is evident in other electoral activities; for instance, in the actual control over party organizations in Texas. This is an ideal situation for the business community. Low voter turnout, limited competition, and a conservative, probusiness perspective among top contenders for political office offer members of the economic elite a great opportunity to work with compatible politicians. Chapter 4 will examine the direct pressure exerted on Texas state government by the business community through elections and lobbying.

★ ★ ★ ★ ★   NOTES

1. Janice C. May, "The Texas Voter Registration System," *Public Affairs Comment,* XVI (July 1970):2.

2. *United States v. Texas,* 252 F. Supp. 234, Affirmed 384 U.S. 155(1966).

3. *Beare et al. v. Preston Smith, Governor of Texas,* 321 F. Supp. 1100 (1971).

4. Office of the Secretary of State, *1982 May Primary Election Analysis* (Austin: Office of the Secretary of State, 1982), Table 11.

5. Ibid.

6. Gregory Curtis, "The Home Vote," *Texas Monthly,* December 1994, p. 5.

7. Figures from the Office of the Secretary of State's World Wide Web page: http://www.sos.state.tx.us

8. Information from the Texas Poll, cited in Thomas R. Dye, L. Tucker Gibson, and Clay Robison, *Politics in America: Texas Edition* (Upper Saddle River, NJ: Prentice-Hall, 2d ed., 1997), p. 766.

9. Information compiled from several sources, including the *Houston Chronicle,* November 7, 1996, 1996–97 *Texas Almanac,* pp. 447–448, Mike Kingston, Sam Attlesey, and Mary G. Crawford, *The Texas Almanac's Political History of Texas* (Austin: Eakin Press, 1992), p. 114, and the Secretary of State's Web page, http:\\www.sos.state.tx.us

10. This profile is drawn from James Dyer, *Texas Poll,* Fall 1989, p. 1, *the Texas Poll,* November 1990, James Dyer and Don Haynes, *Social, Economic, and Political Change According to the Texas Poll* (Austin: College of Communication, University of Texas at Austin, 1987), and "Voter Influx Alters Election Demographics," *The Monitor,* July 15, 1996, p. 1D.

11. Paul Burka, "Primary Lesson," *Texas Monthly,* July 1986, p. 104.

12. Discussed, ibid.

13. James Dyer and Don Haynes, *Social, Economic, and Political Change.*

14. For national efforts by the Republican party, see David Adamany, "Political Parties in the 1980s," in *Money and Politics in the United States,* ed. Michael J. Malbin (Chatham, NJ: Chatham House Publishers, 1984).

15. Dave Denison, "Are We There Yet?" *Texas Observer,* June 13, 1986, pp. 6–8.

16. *Texas Poll,* Fall 1989.

17. Quoted in R. A. Dyer, "Redistricting Aids Incumbents," *Houston Chronicle,* November 7, 1996, p. 36A.

18. *Texas Poll,* Spring 1994.

19. *1982 May Primary Election Analysis,* Table 3.

20. Anthony Champagne and Rick Collis, "Texas," in *The Political Life of the American States,* ed. Alan Rosenthal and Maureen Moakley (New York: Praeger, 1984), p. 142.

21. Ibid.

22. Sam Attlesey, "Cowboy Conglomerate," *Dallas Morning News,* March 25, 1990.

23. Explored more fully in Chandler Davidson, *Race and Class in Texas Politics* (Princeton, NJ: Princeton University Press, 1990), Chapters 2 and 3.

24. George Norris Green, *The Establishment in Texas Politics: The Primitive Years* (Norman: University of Oklahoma Press, 1979), p. 197.

25. Jim Hightower wrote two books on agribusiness: *Eat Your Heart Out: How Food Profiteers Victimize the Consumer* (New York: Crown Publishers, 1975) and *Hard Tomatoes, Hard Times: The Failure of the Land Grant College Complex* (Boston: Schenkman, 1977).

26. Quoted in Peter Elkind, "Cosmic Plowboy," *Texas Monthly,* December 1983, p. 238.

27. Quoted, ibid, p. 154.

28. Quoted, ibid.

29. Nina Butts, "Four Fresh(men) Sing Hiring Improvements," *Texas Observer,* January 13, 1984, pp. 4–5.

30. "Building a Texas Populist Alliance," *Texas Observer,* August 31, 1990, pp. 3–4 and 12.

31. Quoted in the *Texas Observer,* January 11, 1991, p. 21.

32. Michael Parenti, *Democracy for the Few,* 2d ed. (New York: St. Martin's Press, 1977), p. 203.

33. Harry Hurt III, "The Most Powerful Texans," *Texas Monthly,* April 1976, p. 73.

34. Quoted in Griffin Smith, Jr., "Empires of Paper," reprinted in *Texas Monthly's Political Reader* (Austin: Texas Monthly Press and Sterling Swift Co., 1978), p. 34.

35. See David F. Prindle, *Petroleum Politics and the Texas Railroad Commission* (Austin: University of Texas Press, 1981), pp. 170–204.

36. George Norris Green, *The Establishment in Texas Politics,* p. 17.

CHAPTER 4

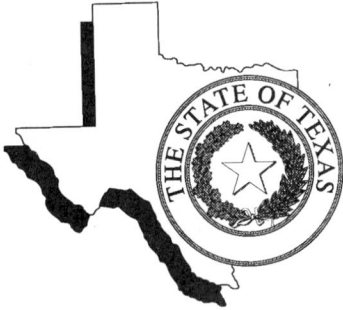

Economic Influences: Campaign Contributions and Lobbying

People and institutions in control of Texas's economic resources exert substantial pressure on officeholders in Texas by making campaign contributions and directly lobbying members of government. In many cases, this process begins with financial support of candidates, especially incumbents, and flows effortlessly into influencing decisions that are made by officials once they are in government. This chapter will first focus on campaign contributions and will then examine various methods used to influence the actions of officeholders in Texas.

★★★★★ CAMPAIGN CONTRIBUTIONS

Money is critical to running an effective political campaign in Texas. Given the geographic size and the tremendous population of the state, the quickest path to the electorate is usually through the media. Consequently, "serious candidates for statewide office find it necessary to raise and spend large sums of money for advertising in the ten major media markets of the state."[1] Media costs, especially for television, are very high. Money must be allocated for hiring advertising firms and for the production of messages, as well as for actual presentation of campaign pitches over the airwaves. Production costs for just one thirty-second television spot are about $5,000. To air a half-minute message over television in the most heavily populated markets—for instance, in Dallas/Fort Worth or Houston—runs about $2,000. Placing a campaign advertisement in the Sunday edition of a large city newspaper costs from $4,000 to more than $20,000 for a full page.[2] Altogether, media expenses consume most of the money spent in campaigns.

In 1990, the Ann Richards's campaign spent $14.5 million to win the governor's race; her opponent, Republican Clayton Williams, exhausted $22 million in his losing effort. All told, this was the most expensive election ever conducted in Texas, a record that prompted former state senator John Montford (Democrat, Lubbock) to remark, "It bothers me how people are going hungry and we're dropping [over $50 million] on a governor's race. We've got some values mixed up here."[3] In 1994, Governor Ann Richards spent nearly $19 million and lost; the expenditures of her successful Republican challenger, George W. Bush, were close to the $13 million mark.[4]

Candidates for statewide offices—for example, lieutenant governor, attorney general, or a seat on the Railroad Commission—aim at raising at least $1 million. In his 1994 race to retain his position as lieutenant-governor, Bob Bullock spent $6.4 million.[5] Judicial candidates do not escape the finance problem. Candidates seeking election to the Texas Supreme Court between 1990 and mid-1994 collectively spent $11.2 million.[6] A typical competitive state senatorial race costs each candidate about $500,000, while a contested seat in the Texas House requires at least $100,000. Interestingly, even uncontested legislative elections attract campaign contributions. In 1992, a total of more than $500,000 was given to 60 legislative candidates who faced no opposition.[7]

Local elections are also expensive. City council races cost candidates in Texas's largest cities from $50,000 to $100,000. It has been reported that candidates contesting county-commissioner races have run up costs of about $40,000 and that even candidates for local school boards incur expenses in the $15,000 range. In 1995, the successful candidate in San Antonio's mayoral election spent $750,000, while contests for recent mayoral races cost $1.8 million in Dallas and about $5 million in Houston.[8]

Sources of Funds

The Texas Election Code requires that all candidates file reports detailing the name and address of each donor upon receipt of any campaign contribution over $50. Likewise, any group or organization contributing more than $100 to a candidate or political party must report the contribution. Under threat of possible civil and criminal penalties, these reports are to be filed at scheduled times, and they are open for public scrutiny. The amount that an individual or organization can give to candidates and parties is *unlimited* in Texas.

Investigations of these disclosure reports reveal that the lion's share of campaign contributions comes from relatively few sources. For instance, in the first six months of 1994, George Bush and Ann Richards each raised about $8 million from a total of 17,263 and 15,546 contributors, respectively. Nearly three fourths of Richards's funds came from about 4 percent, or some 622, of her supporters; similarly, 61 percent of Bush's contributions were provided by 5 percent of his supporters, or about 863 benefactors.[9] The major contributors in Texas are wealthy individuals and resourceful organizations, such as corporate political action committees, professional associations, law firms, and other special-interest groups.

Wealthy Individuals   Candidates may spend their own personal wealth on their campaigns. Republican Clayton Williams committed $8.4 million of his money to his unsuccessful 1990 governor's race. Mostly, however, leading candidates for the governor's post in Texas rely heavily on contributions from wealthy individuals and families. In the 1994 governor's race, 10 percent of all the money contributed to both Richards and Bush came from two dozen donors. Bush's top twelve financial backers included bankers, investors, and computer and insurance executives; his leading contributor was Dallas businessman (and former owner of the Dallas Mavericks) Donald Carter, who gave him $115,000. Ann Richards's top financial supporters were led by Houston lawyer Arthur Schechter ($138,000). Her "fat-cat" donors included business executives, people from the entertainment world, such as rock musician Don Henley ($62,000) and movie director Steven Spielberg ($90,000), and several other lawyers.[10]

Over the years, a few individuals stand out in their generosity to candidates seeking office in Texas. Between 1990 and mid-1994, twenty individuals or families contributed $4.3 million to statewide races. Tyler oil executive Royce Wisenbaker donated $400,500 to Democratic state candidates. Peter and Edith O'Donnell together provided $361,000 to Republican office seekers. The other leading contributors were lawyer Frank Branson and his wife Debbie ($336,689), lawyer John O'Quinn, business executive Connie Armstrong ($322,000), oilman John Cox ($298,279), computer executive John Moores ($289,500), lawyer Joseph Jamail ($284,973), investor Louis Beecherl, Jr. ($259,750), petrochemical executive Virgil Waggoner ($249,150), businessman James Leininger ($227,250), real estate developer James Pitcock, Jr. ($226,500), J. Donald and Latimer Bowen ($199,000), insurance executive Bernard Rapoport ($197,322), Boone and Beatrice Pickens ($196,300), Donald Carter ($194,500), Rex and Betty Houston ($186,691), Robert M. Bass ($183,824), investor Ralph Thomas ($161,000), oilman Ben Fortson ($152,000), and lawyers David Perry and Rene Haas ($143,387). Finally, during this period, Beaumont lawyer Walter Umphrey personally donated $166,297 to state candidates, contributed another $861,915 through his law firm's political action committee, and, in 1990, loaned Ann Richards $230,000 through his Texans Political Action Committee.[11]

Even the most cursory reading of these names reveals the presence of many lawyers among the top donors. More systematic research indicates that between 1990 and mid-1994, lawyers, as a group, contributed nearly $9 million to candidates in statewide Texas races. Most of this money went to Ann Richards's gubernatorial campaigns and to candidates seeking positions on the state's courts.[12]

Political Action Committees (PACs)   Texas law prohibits corporations and labor unions from giving money directly to candidates. However, they, along with other individuals and groups, may form committees, commonly called *political action committees (PACs),* to collect and disburse campaign funds. All PAC donations must be voluntary and the names of contributors must be disclosed if more than $10 per month is given. A PAC has to register if it is composed of ten or more people. PACs can register voters and help mobilize them on Election Day.

The number of political action committees reported in Texas has increased steadily in recent years, rising from 950 in 1982 to more than 1,300 eight years later.[13] Most PACs are loose-knit, ad hoc organizations composed of friends or supporters of a particular candidate. The most important sources of campaign contributions, however, are PACs established by corporations, law firms, and, especially, professional associations comprising doctors, lawyers, teachers, and realtors. The top fifty PACs in Texas contributed more than $10 million to state, local, and out-of-state races in 1990. Six of the top ten of these PACs were formed by professional organizations. The leader was TEXPAC, the political action committee of the Texas Medical Association, which donated $1 million.[14] Fifteen PACs, led by the Bass Brothers ($664,945); Vinson and Elkins ($532,052); the Teamsters Union ($300,500); the American Federation of State, Municipal, and County Employees ($281,427); Dallas law firm Winstead, Seachrest, and Minick ($275,529); Fulbright & Jaworski ($268,841); Texas Real Estate ($263,154); NationsBank ($253,103); and Baker and Botts ($229,950), contributed a total of $6.6 million to all state races conducted between 1990 and mid-1994.[15]

The importance of PACs in financing state elections is especially evident in races for legislative office. In 1985, for instance, senators in Texas received $1.4 million from special-interest groups, most of which were PACs; two years earlier, less than one third of contributions given to senators was PAC money.[16] Correspondingly, between 1983 and 1985, there was a 64 percent increase in PAC donations to candidates seeking seats in the Texas House of Representatives. About half of the total contributions to House races in 1985 came from special-interest PACs.[17]

A substantial portion of PAC money is given to representatives and senators who hold influential posts in the Texas Legislature. In 1988, for example, almost $4.7 million went to 47 legislators who chaired legislative committees; interestingly, only 16 of these chairs faced opposing candidates. Sixty-three percent of this money came from lobbyists and PACs.[18] More than $3.5 million was contributed to committee chairs in 1990; 62 percent of these funds came from PACs, lobbyists, and other special interests.[19] In 1994, 41 percent of the $6 million-plus contributed to the campaign of Lieutenant Governor Bob Bullock, who is the leader of the Texas Senate, was donated by PACs. In the same year, the speaker of the Texas House of Representatives, Pete Laney (Democrat, Hale Center) ran unopposed, yet raised nearly $750,000. About 73 percent of this total came from PACs, the foremost of which were composed of lawyers, businesses, doctors, educators, and real estate interests.[20]

★ ★ ★ ★ ★ # TOWARD LOBBYING

Campaign contributions are often part of a general strategy by donors to pressure, or *lobby*, officeholders and thus to shape Texas laws and policies. For example, races for seats on Texas's courts have attracted a great deal of money from special interests that are likely to have cases pending before the judiciary. Fully 87 percent of the $11 million contributed to winning judges in the 1988 and 1990 Texas Supreme Court elections came from PACs representing doctors, lawyers, bankers, insurance companies, and other special interests. In 1991–92, insurance companies, manufacturers, doctors, and other medical professionals contributed more than $500,000, and lawyers donated another $1.8 million to all candidates seeking election to the state Supreme Court; indeed, the top 25 personal-injury law firms in the state accounted for about 25 percent of all money contributed to Supreme Court races in 1992.[21] The Supreme Court makes the final decision at the state level in civil-law cases, which often involve suits for substantial financial damages from corporations. All sides in these cases have a financial interest in the court's decision and, thus, have a strong incentive to try, through campaign contributions, to bring about the election of judges who may rule in their favor.

Candidates for some administrative officials have also been financially supported by individuals and groups affected by their offices. The leading contenders for the Texas Railroad Commission, for instance, usually receive large donations from petroleum and trucking interests, which are regulated by the Commission. The two incumbents who sought reelection to the Commission in 1994 received at least 50 percent of their campaign contributions from PACs or individuals affiliated with industries regulated by the commission.[22] Commissioner Jim Nugent was specifically accused of voting in cases before the Commission to compensate at least some of his donors, including Phillips Petroleum.[23]

Large campaign contributions may also lead to appointment to an administrative agency. From that position, a donor might be able to influence decisions affecting his or her interests. There has been a pattern in Texas of linkage, which will be discussed in greater detail in Chapter 6, between gubernatorial appointments to key state agencies and donations to candidates running for governor. In 1994, for example, more than one third of the twenty-five most important individual contributors in the state had been appointed by governors (Ann Richards and her predecessors) to major agencies, such as the Boards of Regents of the University of Texas and Texas A&M, the Texas Transportation Commission, and the Parks and Wildlife Commission.[24]

Along a related front, campaign contributors might be assigned lucrative projects by officeholders they helped elect. For instance, four elected Harris County judges have routinely appointed many of their most generous campaign backers to panels that, for a fee, established the price that the state would pay for condemned property. Between 1988 and 1994, these appointees contributed a total of $413,985 to the campaigns of the judges, some 40 percent of all the donations the latter received. During the same time, the fees these donors earned for setting prices on condemned holdings came to nearly $2 million.[25]

Even when campaign contributions do not result in direct policy benefits or appointments to various positions, contributors work toward the election of officeholders with whom they share beliefs and policy perspectives. For example, the aim of the PAC of the Texas Realtors Association, according to its former president, is to elect officials "to run this great state of ours [who will] protect the realtor and the property owner of Texas."[26]

At a minimum, large campaign contributors expect that their donations to successful candidates will ensure access to them after their election. As noted by University of Texas at Dallas political scientist Anthony Champagne, major contributors "can always get their telephone calls answered, and they can always present their case. That doesn't mean they always win their case when they want something from government or want the government not to do something to them, but they can always get access to key decision-makers and present their point of view."[27] Gene Fondren, lobbyist for the Texas Automobile Dealers Association, concurs, noting that his organization "supports candidates who at least will give us an ear in terms of industry issues."[28] Or, in the words of state representative Eddie Cavazos, "If I've got a $1,000 donor on the phone and one who's never given a dime, whose call do you think I am going to take?"[29]

Is it any wonder that contributors who have not supported winning candidates before the election will often rush to their aid after the votes have been tallied? Within weeks of his election as governor in 1994, George W. Bush, even though he had no campaign debt to retire, received $545,755 from 100 contributors who had previously supported Ann Richards exclusively. Among those to jump on board the Bush train late were some of Richards's appointees to major state agencies (for example, university boards of regents), individuals with business pending before the state, and PACs, such as those of the Texas Automobile Dealers Association, the Texas Medical Association, Texaco, the Texas Dental Association, the law firm of Vinson and Elkins, the Teamsters' Local 745 (Dallas), and the Texas Society of CPAs. None of these tardy donors gave less than $10,000 to Mr. Bush.[30] This practice of post-election contributions is widespread in Texas, affecting the judiciary, the state legislature, and other offices in the executive branch of state government.[31] It is a practice, as noted by columnist David Broder with specific reference to Texas, where

> The people or groups that give money after an election, when there is no risk, are almost always people who have a particular interest in ingratiating themselves with an officeholder. Giving a "campaign contribution" to the winner of the last election . . . [blurs] the distinction between a campaign contribution and a personal payoff.[32]

Problem Areas

The ready availability of campaign contributions spills over into the policy-making process in Texas in two ways that raise serious questions about the propriety of these donations. First, candidates who are elected often still have unspent contributions that they can use for personal expenses. Second, the line between making a campaign contribution and deliberately trying to buy a vote sometimes becomes very thin in Texas. Each of these points deserves more elaboration.

Unspent Contributions   It is not uncommon for officeholders to have surplus campaign-contribution money after an election. In 1994, for example, 25 of the 30 members of the Texas Senate had unspent campaign contributions totaling $2.3 million, an average of $91,461 each. About one quarter of the House members had a campaign surplus, led by the Speaker Pete Laney, who had $400,000 in unspent donations.[33]

Until 1991, there were very few restrictions on how officeholders could spend surplus funds. In effect, the money became the personal property of the candidate. According to one report, money was used

> to buy cars, make mortgage payments on condos, and pay salaries to family members. One legislator bought a diamond ring for a special secretary. A judge used campaign money to buy season tickets for the Rockets. One legislator bought expensive boots for his friends. One retiring legislator bought a ranch, paid for with campaign funds.[34]

Officeholders now can spend surplus campaign money only on "ordinary and necessary" Austin living expenses. Sixteen state senators and twenty-six representatives with unspent donations in 1994 used some of their surplus for this purpose, including subsidizing rents (ranging between $1,200 and $2,900 per month) for housing, buying household furniture and tickets to sporting events, and paying for utilities (including cable television), car rentals, parking tickets, and memberships at health clubs.[35] Hence, a clear pathway exists for contributors to provide money to candidates who, after the election, can use it to defray living expenses. "The system," according to the director of Public Citizen (a reform public interest group), "is very ripe for abuse."[36]

Legalized Bribery? Individuals and groups seeking favorable decisions from elected policy makers in Texas can use campaign contributions as inducements, sometimes approaching the point where the offer of cash looks very much like a bribe. For example, a major ruckus occurred during the 1989 legislative session when millionaire Lonnie "Bo" Pilgrim, head of the Pilgrim's Pride processed-chicken company, walked onto the floor of the Texas Senate and promised a $10,000 check to any senator who voted to change the workers' compensation law. Nine senators apparently accepted the offer.[37] On the surface, this transaction appears to be blatant bribery, a criminal offense in Texas. However, Pilgrim claimed that he was simply giving campaign contributions to the senators. Prosecutors agreed and did not pursue any legal action against him, leading Travis County district attorney Ronnie Earle to proclaim that "right now it's not against the law to bribe a public official in Texas, and that's an intolerable situation."[38]

★★★★★ DIRECT LOBBYING

Campaign contributions are the first step taken by outside interests in developing links with political decision makers. Once the latter are in office, the process of applying pressure directly on them begins. Lobbying occurs both in the informal milieu of a social gathering or a personal conversation and in the formal setting of a legislative committee hearing, an administrative session, or a judicial trial. Groups are successful at lobbying if they can translate their wishes into actions on the part of officeholders. The most effective tactics of lobbying are cultivating and maintaining personal contact with officials, supplying decision makers with research, and grassroots mobilization.

Personal Contact

One method of achieving continuous personal contact with decision makers is to hire people to nourish close connections with them and to closely monitor the ongoing business of the political system. According to one highly regarded lobbyist, Russell Kelley, whose clients have included American Airlines, the Texas Soft Drink Association, the Texas Association of Bank Holding Companies, Sprint, Ross Perot, Texaco, and West Publishing Company (now owned by International Thomson Publishing), "Nothing takes the place of personal contact."[39] Professional lobbyists are most evident in the legislative segment of government.

The opening of legislative sessions attracts scores of lobbyists to Austin. Texas law requires people to register as lobbyists, and pay the state a fee of $300, if during a calendar year they are paid $1,000 or more to lobby state officials or spend over $500 to gain favor with them. By the time the legislative session is over, some 1,200 to 1,600 people are registered as lobbyists in Texas. An overwhelming number of them represent big business or major economic interests.

Efforts to influence legislators cost lobbying interests between $1.2 and $2 million a year. These days, most of this money is spent in underwriting the costs of events, such as picnics, outings, and special days, to which legislators are invited to partake of food, beverages, and entertainment. Businesses and economic groups are the principal sources of lobbying money. For instance, Anheuser Busch, makers of Budweiser beer, spent $167,000 on its "Texas Legislative Outing," conducted in Austin a few weeks after the 1993 legislative session opened. Moreover, about one third of all money dedicated to lobbying legislators that year came from eight business interests. Southwestern Bell alone accounted for two thirds of *all* lobbying expenses—some $5.7 million—recorded in 1993.[40]

To facilitate access to policy makers, groups and individuals often hire former state officeholders as their lobbyists. During recent legislative sessions, more than 50 former members of the legislature, including five former speakers of the Texas House (see Highlight 4–1 for one example), have

★ ★ ★

Highlight 4–1: Lobbying and Former House Speaker Gib Lewis
When the Dallas/Fort Worth International Airport wanted to expand and met resistance from its municipal neighbors, it hired the former speaker of the Texas House, Gib Lewis, to lobby for a state law to circumvent the need for local approval for construction of new runways to begin. The airport board chairman justified paying Mr. Lewis $110,000 by saying, "I don't think there's any question that he has relationships down there [Austin] that cannot be duplicated." Tom "Smitty" Smith, director of Public Citizen in Texas, concurred that "there is probably no lobbyist as powerful" as Gib Lewis. A member of the Dallas City Council, commenting on Lewis's six-figure contract, stated, "The way I figure it, that's about $10,000 for booze, $10,000 for other entertainment, $20,000 for political contributions, and $1,000 an hour for Mr. Lewis."[1] In any event, the legislature was persuaded to enact a law allowing airport expansion without the cooperation of surrounding cities.

Notes
1. Quoted in J. Lynn Lunsford, "D/FW Airport Likely to OK Lewis' $110,000 Contract," *Dallas Morning News*, January 30, 1993, pp. A-1 and A-14.

registered as lobbyists.[41] Ex-legislators are valuable because they are quite familiar with the formal and informal procedures of the legislative process and are usually on a first-name basis with current members. Becoming a lobbyist is, for some legislators, an attractive career change. Rayford Price, who jumped from the legislature to the lobby, contends that "it's more fun being in the Legislature, but it is more remunerative being out of it."[42]

Some lobbyists who attempt to shape legislation also hold appointed positions with state agencies. Nineteen of the lobbyists registered in 1996 served as unpaid state officials, including lobbyists Don Adams, a former member of the legislature, and Bill Clayton, former speaker of the Texas House, both of whom sit on the State Aircraft Pooling Board. Clayton also is a member of the Board of Regents of Texas A&M University.[43] Demonstrating that turnabout is fair play, between 1991 and 1993, sixteen members of the Texas Legislature were paid to lobby administrative agencies. Collectively, this group of legislator-lobbyists collected $680,000 for their time and effort.[44]

A variety of techniques are used to engage in personal contact with officeholders. A few well-heeled lobbyists own or lease hunting grounds and fishing lodges used by legislators for rest, recreation, and sport.[45] Some have also showered legislators and their staff with gifts, such as golf bags, free movie passes, and tickets to sporting events, and arranged special meals in exclusive clubs to bring their clients together with key legislative players. Indeed, such special dinners were once so common that a veteran lobbyist complained that "in order to take a senator to dinner now it's a two-week wait."[46] Legislators during recent sessions could, if they chose, start their day with a breakfast at Austin's Driskill Hotel, followed by a coffee break in the cafeteria in the Texas Employment

Commission building, lunch at the private Austin Club (by invitation only) or, on Tuesday and Wednesdays, at the office of the Texas Trial Lawyers Association, and dinner at several Austin restaurants—all at the expense of several lobbying organizations. On Tuesdays during the legislative session, they could attend Speaker's Night at the Broken Spoke, "a South Austin honky-tonk where a different lobbyist buys the beer and pays for the band."[47]

Observers of the Texas Legislature are divided over the propriety of the tactics used by lobbyists to personally pressure legislators. One group portrays the typical lobbyist as a conscientious, public-spirited citizen who courts legislators in an above-board, low-keyed, businesslike manner.[48] According to this view, the effective lobbyist provides legislators with correct answers to political questions. When asked, most state legislators, including those in Texas, say that the most successful lobbyists are those who perform this informational service.[49]

Another group paints a much darker picture of the lobbying process in Texas. They contend that money—along with the favors that it can buy—flows without much legal or ethical restraint between some lobbyists and a few legislators. The following pieces of evidence lend some plausibility to this negative view.

In 1969, Houston financier Frank Sharp offered several key state officials, including the speaker of the house and the governor, financial inducements in exchange for favorable legislation.[50] These officeholders made handsome profits and the bill desired by Mr. Sharp was enacted by the legislature (but not signed by the governor). Four individuals, including the speaker, were found guilty, in what became known as the *Sharpstown Bank scandal*, of accepting bribes and were given probation for their crimes.

A cloud reappeared over the legislature in 1980 when Speaker of the House Bill Clayton was accused of accepting money in exchange for his support in awarding a state contract to an insurance company. Mr. Clayton was indicted by a Harris County grand jury, but was later exonerated by a Houston jury, even though some incriminating conversations between Clayton and his benefactors had been taped by the FBI and entered as evidence.

Mr. Clayton's successor to the speaker's post, Gib Lewis, pleaded no contest in 1983 and paid an $800 fine after failing to disclose on his personal finance statement that he had a business relationship with a horse-racing lobbyist. In 1990, he was indicted by a Travis County grand jury on two charges arising from his not reporting receipt of a gift and from the fact that a law firm had paid his delinquent property taxes.[51] He entered a plea of no contest to two misdemeanor charges, paid a fine of $2,200, and chose not to seek election in 1992. Incidentally, Lewis paid his lawyers $5,000 from unspent campaign contributions.[52]

Questionable lobbying expenditures have permeated the legislature in recent years. Important legislative leaders, such as chairs of committees, have visited Europe, Japan, Mexico, and Hawaii, skied in Utah, watched championship boxing in Las Vegas, and attended prestigious golf tournaments—all expenses paid by lobbyists. Travis County district attorney Ronnie Earl contends that "these trips are pure and simple, a gift of a very large amount of money to curry the favor of the legislator."[53]

Supplying Research

Officeholders in Texas frequently find themselves without adequate information about policy matters. Interest groups often step into the gap, offering to collect, assemble, and analyze information for policy makers and, in so doing, move into an advantageous position in the influencing of policy decisions. The most interesting example of a private interest group's gaining access to Texas officials through performing this informational task is the Texas Research League (TRL).

The TRL was organized in 1952 to engage in public policy research if asked by the state government. Every request must be approved by the League's executive committee and its board of directors. Approved studies are carried out by a full-time paid staff. Over the last four decades, the TRL has studied and made recommendations in a large number of policy areas affecting Texas, including economic development; education; vocational rehabilitation; medical assistance for the poor and elderly; health care; the state library; the Railroad Commission; the Parks and Wildlife Commission; the overall administration of local, county, and state government; the state retirement system; housing; law enforcement; and roads and highways. The main focus of the TRL's work, however, is tax policy; that is, the question of who is going to pay what for which state services. Obviously, government in Texas has taken extensive advantage of the "free" information services offered by the League: "The TRL's staff has turned out enough reports to fill no less than seven shelves—floor to ceiling—in the Legislative Reference Library."[54] One observer states that "in effect, the league functions as a research arm of the state, and its staff will often sit at the right hand of the committee chairman in the legislature."[55]

The initial push for creating the TRL came from big business; Hines Baker, former chairman of Humble Oil (now Exxon), acted as one of the driving forces behind its establishment.[56] Its fifteen-person executive committee mostly contains prominent people associated with oil and natural gas companies, public utilities, industrial firms, and major banks. The remaining 150-plus members of its board of directors constitute much of the honor roll of the economic executives working in Texas. Its annual budget surpasses the million-dollar mark. Where does the money come from?

No one knows for sure. Since the League is chartered as a nonprofit, nonpolitical educational corporation, it is not legally obliged to disclose its funding sources, and it consistently refuses to volunteer this information.

At a minimum, some of the money comes from fees paid by the 1,000 or so members of the TRL. A business membership—and 90 percent of its members are businesses—costs $150 per year; individuals contribute $100 per year. Because of the League's business affiliations, some people, including a sprinkling of political officials in Texas, have questioned the objectivity of its work. One critic, for instance, says the following about its studies:

> At its best the TRL is a valuable source of well-organized and carefully refined information on Texas state and local government finance. The problem is that what public officials, private individuals and the general public get to see of that information is selected, manipulated and presented to the beat of the League's drummers—the elite of Texas business and industry. Except for rare occasions of outright misrepresentation, . . . TRL tells the truth and nothing but the truth—but seldom tells the whole truth. Indeed, some of [its] most insidious works exhibit an ingenious combination of relevant, irrelevant and omitted truths.[57]

Others, including some governors of Texas, have heaped bouquets of praise on the work of the TRL. For example, Dolph Briscoe, when governor, told League members,

> For many years this organization has made important contributions to the future progress of our State through its in-depth studies of the pressing problems which have faced State government. The programs you have undertaken, and the resulting evaluations, have led to a better understanding of the functions and effects of government operations.[58]

Regardless of the possible bias of its work, the Texas Research League certainly has access to officeholders. At the very least, its reports draw official attention and some have been incorporated into public policy. Its recommendations often set the agenda for the state's political decision makers. By providing information, the TRL links the interests of its members to the operations of the state government. Commenting on its political and economic power, one observer argues that "it is through . . . organizations like the TRL that the modern corporation exercises its domination of the political as well as the economic arena."[59]

Grassroots Lobbying

Effective lobbying groups are able to activate their members, and perhaps the public at large, virtually on the spur of the moment. Demonstrations of grassroots support for a group's position often impress officeholders, who, especially if they are elected, must reckon with the political implications of an opinionated, mobilized, large body of citizens. There are signs that interest groups in Texas are expanding their use of grassroots campaigns to lobby members of state government.

For example, in 1992, the Texas Bankers Association (TBA) created the Legislative Network to improve the legislature's image of the state banking community. According to a TBA spokesperson, "the objective of the Legislative Network is to have Texas bankers contact all 181 state legislators . . . at least three times in 1992 and at least two times yearly afterward to discuss important Texas banking issues. . . . Once a relationship is established with a legislator, it is easier to ask him to vote in the best interests of the state's banking community." A banker is selected to serve as an area leader in each of the state's thirty-one senatorial districts. Every district has a panel of four to six local bankers who have the responsibility of "contacting their assigned legislator and arranging meetings with area bankers and other influential community leaders."[60]

In 1993, Southwestern Bell spent nearly $4 million on lobbying, most of which went to CONNECTEXAS, a mass media campaign and mobilization effort aimed at persuading the legislature to deregulate the telephone industry in Texas. Among other things, deregulation would allow Southwestern Bell to develop a fiber optic network, making it possible for the company to transmit images and information directly into people's homes. As part of this campaign, Southwestern Bell transported 6,000 of its employees from all over Texas to Austin to demonstrate collective support for deregulation. According to one participant, the employees were in Austin "hoping maybe we get some attention by coming out in force like this."[61]

Southwestern Bell, along with fifty-seven other telecommunications firms, also mounted an extensive television, newspaper, and magazine blitz to convince the public that it should support the company's deregulation plan. The state's Public Utility Commission was portrayed as hampering the development of the telecommunications industry in Texas through its restrictive rate policies. The public was encouraged to pressure the legislature to change this regulatory climate. Thirty-second advertisements, costing around $500,000 a week, were aired on television throughout the state. Highly visible ads were placed in major daily newspapers. A glossy eight-page special supplement was included in the *Texas Monthly* magazine. Readers and viewers were invited to call an 800 number to register their support and to inquire about the proposal. Some 650 ranchers, farmers, business people, educators, and religious leaders were chosen by their local phone companies and invited to attend a one-day conference in Austin to discuss telecommunications policy; telephone interests paid $200,000 to cover all expenses.[62]

Southwestern Bell did not immediately achieve all its objectives, mainly because cable companies, newspapers, and consumer groups, which were troubled about the telephone company's plans to enter the entertainment and information markets, fought deregulation. The legislature decided to defer any decisions for two years, pending completion of a comprehensive study of the issue, and promised Southwestern Bell that most of its rates would be frozen during the interim, certainly a measure of the success of CONNECTEXAS.

WELL, YOU MAKE DEREGULATING PHONE RATES SOUND PRETTY GREAT...

HOW 'LL IT AFFECT ME?

TEXAS CONSUMER

BEN SARGE

Sargent © 1988 *Austin American-Statesman.* Reprinted with permission of UNIVERSAL PRESS SYNDICATE. All rights reserved.

The Texas Good Roads Association (TGRA) has set the standard for effective grassroots lobbying in the state. Whenever the state's commitment to highways as the principal component of transportation policy appears to be in danger of changing, the TGRA unleashes a media campaign. In addition, the association can count on its more than 2,000 members, who are mostly connected with interests that benefit from highways (such as oil companies; insurance and road construction firms; and the trucking, bus, and automobile industries) to vocally remind officeholders of the value of roads and highways. The presiding officers of the TGRA have often been media people, who constitute a useful asset if the political and economic priorities of the organization are called into question.[63]

★ ★ ★ ★ ★   ## EFFECTIVENESS

The ability of wealthy individuals, economically powerful corporations, and professional associations to financially support campaigns and lobbying efforts gives these actors unrivaled influence in Texas state government and politics. This is a conclusion reached by such people as the authors of a major textbook on Texas politics, who note, "Business groups and associations . . . tend to dominate the lobbying scene and command unmatched influence in the policy-making process."[64] The national director of the Baptist Church's joint committee on public affairs tersely told the Texas Conference of Churches in 1981, "Texas legislatures have been held hostage by the corporate lobby for decades."[65] A recent *Dallas Morning News* survey about the Texas Legislature, which included legislators, chairs of committees, legislative staff, political observers, and lobbyists, concluded that "a small coterie of insiders, operating on big money and personal contact, still helps determine the taxes, laws and regulations that touch every Texan."[66]

To be sure, interests other than the rich and economically influential have had some effect on the shaping of state policy. Probably the most successful example has been the Industrial Areas Foundation, a consortium of various community-based organizations, including COPS of San Antonio, Interfaith Sponsoring of Austin, Houston's Metropolitan Organization, Valley Interfaith of the Rio Grande Valley, the Dallas Interfaith Sponsoring Committee, and the El Paso Interreligious Sponsoring Organization (EPISO). Its most notable policy achievements have been a successful court challenge to the method used by Texas to finance its public school system, the enactment of an indigents' health care system, and the passage of a constitutional amendment that brought water to many *colonias* located along Texas's border with Mexico.

The organizational base of the Industrial Areas Foundation is at the grassroots level, principally in the Hispanic community. Each component group of the Foundation has mobilized its members by appealing to their common cultural ties, the relative poverty of Hispanics, the lack of state services for poor Hispanics, and the possibility of political success. The rise in the state's Hispanic population and the drive to register Latino voters have not gone unnoticed by some state political leaders. Recognizing the growing political force of Hispanics, key officeholders have courted the support of the Industrial Areas Foundation and have advanced and implemented several of its policy suggestions.

Other groups have also confronted the business lobby in Texas and, on occasion, have won. The Texas Consumers Union, for example, has opposed electric companies before the Public Utility Commission (PUC) and scored some victories, including the creation of a public counsel to represent consumers' interests before the commission and the requirement that electric companies obtain PUC approval before they pass on higher costs for fuel to their customers. Sometimes industrious individuals, aggrieved by a business practice, come to Austin and pressure officeholders; occasionally they win. Mrs. Dianna Loper of Houston was angry at a health spa that solicited her membership, took her money, and never opened for business. She soon discovered that she had no legal recourse in Texas and promptly undertook to remedy this situation. She first uncovered the names of 1,000 women in Houston who had also been victimized by shady "health spa" operators. She personally visited the offices of legislators and "after doggedly pressing her case, eventually won passage of a bill requiring spas to place pre-opening sales money in escrow. If a spa doesn't open, . . . the customer gets the money back."[67]

Nonetheless, these groups find it difficult to compete with business organizations. Without much money, they can achieve political influence only by representing a substantial number of people and by investing a great deal of time in the lobbying effort. As noted by the executive director of Common Cause of Texas, "the amount that lobbyists spend in just three weeks is four times my annual budget."[68] Irving-based Exxon, for example, has enough resources to maintain a fully staffed office in Austin to monitor policy developments and maintain membership in the Texas Research League and the Texas Association of Taxpayers, a group that lobbies the state on behalf of Texas's largest property holders, as well as being a major force in industrywide petroleum organizations such as the Texas Mid-Continent Oil and Gas Association, whose 3,000 members are dedicated to the protection and expansion of oil producers. With such an elaborate network of lobbying within its corporate empire, it is no wonder that "Exxon is [considered] most active in the politics and economy of the state."[69]

Moreover, traditionally, Texas politics has not been very hospitable to nonbusiness lobbying. Consequently, in the words of Representative Mike Toomey (Republican, Houston), these interests do not operate in "a favorable climate for their views. That, combined with a lack of resources, makes them minor players in the political process."[70] Finally, concerted efforts have been made recently to bring together various corporate interest groups, particularly the Chamber of Commerce, the Texas Association of Business, and the Texas Research League, so that the business community will speak to policy makers and to the public with one voice.[71]

★★★★★ CONCLUSION

Elections are expensive in Texas. Candidates are constantly seeking money to campaign effectively, especially through the mass media. Wealthy individuals and organizations are the prime sources of contributions, which are not legally limited in Texas, and, as such, they are influential in the politics of the state. As noted by Ken Ross, lobbyist for the Texas Medical Association, "there is no question that money in the campaign process is influential. Why else would we [give] it?"[72] At a minimum, large campaign donations gain their contributors access to officeholders.

Influence is furthered by constant personal contact with political officials. Well-organized groups have the resources to hire lobbyists to present their cases personally to officials. The web connecting campaign contributions and direct lobbying is tangled and, as shown in Highlight 4–2, can be quite effective in shaping policy. Moreover, providing research to officeholders and mobilizing public support at the grassroots level are important lobbying tools.

★ ★ ★

Highlight 4–2: Tobacco and Lobbying

In 1993, the Texas Legislature enacted a law that denies people the right to sue manufacturers for damages if they used a product that was known to be dangerous. Hence, for example, as long as cigarette companies adequately warn their customers of the potential hazards of tobacco, they are immune from future suits brought by ill smokers in Texas. One of the keys to the passage of this bill was the support of the leader of the state senate, Lieutenant Governor Bob Bullock. Bullock was instrumental in designing the bill behind the scenes and shepherding it through the legislature. The tobacco industry lobbied heavily for this measure.

Between 1990 and mid-1992, the PAC of tobacco giant Philip Morris contributed more than $75,000 to various political officials, including $15,000 to Bob Bullock's campaign. RJR Nabisco, another leading tobacco manufacturer, gave $5,000 to Bullock in 1992.[1] In the words of Dr. Alan Blum, founder of the antismoking group Doctors Ought to Care, "Bob Bullock takes money from the tobacco industry and says they can do business any way they please."[2] Tobacco companies also had forty lobbyists, including former legislators and the son of a longtime personal friend of Bob Bullock, working the legislature. Another physician, Dr. Joel Dunnington of the University of Texas System M.D. Anderson Cancer Center in Houston, attributed the legislative success of manufacturers to "money—money in the form of Philip Morris, the Tobacco Institute, and R. J. Reynolds. They have a tremendous amount of money."[3]

Notes

1. *Texas Observer,* March 26, 1993, pp. 3–4, and Bruce Hight, "Tobacco Industry's Influence Felt by Texas Legislators," *Austin American-Statesman,* February 8, 1993, pp. A-1 and A-8.
2. Quoted in Charles B. Camp, "Business Anticipates Victory on Tort Reform Bills," *Dallas Morning News,* February 20, 1993, p. A-16.
3. Quoted in Bruce Hight, "Tobacco Industry's Influence Felt by Legislators," p. A-8; also see the *Texas Observer,* March 26, 1993.

Overall, members of the economic elite are in the best position to be effective lobbyists. Consequently, many legislators, administrators, and judges—enough to have a major impact on the governing of the state—are deeply indebted to these interests. Economic issues dominate the agenda put before the political institutions of Texas. Other concerns and interests—for instance, those affecting the poor, workers, minorities, and consumers—are overshadowed by the attention paid to the requests, desires, and preferences of those who own and operate the principal means of production and distribution in Texas.

★ ★ ★ ★ ★   # NOTES

1. Charles W. Wiggins, Keith E. Hamm, and Howard Balanoff, "The 1982 Gubernatorial Transition in Texas: Bolt Cutters, Late Trains, Lame Ducks, and Bullock's Bullets," in Thad L. Beyle, ed., *Gubernatorial Transitions* (Durham, NC: Duke University Press, 1985), p. 379.

2. Richard H. Kraemer and Charldean Newell, *Texas Politics* (St. Paul, MN: West Publishing Co., 5th ed., 1993), p. 178.

3. Quoted in Mike Hailey, "'90 Election Costs Might Spur Reforms," *Houston Post,* November 11, 1990, p. A-22. Former Senator Montford actually used the figure of $35 million, which was the correct amount at the time of his statement. I have substituted the figure actually spent in the governor's race.

4. George Kuempel, "Richards' Campaign Ends $150,000 Short," *Dallas Morning News,* January 19, 1995, and Wayne Slater, "Governor Pays Campaign Debt; Cash Left Over," *Dallas Morning News,* July 18, 1995.

5. Ben Wear, "Ethics Law Allows Legislators to Live on Campaign Funds," *Austin American-Statesman,* April 23, 1995.

6. Wayne Slater, "Fuel for the Political Fires," *Dallas Morning News,* June 3, 1994.

7. Ken Herman, "For Unopposed Candidates, War Chest a Real Cash Cache," *Houston Post,* October 13, 1992, pp. A-1 and A-12.

8. Thomas Dye with L. Tucker Gibson, Jr., and Clay Robison, *Politics in America: Texas Edition* (Upper Saddle River, NJ: 1997), p. 777.

9. "Big Donations Fuel Richards, Bush Campaigns," *Austin American-Statesman,* July 29, 1994.

10. Wayne Slater, "Big Donors Fuel Governor's Race," *Dallas Morning News,* November 3, 1994.

11. Wayne Slater, "Fuel for the Political Fires."

12. Wayne Slater, "Lawyers' Donations Assailed," *Dallas Morning News,* September 14, 1994.

13. Interstate Bureau of Regulations, *State Political Action Legislation and Regulation: Index and Directory of Organizations* (Westport, CT: Quorum Books, 1984), and Ken Herman, "Speaker Ally Files Bill to End PACs, Lift Corporate Ban," *Houston Post,* March 5, 1991, p. A-11.

14. Ken Herman and Mike Hailey, "Texas PAC-ed House, Senate," *Houston Post,* October 29, 1990, p. A-9.

15. Wayne Slater, "Fuel for the Political Fires." The $861,915 contributed by the PAC of the law firm of Provost and Umphrey was not included here because it was incorporated into the text discussing contributions made by Mr. Walter Umphrey, mostly to Ann Richards.

16. Figures reported in George Kuempel, "PACs Hike Funding to State Senators, Citizens Group Says," *Dallas Morning News,* July 12, 1986.

17. Figures reported in Edward M. Sells, "Group Cites 'PAC-ed' House," *San Antonio Light,* July 24, 1986.

18. Laylan Copelin and Mike Ward, "Lawmakers Live High on Donations," *Austin American-Statesman,* August 27, 1989.

19. Ken Herman and Mike Hailey, "Texas PAC-ed House, Senate."

20. Wayne Slater, "Key State Leaders Get Big Money from Special-Interest Contributors," *Dallas Morning News,* January 16, 1995, and Ben Wear, "Ethics Law Allows Legislators to Live on Campaign Funds," *Austin American-Statesman,* April 23, 1995.

21. Mary Lenz, "Law Firms Top Donors to Justices," *Houston Post,* October 7, 1992, p. A-13, and Cleo Beard, "Campaign Reform Gains Support," *Lubbock Avalanche-Journal,* March 28, 1993, p. A-13.

22. Ben Wear, "Regulated Donating Heavily to Regulators," *Austin American-Statesman,* September 11, 1994.

23. Kathy Walt, "Nugent Accused of Selling Votes to Special Interests," *Houston Chronicle,* October 19, 1994.

24. Wayne Slater, "Fuel for the Political Fires."

25. "Contributors to Harris Judges Get High-Paid Posts, Report Says," *Austin American-Statesman,* June 12, 1994, p. B-5.

26. Quoted in Rod Davis, "The Sessions' Worst Lobby," Texas Observer, June 17, 1977, p. 22.

27. Quoted in Wayne Slater, "Big Donors Fuel Governor's Race."

28. Quoted in Wayne Slater and George Kuempel, "White's '86 Run Fueled by Large Contributions," *Dallas Morning News,* March 23, 1986.

29. Quoted in the *Texas Observer,* June 28, 1991, p. 24.

30. Wayne Slater, "'Late Train' Donations Aid Bush," *Dallas Morning News,* February 14, 1995.

31. See, for other recent examples, Michael Totty, "The Late Train: The Elections Are Over—And the Fund Raising Is Hot," *Wall Street Journal,* December 7, 1994, and Marc R. Masferrer, "Rusling Racks Up $34,000 After Vote," *Waco Tribune-Herald,* January 22, 1995.

32. David Broder, "Congress Should Address Campaign Funding," *El Paso Times,* November 20, 1978, p. 6-A.

33. Ben Wear, "Ethics Law Allows Legislators to Live on Campaign Funds," *Austin American-Statesman,* April 23, 1995.

34. "Nut Case," Corpus Christi Caller Times, September 24, 1994.

35. Ben Wear, "Ethics Law Allows Legislators to Live on Campaign Funds."

36. Tom "Smitty" Smith, quoted ibid.

37. Mark Toohey, "Big Bucks were Spent to Influence Legislation, Records Show," *Houston Chronicle,* July 23, 1989, and Roberto Suro, "Lobbying Becomes Bolder in Texas," *New York Times,* July 23, 1989.

38. Quoted in Wayne Slater, "Travis DA Urges Law Overhaul," *Dallas Morning News,* September 23, 1989.

39. Quoted in Virginia Ellis, "We Don't Do Bars: Austin's Best Play by New Set of Rules," *Dallas Times Herald,* March 1, 1987.

40. See Mike Ward and Jeff South, "Texas Government Still Draws Millions in Lobby," *Austin American-Statesman,* March 2, 1994, pp. A-1 and A-6.

41. Mike Ward, "Ex-Legislators Find Lobbying a Natural Turn," *Austin American-Statesman,* November 15, 1992, p. A-1.

42. Quoted in Felton West, "Ex-Legislators Find it Greener on Lobbying Side of Austin," *Houston Post,* January 30, 1985.

43. Ken Herman, "List of Lobbyists Includes 19 Who Still Hold State Positions," *Austin American-Statesman,* November 3, 1996.

44. Tom "Smitty" Smith, "Capitol Needs Thorough Cleaning," *San Antonio Express-News,* July 15, 1995.

45. Wayne Slater and George Kuempel, "Texas' 'Third House,'" *Dallas Morning News,* March 29, 1987.

46. Anonymous source quoted in Wayne Slater and George Kuempel, "Party Time," *Dallas Morning News,* March 30, 1987.

47. Ibid.

48. This is the conclusion suggested in most standard textbooks on Texas politics. For one assertion of this view, see Richard West, "Inside the Lobby," reprinted in *Texas Monthly's Political Reader* (Austin: Texas Monthly Press and Sterling Swift Publishing, 1978).

49. See ibid. and Harmon Zeigler and Michael Baer, *Lobbying: Interaction and Influence in American State Legislatures* (Belmont, CA: Wadsworth, 1969), p. 191.

50. See Harvey Katz, *Shadow on the Alamo* (Garden City, NY: Doubleday, 1972), and Sam Kinch, Jr. and Ben Procter, *Texas Under a Cloud* (Austin: Jenkins Publishing Company, 1972).

51. Reviewed in "The Best Ethics Money Can Buy," *Texas Observer,* January 11, 1991, pp. 3–4.

52. Ken Herman, "Lewis Paid Law Firm with Contributions," *Houston Post,* July 20, 1991, p. A-29.

53. Quoted in Mike Ward, "Gifts Commonplace for Key State Officials," *Austin American-Statesman,* July 13, 1989.

54. *Texas Government Newsletter,* November 24, 1975, p. 2.

55. Clifton McCleskey, Allan Butcher, Daniel E. Farlow, and J. Pat Stephens, *Government and Politics of Texas,* 6th ed. (Boston: Little, Brown, 1978), p. 176.

56. The origins of the League are discussed in Ronnie Dugger, "Researching the Researchers," *Texas Observer,* February 7, 1963, pp. 3–9, and John Muir, "Information Is Power," *Texas Observer,* August 9, 1974, pp. 14–16.

57. Personal communication from Craig Foster, former executive director of the Public Education Resource Equity Center, Austin, Texas. Reprinted by permission.

58. Quoted in the Texas Research League, *Annual Report,* 1978, p. 6.

59. John Muir, "Information is Power," p. 15.

60. Joe Pickerill, "TBA's Legislative Network Fights for Respect," *Texas Banking,* May 1992, p. 21.

61. The quotation is from Southwestern Bell employee Brenda McWilliams, who traveled from Lubbock to participate in the rally. Mary Alice Robbins, "Thousands Rally for Phone Company Deregulation," *Lubbock Avalanche-Journal,* April 14, 1993, p. A-7.

62. Sylvia Moreno, "Phone Companies Lobby for Reduced Regulation," *Dallas Morning News,* March 22, 1993, pp. A-1 and A-10.

63. For an interesting example of the grassroots effectiveness of the Texas Good Roads Association, see Griffin Smith, Jr., "The Highway Establishment and How it Grew, and Grew, and Grew," reprinted in *Texas Monthly's Political Reader* (Austin: Texas Monthly Press and Sterling Swift Publishing, 1978).

64. James E. Anderson, Richard W. Murray, and Edward L. Farley, *Texas Politics: An Introduction,* 2d ed. (New York: Harper and Row, 1975), p. 93.

65. James Dunn, quoted in "Baptist Director Criticizes Lobby," *El Paso Times,* February 8, 1981, p. 4-C.

66. Wayne Slater and George Kuempel, "Texas' 'Third House.'"

67. Wayne Slater and George Kuempel, "Public-Interest Lobbyists Find Persistence Sometimes Pays," *Dallas Morning News,* March 30, 1987.

68. Pam Fridrich, quoted in Mike Ward, "Stricter Rules Sought on Lobbyists' Gifts," *Austin American-Statesman,* July 14, 1989.

69. Harry Hurt III, "The Most Powerful Texans," reprinted in *Texas Monthly's Political Reader* (Austin: Texas Monthly Press and Sterling Swift Publishing, 1978), p. 15.

70. Quoted in Wayne Slater and George Kuempel, "Public-Interest Lobbyists Find Persistence Sometimes Pays."

71. See Dale Rice, "Corporate Harmony," *Dallas Times Herald,* February 22, 1988.

72. Quoted in Debbie Graves, "Legislators Draw Fire for Gifts from Special Interests," *Austin American-Statesman,* July 24, 1986.

PART III

Political Institutions

Political decision makers can be more easily swayed if political institutions can be easily penetrated by outside interests. In a fully democratic society, political institutions would be accessible to all citizens. If only a few groups can pass through the institutional walls surrounding political decision makers, democracy is weakened. This part of the book examines the major political institutions created to govern the state of Texas. Chapter 5 investigates the legislature. Chapter 6 focuses on the state's chief executive officers and its administrative system. Chapter 7 examines the judiciary. Beyond describing the actual workings of these institutions, each chapter emphasizes the access to the inner operations of state government by the holders of economic power in Texas.

CHAPTER 5

The Legislature

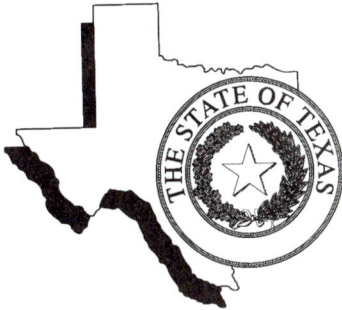

The chief function of any legislative body in the United States is to enact laws that are binding on the population living within its jurisdiction. State legislatures are mostly involved in formulating policy in the areas of education, transportation, criminal justice, welfare, the regulation of social and economic behavior, and the raising of revenue to finance these activities. In addition, state legislatures play a key role in establishing administrative agencies, overseeing their operations, selecting their personnel, and terminating their existence. On rare occasions, legislatures judge the improprieties of their own members or of other officeholders (for instance, the governor). Finally, the process of amending the state constitution begins in the legislature.

[handwritten: 31 = Senate = 4 yr terms]
[handwritten: 150 = House = 2 yr terms]

★★★★★ COMPOSITION *[handwritten: can serve any # of terms.]*

The Texas Legislature has 181 members: 150 in the House of Representatives and 31 in the Senate. Representatives are elected every two years from 150 geographic districts, each of which should ideally contain 117,000 residents. Senators serve four-year terms; about half of the Senate is chosen in each general election. Each senator represents one geographic area of the state. The ideal population size of a senatorial district would be 566,000.

Texas is not among the twenty-one states that have imposed fixed limits on the number of terms that legislators can serve. Practically speaking, terms are limited in Texas anyway, because it is rare to find any member of the House or the Senate who has been in office for more than ten years. During 1995, for instance, only 22 percent of Texas's 181 legislators had continuously held the same position for a decade or more; 58 percent had first been elected in 1991.[1]

[handwritten margin notes, top: " Reprensentative = 21 yrs old, A tx resident for 2 consecutive yrs. * Senate = 26 yrs old, a resident for 5 consecutive years"]*

Eligibility

[handwritten left margin: "Must both be a US citizen & one yr residency in the House or senatorial district."]

On the surface, most Texans are eligible to hold legislative office. A member of the House must be at least 21 and a Texas resident for two consecutive years prior to election. A senator must be at least 26 and have been a resident for five continuous years before election. United States citizenship and a one-year residency in the House or Senatorial district are the only additional major formal requirements.

In reality, however, only a few citizens can afford to sit in the Texas Legislature. As noted by John Hildreth (director of the Consumers' Union, southwest division), "we might as well point out in the Constitution that to run for the Legislature you must first be wealthy, be in a business or a law firm where your partners will cover for you while you're gone because they feel it's in the best interest of the firm, or be owned lock, stock and barrel by the [business] lobby."[2] The principal reasons for this situation are the high cost of waging an effective campaign for legislative office in Texas (as discussed in Chapter 4) and the low salaries paid to legislators.

Background of the Membership

The members of the Texas Legislature are not representative of the state's population. The general population is evenly divided between men and women, but only 18 percent of the legislature (33 legislators) are women. Although non-Hispanic whites constitute about 57 percent of the state population, they make up 71 percent of the legislature. Hispanics account for 28 percent of the state's population, but only 19 percent of the legislature. Nearly 12 percent of Texans, but only 9 percent of the legislators, are African Americans.

Forty-four percent of the members come from a business background, 30 percent are lawyers, 6 percent are farmers or ranchers, 4 percent are educators, and 3 percent are from the medical profession—hardly representative of the occupational profile of Texas society at large. About 75 percent are incumbents.[3] Their average age is 46. A majority have graduate or professional degrees. In short, the typical legislator is a middle-aged, middle-class, well-educated, white (non-Hispanic) male with prior experience in the legislature.

Compensation

Salaries for Texas legislators are set at $7,200 per year. By comparison with those paid in other states (especially industrialized ones), legislative salaries in Texas rank near the bottom. For instance, state legislators in California are paid $52,500 per year; in New York, they earn $57,500. Legislative salaries in Texas have not increased over the past three decades. An attempt to raise salaries to $23,358 was defeated by Texas voters in 1988. Currently, the Texas Ethics Commission can increase the pay of legislators, subject to voter approval.

Legislators also receive a supplemental daily allowance of $95 for the first 120 days of the legislative session. This per diem is allocated to cover lodging, meals, and related expenses. Legislators are also reimbursed for some expenses incurred in traveling between their districts and Austin. In 1991, legislators increased their own retirement benefits. If a legislator retires at age 50 after serving in office for twelve years, he or she can collect $13,632 per year. Retirement salaries increase with length of time spent in office, reaching more than $40,000 per year for legislators past age 60 who have held office for more than 30 years.[4] Texas's retirement system is third best among all state legislatures.

Assistance

Most Texas legislators, especially members of the House, find it financially difficult to hire competent full-time staff. During the 1980s, representatives in the House received $6,500 per month to operate their offices during the regular session and $5,500 per month during the interim between sessions. The most that representatives could pay a member of their staff each month was $2,000. Senators were allocated slightly more money. At best, legislators can hire two, perhaps three, full-time aides.

To stretch their assistance allowances, some members of the legislature pool their resources and hire aides whose services they share. The House Study Group was one such pooling arrangement. In 1986, 133 representatives and 15 senators each paid $250 from their allowances to fund this group. The following year the House Study Group was restructured to become a permanent administrative department of the House. It was given a new name—the House Research Organization—and a fifteen-person steering committee. The House Research Organization is financed for a year under a budget formulated by the steering committee. It currently has an annual budget of $675,000, about 20 percent of which comes from outside subscriptions to its publications.[5] In 1991, the Senate created the Senate Research Center, a counterpart of the House Research Organization.

Legislators can also draw on the technical and legal expertise of organizations especially created by the legislature to perform information services for its members. One such organization is the Legislative Council. The council is composed of fifteen legislators (ten from the House and five from the Senate), who appoint an executive director and a permanent staff. Legislators solicit the council for advice and assistance in drafting laws. Indeed, about three fourths of all bills introduced in the legislature each term are prepared by council staff. The Legislative Reference Library, located in the state capitol building, is a vital source of information for legislators and their aides. The library contains more than 30,000 documents. Finally, information concerning legislative activities, such as the status of bills, and committee schedules, functions, and members, is accessible over the World Wide Web at http://www.capitol.state.tx.us. Even with these various types of assistance, individual legislators find it difficult to fully inform themselves about all issues that pass before the legislature. One result is that they welcome outside-interest groups that offer research assistance. The success of the Texas Research League (Chapter 4) in legislative matters, especially those involving taxation, is a prime example of a group's obtaining access to the legislature by providing research services to Texas's lawmakers.

★★★★★ PROCEDURES

Texas legislators confront a complicated maze of formal and informal rules and procedures during the lawmaking process. Some of these obstacles are established by the Texas Constitution, while others are formulated by the legislature itself. Figure 5–1 presents a thumbnail sketch of the legislative path a bill must follow in order to become law in Texas.

The first step in enacting a law is the introduction of a bill. Only members of the legislature can officially offer proposals. Bills may be introduced either in the Senate or in the House (or in both chambers simultaneously). However, bills that require new revenue to be raised must be

✪ **FIGURE 5–1**
How a Bill Becomes Law

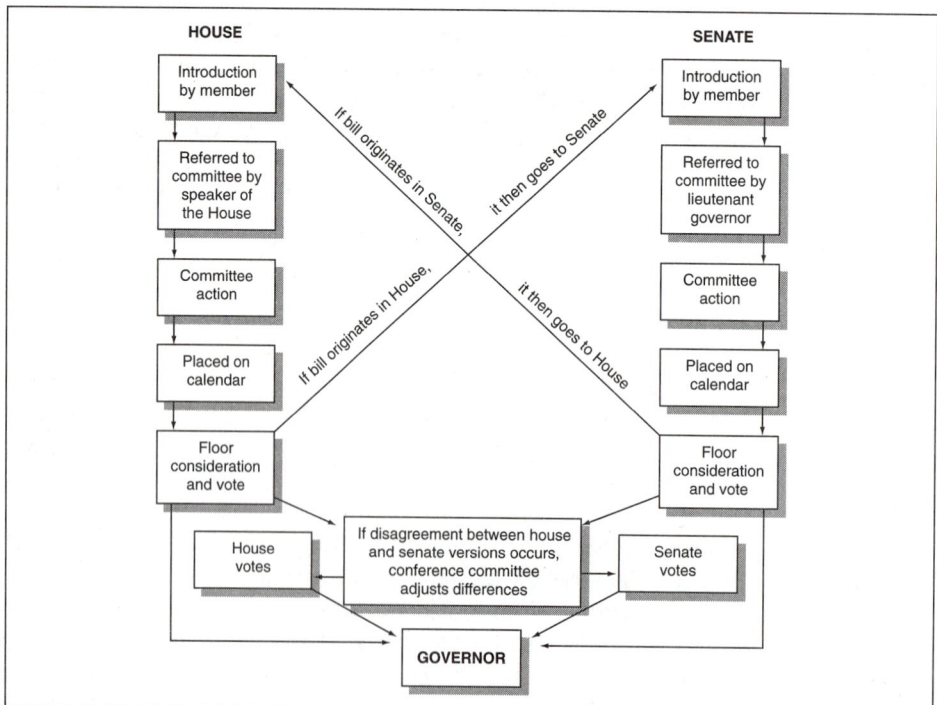

considered by the House first, and, in practice, most proposals start in this chamber. Most bills are introduced during the first sixty days of the session. After that, any bill, other than a local bill or one pertaining to an emergency declared by the governor, must be approved by a four fifths vote to be introduced. A member ordinarily provides thirteen copies of the proposal to the clerk of the House or to the secretary of the Senate to formally initiate the process. The bill is given an official number and the title of the bill is read to the Senate or House membership by the chief clerk; this is the *first reading* of the measure. More than 4,000 bills have been introduced in recent regular legislative sessions.

The presiding officer of the House or of the Senate assigns the bill to a standing committee. In the Senate, the lieutenant governor forwards bills to committees; in the House, the Speaker of the House has this duty. The committee assignment is announced at the first reading. Each presiding officer has some discretion in choosing the committee to which a bill is sent. If, for instance, the Speaker is dissatisfied with the work of the committee that first received a bill, he or she can unilaterally reassign the measure to another committee. A majority of the House membership can overrule the Speaker's choice of committee, but this rarely occurs.

Standing Committees

During the Seventy-Fifth Legislature (1997-98), there were thirty-six standing committees in the House: thirty were structured around substantive topics (for example, appropriations, business and commerce, agriculture, criminal justice, public and higher education, insurance, energy, and transportation) and six were organized to facilitate the flow of business in the House. The Senate had thirteen standing committees and one procedural committee. Table 5-1 lists the House and Senate committees that existed during the Seventy-Fifth session (1997–98). Observers identify Appropriations, State Affairs, Ways and Means, and Calendars as the most important House committees. Finance, State Affairs, and Jurisprudence are the top three Senate committees.

A standing committee is composed of a relatively small number of legislators, between seven and twenty-seven. Most substantive committees in the House have nine members; procedural committees usually have eleven. In the Senate, most committees have eleven or fewer members. Subcommittees are rare in the Texas Legislature; in the Seventy-Fifth legislative session, for instance, only the Senate's natural resources committee had subcommittees (two, each with five members) and the House's appropriations committee had nine subcommittees.

Each committee has almost complete control over matters brought before it. The committee may choose to hold open hearings, during which members of the public are invited to present their views on the bill. If a public hearing is called during the regular session, notice must be posted five days before the event. Committees also have the option of conducting

★ **TABLE 5–1**
Standing Committees in the 1997–1998 Texas Legislature

House	Number of Members
Substantive Committees	
Agriculture and Livestock	9
Appropriations	27
Business and Industry	9
Civil Practices	9
Corrections	9
County Affairs	11
Criminal Jurisprudence	9
Economic Development	9
Elections	9
Energy Resources	9
Environmental Regulation	9
Financial Institutions	9
Higher Education	9
Human Services	9
Insurance	9
Judicial Affairs	9
Land and Resource Management	9
Licensing and Administrative Procedures	9
Natural Resources	9
Pension and Investments	9
Public Education	9
Public Health	9
Public Safety	9
State Affairs	15
State, Federal, and International Relations	9
State Recreational Resources	9
Transportation	9
Urban Affairs	11
Ways and Means	11

a formal session, without public participation, during which a vote will be taken or a work session will be held without public input or a formal vote. In deciding a bill, the committee can approve a measure (either unchanged or with amendments), reject it, or let it die of neglect. During recent regular sessions, only about 20 percent of the bills introduced in the legislature have been enacted into law; most (about 67 percent) have never advanced beyond the committee stage.

Generally, only bills approved by a majority of the committee move ahead, although it is possible for the full membership of each legislative chamber to force a measure out of a recalcitrant committee. For instance, in the House, a committee can be ordered to discharge a bill if (1) the committee has held the measure for six working days and (2) two thirds of the members in the first seventy days of the session, and a simple majority thereafter, vote to remove the item from the committee's jurisdiction. How-

★ **TABLE 5–1** **Continued**

House	Number of Members
Procedural Committees	
Calendars	11
General Investigating	5
House Administration	11
Local and Consent Calendars	11
Redistricting	11
Rules and Resolutions	11

Senate	Number of Members
Substantive Committees	
Administration	7
Criminal Justice	7
Economic Development	11
Education	11
Finance	13
Health and Human Services	11
Intergovernmental Relations	11
International Relations, Trade, and Technology	9
Jurisprudence	7
Natural Resources	11
Nominations	7
State Affairs	13
Veteran Affairs and Military Installations	5
Procedural Committee	
General Investigating	5

ever, it is difficult to invoke these procedures; hence, committee control over legislative matters is almost absolute.

The chair is the most influential member of each committee. The chair can decide what bills the committee will consider, when it will meet, and whether to hold a public hearing on a given bill. Chairs also appoint the chairs and other members of most subcommittees, if they are deemed necessary, and decide whether a bill is to be sent to a subcommittee.

If a committee decides to take action on a bill, it may issue a report that states its recommendations, tells how committee members voted on the measure, gives a detailed analysis of the bill, and, if applicable, of its fiscal impact. The report is printed and given to other legislators in the Senate or House. Before all members of either chamber debate the bill, it must be scheduled for discussion on the floor. Because of the larger size of its membership, the scheduling of floor debate in the House is much more formal than in the smaller Senate. The rules of the House authorize the Calendars Committee or the Committee on Local and Consent Calendars to channel the flow of legislation from the standing committee to full debate of the measure.

The Committee on Local and Consent Calendars handles minor bills. Measures that affect only one of Texas's 254 counties are placed by the committee on the local calendar. Bills that are noncontroversial are placed on the consent calendar. For a bill to be put on either of these calendars, it must receive unanimous support from the members of the standing committee that originally deliberated its fate. Most minor bills end up on the consent calendar. All other bills emerging from the House standing committees must be sent to the Calendars Committee.

The Calendars Committee has thirty days to decide the calendar position of a bill. Since 1993, the committee's vote has been a matter of public record, a major departure from the past, when its deliberations took place behind closed doors. Previously, it was not unusual for a majority of standing committee members to pass measures to please their constituents, knowing full well that the Calendars Committee would quietly and secretly kill these measures.

The Calendars Committee can assign a bill to the emergency calendar, the major state calendar, or the general state calendar. Most bills are placed on the major state calendar. A bill's position on the calendar is usually determined by the date it emerges from the standing committee: the earlier a bill is reported out of committee, the sooner it is scheduled for debate. The Calendars Committee, however, can exercise some discretion in selecting the appropriate calendar for the bill and in placing it on that calendar. Because it possesses this power, the Calendars Committee is considered one of the most important committees in the House.

In the Senate, local and noncontroversial bills are scheduled for full Senate consideration by the Administration Committee. All other bills are sent directly to the Senate floor. At this stage, either in the House or the Senate, the bill is given a *second reading* before the full membership of the chamber, and floor action can commence.

Floor Action

In the senate, bills are simply scheduled for floor discussion in the order in which they are reported out of committee. However, this sequential arrangement can be altered by suspension of Senate rules. The bill's sponsor must notify the presiding officer of the chamber (the lieutenant governor) of his or her intention to change the calendar. Assuming the presiding officer concurs, the call for suspension must be approved by four fifths of the senate during the first sixty days of the legislative session or by two thirds during the remainder of the term. In recent sessions, a bogus bill has been introduced in the Senate on the first day. This bill stays in the Number One position throughout the session; no attempt is made to pass it. Thus, to consider any other bill—any bills that are real—

requires a suspension of the rules and means that a minority of between seven and eleven senators can block a motion to suspend and prevent the passage of bills.

Once a bill is on the floor of the House or the Senate, discussion of its merits is open to all legislators. Debate is more restricted in the House. Members are allotted ten minutes to present their views; the floor leader of the bill is allocated twenty minutes for introduction and twenty more for summation. More time can be authorized by a majority vote. Senators can talk as long as they wish (or are able). Unlimited discussion opens the door for attempts to filibuster a bill.

The term *filibuster* refers to the deliberate effort to kill or seriously hurt the chances of a bill through endless discussion. It is a tactic usually employed by opponents of the bill who are in the minority. The longest filibuster in Texas history is forty-three hours, a record set in 1977 by Senator Bill Meier (Democrat, Euless). A filibustering senator must speak to points germane to the bill and must remain at his or her desk during the entire filibuster. There are no breaks for food, drink, sleep, or other needs. When, during the 1993 legislative session, Senator Gonzalo Barrientos (Democrat, Austin) filibustered for eighteen hours, it was alleged that he was equipped with an "astronaut" kit to overcome the need to leave the Senate floor to use the men's room.[6]

Once a member has finished speaking, he or she must yield the floor to the presiding officer and thus cannot turn the debate over to a like-minded colleague. The presiding officer can then recognize a supporter of the measure and thereby short-circuit a prolonged filibuster attempt. Alternatively, a filibuster may be ended by invoking *cloture*. A cloture motion requires a two-thirds vote to pass and is rarely successful.

Third reading

Amendments to the bill may be made during floor debates. Acceptance of an amendment requires a majority vote in both the House and the Senate. After debate, and possibly with amendments added to it, the bill has its *third reading.* Amendments may be proposed on the third reading, but they require a two-thirds vote for passage.

Approval of a bill on both the second and third readings requires a simple majority vote in both the Senate and the House. In recent sessions, members of the House have often voted by division, which means that their votes are tabulated by computer, aggregated, and then vanish from the tote board in the chamber. No public record is kept that matches a vote to the legislator who cast it. Other votes are recorded, thus permitting the public to see how their representatives voted. It has not been uncommon for legislators to cast votes on behalf of absent colleagues. Although the rules require that a member be on the floor, or in a room adjacent to the chamber, to vote, the votes of legislators who are not even in the city of Austin have been recorded and counted. Indeed, new meaning was given to the term *ghost voting* in 1991 when the vote of a dead member of the house was tabulated, continually, until his body was discovered.

Conference Committees

Because the legislature is bicameral, all bills must have the consent of both chambers to become law. It is likely, however, that the two chambers will pass different versions of the same bill. These differences must be reconciled. A special ad hoc committee, known as a conference committee, is established each time such a conflict occurs. Every conference committee has ten legislators: five from the House and five from the Senate.

Since 1973, conference committees have been denied the right to substantially rewrite any bills approved by either the House or the Senate. A majority of the delegation sent from each chamber must agree on a common version of the bill. The conference committee's report is then presented for consideration by all members of the legislature. Legislators can approve the report, reject it, or return it to the conference committee for further work; they cannot amend the measure. Considering the fact that most legislation is actually formulated in the latter part of the session, there is little time for the full membership to do anything but accept the conference committee's version of a bill. Hence, the conference committee is very important in the enactment of laws in Texas. After the legislature approves a bill, that bill is sent to the governor for consideration; this process will be discussed in the next chapter.

Scheduling Constraints

The passage of legislation in Texas requires the clearing of a large number of hurdles within a short period of time. The legislature is constitutionally authorized to be in regular session for only 140 consecutive days, once every two years. The governor may call special thirty-day sessions, but only items specifically designated by the governor may be placed on the agenda of the special session. On the average, at least one special session is called in every two-year period. The Seventy-First Legislature (1989–90) was called into special session a record-breaking six times; all told, that legislature met for 276 days.

During the regular legislative session, a fixed schedule regulates the flow of business. The first thirty days are devoted to the introduction of bills, the approval of the governor's recess appointees (by the Senate only), and action on emergency appropriations requested by the governor. The second thirty-day period is dedicated to committee hearings on legislative proposals and consideration of emergency items. Only the last eighty days are left for legislative action on pending bills. No bills can be introduced after the first sixty days of the session. (However, these constitutionally established rules can be suspended in either chamber.)

Traditionally, a logjam of bills clogs the legislative session at its conclusion. Until recently, more than half the bills approved by the House, for instance, were passed in the last three days of the session. The result was a frenzy of activity and a substantial amount of uninformed voting. In 1993, Speaker of the House Pete Laney introduced a new timetable. If a bill is introduced first in the House, it must be approved no later than ten days before the session's end; House bills of major importance must be enacted within seventeen days of closing the session. Bills originating in the Senate must be approved by the House six days prior to termination. The last few days of the session are devoted to consideration of Senate amendments to House bills and conference committee reports.[7]

★★★★★ POWERS OF THE LEGISLATIVE LEADERSHIP

The process of converting an idea into legislative policy in Texas is a cumbersome, tortuous, often frustrating exercise. The probability of enacting a bill is enhanced greatly, however, if the leaders of the House and Senate favor and advocate its passage. The dominant figure in the House is the Speaker; the equivalent in the Senate is the lieutenant governor, who bears the constitutionally created title of President of the Senate.

The Speaker is elected by the 150 members of the House at the beginning of each regular session; selection requires majority support. Until the

I KNOW IT SEEMS LIKE JUST A RICH, COMPLEX URBAN STATE NOW, MAW, BUT WITH ENOUGH GRIT, HARD WORK AN' SHEER OBTUSENESS, WE CAN BY GOD TRANSFORM IT INTO A POOR, IGNORANT BACKWATER....

TEXAS HOUSE OF REPRESENTATIVES

BEN SARGENT

1970s, speakers customarily served for two terms or four years. Representative Bill Clayton broke with tradition and stayed as Speaker for four sessions, from 1975 to 1982. His successor, Gib Lewis, held the post for ten years. The current Speaker, James E. "Pete" Laney (Democrat, Hale Center), was first selected for this position in 1993. The lieutenant governor is elected every four years by the voters of Texas. Bill Hobby held this position from 1973 until his retirement from Texas politics in 1990. He was succeeded by Bob Bullock, former comptroller of public accounts.

The Speaker and the lieutenant governor are the presiding officers of their respective chambers. As such, they have a great deal to say about the day-to-day process of legislation and they determine much of the agenda facing the legislature. The leaders also, as we have mentioned, assign bills to committees. In the House, this means, in the words of a former speaker, that the leader "can do much to pass a bill he favors by sending it to a 'friendly' committee, one in which it is likely to receive favorable treatment by the chairman and a majority of the members."[8]

The legislative leaders also make, and rule on, procedural matters. In so doing, they exercise some control over legislative proceedings. When Gib Lewis began his tenure as Speaker, for instance, he instructed the Calendars Committee to schedule for floor debate only bills that were guaranteed to pass. At the beginning of the 1993 session, Pete Laney again reduced the number of House committees, removed the cloak of secrecy that shrouded the work of the Calendars Committee, and reorganized the scheduling of consideration for bills.

As presiding officers, the legislative leaders can choose to recognize members for participation in debate and discussion. Thus, they can, if they wish, prevent a legislator from taking the floor to offer amendments, to propose suspension of the rules, or to air unwelcome views. If the Speaker, for instance, "knows that a certain member is going to say something on the floor of the House and he does not wish to have it said, [he or she] can simply fail to recognize that member."[9]

In the Senate, the lieutenant governor has the power to greatly influence whether a bill will reach the floor of the chamber, and the authority to determine the specific order in which bills will be considered by the Senate. The lieutenant governor can vote in the case of a tie, and, if the chamber is meeting as a committee of the whole, can vote on all issues. The Speaker is a duly elected member of the House and can vote on all matters. Both leaders must sign all bills and resolutions before they can take effect.

The leaders also have significant influence on the appointment of members to the standing committees. In the House, the Speaker appoints the chair and vice-chair of each standing committee and also selects half the members of each committee; the remaining committee positions are filled through self-selection on the part of the legislators, and seniority determines the order in which these preferences are accommodated. The lieutenant governor appoints the chairs of Senate committees and about two thirds of the members of each committee; the other third is allotted on the basis of seniority. Reflective of the fact that Republicans held seventeen seats in the thirty-one-member senate, in 1997 Bob Bullock appointed a majority of Republicans to ten of the thirteen committees in that chamber. However, he selected Democrats to chair eight of those committees.

The legislative leaders also choose the five members from within their respective chambers to serve on conference committees. They can also appoint members to select committees and to direct committees to conduct studies during the interim between legislative sessions.

The lieutenant governor and the Speaker appoint the principal members of four organizations established to assist the legislature in its work. They also serve as the chief officers of each of these agencies. The four major legislative assistance agencies are the Legislative Council, the Legislative Audit Committee, the Legislative Education Board, and the Legislative Budget Board. The Legislative Council helps legislators in drafting bills and researching topics. The Legislative Audit Committee investigates the expenditures of any state administrative agency. The Legislative Education Board oversees the legislative interest in, and especially its financial obligation to, the public schools of Texas. The ten-member Legislative Budget Board (LBB) recommends to the legislature what the state should fund and at what price.

Sargent © 1989 *Austin American-Statesman*. Reprinted with permission of UNIVERSAL PRESS SYNDICATE. All rights reserved.

The most important of these agencies is the Legislative Budget Board. The lieutenant governor chairs the LBB and the Speaker serves as vice-chair. Each can make two appointments to the LBB. Some eighteen months before the beginning of the regular session, the LBB prepares a detailed operating budget for the state. After the session begins, the LBB's recommendations are forwarded to the Senate Finance Committee and to the Appropriations and Ways and Means Committees of the House. As we will discuss in Chapter 6, the governor's office has some voice in the budgetary process, but the legislative leaders usually have a greater say in budgetary matters.

In short, each of the legislative leaders possesses many resources that can be easily converted into political power. Indeed, the leaders are very much aware of their power base. Former Lieutenant Governor Bill Hobby notes that "today, the office of lieutenant governor is one of the most important in Texas government."[10] Former House Speaker (and lieutenant governor) Ben Barnes asserts bluntly that "a Speaker who uses the office fully can virtually determine what does and what does not become law in Texas."[11] Many members of the legislature agree. Commenting on Bob Bullock, Senator David Sibley (Republican, Waco) remarks

> He can reward or punish you. He can praise you or put you in the fear of God. He can persuade you with facts, he can appeal to your better instincts, or he can just flat come out and scare the hell out of you.[12]

Susan Weddington, vice-chair of the Texas Republican party, speaking of Pete Laney, states that "generally what ends up coming to the [House] floor is what the speaker wants to come to the floor, and all else simply vanishes."[13]

Political influence in the legislature is thus distributed along hierarchical lines. The presiding officer of each chamber exercises the most influence over legislation. A team composed of committee chairs and legislative aides surrounds the leader. Other legislators who wish to curry favor "go along to get along." The minority of legislators not on the leader's team, or not wishing to join it, are relegated to positions of secondary importance. According to former Speaker Barnes, "House members who have opposed the Speaker are likely to get assignments on the least active committees and be placed in roles where they can do him the least harm."[14]

★★★★★ ECONOMIC ELITES AND THE LEADERSHIP

There are many signs of a direct relationship between legislative leaders and wealthy individuals and corporations in Texas. The need for campaign contributions links aspirant leaders to well-heeled backers. Candidates for lieutenant governor campaign statewide for that office. The minimum cost of an effective campaign exceeds $1.5 million. A candidate for the Speaker's position must first be elected from a district, then be selected by a majority of other legislators. It is estimated that this latter election costs about $100,000. In consequence, in the words of former Speaker Barnes, "a candidate for Speaker must be acceptable to lobbying interests, especially those representing clients who are a prime source of political contributions in the state."[15]

Ben Barnes became Speaker in 1965 and held that position until 1970, when he was elected lieutenant governor. Before entering politics, he had no steady source of income; while he was in the legislature, his monthly salary was $400. Yet by 1971, "Barnes had business interests in radio stations at Grand Prairie and Abilene, several Holiday Inns, a multi-million-dollar shopping center, and an apartment complex in Brownwood, numerous stock investments, and 863 acres in valuable farm land."[16] Obviously, once in office, he had established connections with wealthy interests, including the Texas Manufacturers Association, developers, oilmen, and bankers.

Gus Mutscher, Barnes's successor as Speaker (1968–72), received financial support from several economic interests, including the beer lobby. Mutscher apparently did not forget his contributors: "According to those who financed the sailing of the Mutscher ship . . . , he never failed to serve his angels—from small things such as intervening with state agencies to larger matters such as passing crucial pieces of legislation."[17]

One year during his tenure (1975–82) as Speaker, Bill Clayton collected $62,000 from wealthy people and organizations for his office expense account. Much of this money was used to pay for the rental of an airplane from a company in which Clayton owned 100 percent of the stock, to entertain, and to hire staff, including the pilot of the plane.[18]

While in office, former lieutenant governor Bill Hobby amassed a great deal of money for his office expense account and spent it on a variety of items, including his Austin apartment, food and beverages, Christmas cards, and travel. Much of this money came from the PACs of large corporations, banks, law firms, professional associations, and real estate organizations.[19] In 1986, Hobby received $1.8 million in campaign donations, 69 percent of which was provided by lobbyists and PACs.[20]

Speaker Gib Lewis (1982–93) received substantial contributions from wealthy Texans in his initial efforts to win the Speaker's post. He clearly confirmed his economic commitments in a speech delivered to the Texas Association of Business in 1983, when he said, "What is good for business is good for Texas."[21] In 1986, Lewis raised almost a million dollars in campaign contributions: "80 percent came from special-interest political action committees and individual lobbyists."[22]

Current Speaker Pete Laney has received substantial financial support. Between 1990 and 1992, although he ran unopposed, he raised about $100,000 in campaign contributions, nearly 90 percent of which came from lobbyists, special interests, and PACs (such as the PACs of Houston Industries, Texas Utilities, Southwest Public Service, Continental Telephone, MCI, and GTE). In 1990, "not a penny in direct contributions [came] from anyone listing an address in his district."[23] In 1993–94, though he again ran unopposed, Laney received substantial contributions, almost three fourths of which were donated by PACs representing medical, legal, utility, oil and gas, real estate, and banking interests.[24] Facing Republican opposition in 1996, Laney raised nearly $1 million in contributions, most of which came from PACs and wealthy individuals.[25]

In his run-up to reelection in 1994, Lieutenant Governor Bob Bullock received $6.4 million from his benefactors. At least 41 percent of these funds came from PACs; the biggest donors represented casinos, bankers, organized labor, telecommunications, lawyers, and real estate interests.[26] Bullock was so flush with money that he could afford to contribute $400,000 to candidates for legislative office in what a spokesperson for him described as an effort "to help elect people who can deliver politically."[27]

Well-heeled economic interests also contribute to the chairs of legislative committees. In 1988, the chairs of 47 committees collected $4.7 million in campaign contributions, most of which came from PACs and lobbyists.[28] This pattern was repeated in the 1990 elections.[29] Between 1994 and 1996, 55 percent of the $5.3 million given to the chairs of the thirteen substantive committees in the Senate was contributed by PACs, most of which apparently represented business interests.[30]

★★★★★ CONCLUSION

The Texas Legislature is a weak political institution. Legislators are poorly paid, understaffed, and forced to resolve an enormous amount of business in a very short time. These limitations not only restrict the activities of the legislature, but also make it open to outside influence. In effect, well-organized economic interests can exert a great deal of pressure on the legislative process. This may partially account for the fact that the legislature is not very well regarded by the public, a majority of whom rate the performance of the legislature as no better than fair.[31]

The bridge between economic elites and the legislature is easily crossed. Most traffic flows through the legislative leadership and the chairs of committees. The leaders orchestrate much of the business conducted by the legislature. Through financial connections and ideological similarities, the leadership is usually closely allied with the state's economic leaders.

★★★★★ NOTES

1. Gary M. Halter, *Government and Politics of Texas* (Madison, WI: Brown and Benchmark, 1997), p. 98.
2. Quoted in Jim Warren, "PACs Throwing Their Weight Around in Austin," *Laredo Morning News,* March 23, 1986.
3. Profile of members of the Seventy-Fifth Legislature (1997-98), Clay Robison, "Taxing Matters," *Houston Chronicle,* January 12, 1997, p. 1D.
4. David Elliot, "Observers Shame Former Legislators for Perceived 'Revolving-Door' Plan," *Austin American-Statesman,* February 6, 1993, pp. A-1 and A-19.

5. Dave McNeely, "House Group Would Like Stability to Do Its Research," *Austin American-Statesman,* February 7, 1993, p. A-3.

6. *Austin American-Statesman,* April 28, 1993, p. B-3.

7. Laylan Copelin, "Laney Jolts House with Reform Plan," *Austin American-Statesman,* January 16, 1993, pp. B-1 and B-3.

8. Ben Barnes, "The Speaker's Office Seat of Power," in *Governing Texas: Documents and Readings,* 3d ed., Fred Gantt, Jr., Irving O. Dawson, and Luther G. Hagard, Jr. (New York: Crowell, 1974), p. 135.

9. Ibid.

10. Bill Hobby, "The Lieutenant-Governor's Job: An Incumbent's View," in Gantt, Dawson, and Hagard, *Governing Texas,* p. 131.

11. Ben Barnes, "The Speaker's Office," p. 134.

12. Quoted in Bruce Hight, "Genius or Hypocrisy? Bullock's Tactics Prove Effective in Legislature," *Austin American-Statesman,* April 26, 1993, p. A-1.

13. Quoted in Stuart Eskenazi, "Speaker Laney Walks Slowly, Hides Big Stick," *Austin American-Statesman,* January 1, 1997.

14. Barnes, "The Speaker's Office," p. 135.

15. Ibid., p. 138.

16. Sam Kinch, Jr., and Ben Proctor, *Texas Under a Cloud* (Austin: Jenkins Publishing Co., 1972), p. 84, and Harvey Katz, *Shadow on the Alamo* (Garden City, N.J.: Doubleday, 1972), p. 102.

17. Kinch and Proctor, *Texas Under a Cloud,* p. 66.

18. Jaime Murphy, "An Audit of Accounts Receivable," *Texas Observer,* September 9, 1978, pp. 9–10.

19. Ibid.

20. Wayne Slater and George Kuempel, "Texas' 'Third House,'" *Dallas Morning News,* March 29, 1987.

21. Quoted in "Lewis and Company Protect the Status Quo," *Texas Observer,* June 24, 1983, pp. 12–14.

22. Wayne Slater and George Kuempel, "Texas' 'Third House.'"

23. Ken Herman, "Laney Gets Most of His Campaign Funds from PACs," *Houston Post,* March 3, 1991, pp. A–27 and A–28, and Wayne Slater, "Lobbyists, PACs Give Heavily to Likely New Texas Speaker," *Dallas Morning News,* January 12, 1993, pp. A–1 and A–10.

24. Wayne Slater, "Key State Leaders Get Big Money from Special-Interest Contributors," *Dallas Morning News,* January 16, 1995.

25. Stuart Eskenazi and Jeff South, "Laney Hauls in Campaign Cash He Doesn't Need," *Austin American-Statesman,* August 21, 1996, and Stuart Eskenazi, "Speaker Laney Walks Softly, Hides Big Stick."

26. Wayne Slater, "Key State Leaders Get Big Money from Special-Interest Contributors."

27. Michele Kay, "Bullock Often Gives What He Receives in Campaign Donations," *Austin American-Statesman,* November 4, 1994.

28. Laylan Copelin and Mike Ward, "Lawmakers Live High on Donations," *Austin American-Statesman,* August 29, 1989.

29. Mike Hailey, "Panel Chairmen Say PACs Don't Influence Their Actions," *Houston Post,* March 3, 1991, p. A–28, and Ken Herman and Mike Hailey, "Texas PAC-ed House, Senate," *Houston Post,* March 3, 1991, pp. A–21 and A–23.

30. Stuart Eskenazi, "Group Hints Texas State Senators Controlled by Business Interests," *Austin American-Statesman,* June 6, 1996.

31. *Texas Poll,* July 1985; this finding appears often.

CHAPTER 6

The Executive Branch

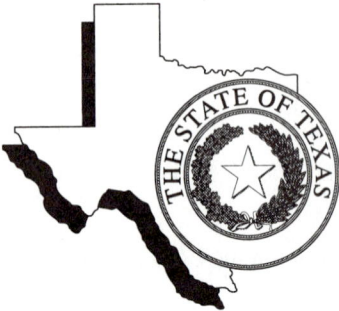

Public policy rarely becomes effective automatically. The executive branch of government is composed of administrative units established to carry out policy directives. Frequently, executives and administrators have discretion in implementation that goes beyond simple application; indeed, these actors often add new rules and adjudicate disputes that arise under the new policies. Rule implementation, rule making, and rule adjudication are thus usually within the legitimate authority of executives and administrative bodies. This chapter explores the executive branch in Texas, identifying the key administrative units and executives, their powers, and the linkage between economic influentials and this branch of government.

★ ★ ★ ★ ★ ## BACKGROUND

The executive branch of government has grown tremendously in the last half century. In Texas, there are so many administrative units that it is difficult to establish their exact number. One reliable source counts roughly 160 administrative units in the state;[1] an equally trustworthy estimate places the number nearer to 180.[2] All told, more than 230,000 full-time positions are available within the executive branch of state government.

There is great variation among the state's administrative agencies. Many of these differences are rooted in their origins, importance, and independence of the federal government. Fewer than 10 percent of the state's administrative units were established by the Texas Constitution: the legislature and the governor created the rest. A few are virtually inactive, others operate only sporadically, and the remainder are continually involved in administration. Federal assistance, usually in the form of money, supports some of these bodies, while others are funded solely by the state. In the budget for the 1996–97 biennium, the state legislature allocated money for more than 180 administrative boards, commissions, departments, and agencies, including state colleges and universities.

It would be a mindless (and perhaps impossible) exercise to describe all the activities of every administrative official and agency in Texas. Instead, a brief discussion of the major administrative positions follows, beginning with elected officials and going on to appointed ones.

★★★★★ ELECTED EXECUTIVES

The statewide electorate chooses some of the key executives in Texas. The state constitution authorizes the election of the governor, the attorney general, the comptroller of public accounts, and the commissioner of the General Land Office.[3] State law has further called for the election of the commissioner of agriculture and the members of the Railroad Commission and the State Board of Education.

The Governor

The governor of Texas is elected to a four-year term and there is no limit on the number of terms he or she may serve. The governor is the state's most visible officeholder: "To most citizens of Texas, the office of governor of Texas more than any other office is the epitome of state government."[4] This perceived importance is reflected by the fact that the governor receives an annual salary of $99,122, a mansion in which to live and a staff to maintain it, a generous expense account, and access to state-owned cars and planes. Moreover, Texans are more likely to recognize and express an opinion about the governor than any other state official. Yet regardless of high compensation and public recognition, the chief executive of Texas is rated among the weakest of all state governors. The most recent study ranks only South Carolina's governor as less formally powerful.[5] However, in the actual process of governing, the governor of Texas does possess some powers that make him or her an influential player in the making of policy and the implementation process.

Legislative Powers   The governor's major source of strength lies in his or her relationship with the legislature. By constitutional mandate, at the beginning of each regular session and on retirement from office, the governor must address the legislature and inform it of the "state of the state." The chief executive usually takes advantage of the opportunity to address the legislature on the first day of its session to present a set of policy proposals. In 1997, for example, Governor Bush's State of the State address to the legislature stressed property tax reform as the most important policy issue facing Texas.

The Texas Constitution also gives the governor the power to call *special sessions* of the legislature. These sessions last thirty days, and the governor can keep calling sessions indefinitely. During special sessions, the rule is that legislators must address only topics placed on the legislative agenda by the governor. Although they frequently stray from this rule, a simple point of order can easily bring legislators' attention back to the governor's stated priorities.

The governor's most potent legislative weapon is the *veto*. Every bill enacted by the legislature must be sent to the governor's office for approval. The governor can sign the bill, thus making it the law of the state, reject it by exercising veto power, or let it become law without a signature. With respect to the appropriations bill (the state budget), the governor has an *item veto*; that is, the power to invalidate any specific budgetary line in that bill. The governor has ten days during the legislative term—twenty days if the session ends—in which to act. If the governor does not do anything about a bill within these time frames, it automatically becomes law.

The legislature, if it is still in session, can override the veto by a two-thirds vote of members in each chamber. Compared with most other states, the number of votes needed to overrule the governor's veto is high in Texas. During her term in office, Ann Richards rejected sixty-two bills and resolutions. Her successor, Governor Bush, vetoed twenty-four bills during the Seventy-Fourth Legislative session. The governor's veto is usually final, often because the legislature has stopped meeting when it occurs and thus cannot override it. Only one veto—Governor Bill Clements's rejection of a minor matter in 1979—has been overridden by legislative action in the last sixty years.

Administrative Powers

The constitution names the governor the chief executive officer of the state, but fails to provide sufficient resources for him or her to exercise the powers implied by this title. The foremost administrative weapons at the disposal of the governor are his or her appointment, budgetary, military, police, and judicial powers.

Appointment Powers   During any four-year period in office, a governor can expect to make more than 4,000 appointments, yet several factors prohibit the governor from fully controlling administrative behavior through these appointments.

First, to become effective, many appointments require the consent of two thirds of the Senate. Although it is very likely that the Senate will accept the governor's selections, rejection has occurred. At a minimum, the Senate's role in the nomination process guarantees that at least some of the governor's nominations will be carefully scrutinized by legislators. Moreover, the governor's recommendation must be approved by the senator representing the district in which the nominee resides. This practice is called *senatorial courtesy*. Without the approval of the appropriate senator, the Senate will not confirm an appointment.

Most gubernatorial appointees take office before their selection is confirmed by the legislature. Governors frequently make appointments while the legislature is in recess, on the assumption that the legislature will confirm the nomination when it next meets. Often, however, the next convening of the legislation is the result of a called session and, because of the crush of business, confirmations are not made. As a result, administrators may serve a substantial length of time in office before the Senate formally approves their appointment. In 1990, the attorney general issued an opinion advising that if a recess appointment is not confirmed during the subsequent legislative session—even if it is a special session—the administrator must relinquish his or her position.

Second, many appointed officials serve six-year terms, and vacancies occur at staggered two-year intervals. The governor's four-year term makes it impossible for him or her to appoint all administrators unless he or she is reelected. Until recently, many administrative appointments took place at the end of the calendar year, thus allowing defeated or retiring governors the luxury of lame-duck appointments and depriving their successors of the opportunity to make these selections. Since 1983, however, governors are required to nominate appointees before November 1 in an election year. In addition, the terms of many appointed positions now expire in February of odd-numbered years.

Third, the governor often has a small pool of people from which to fill administrative positions. Special requirements for administrative positions are sometimes set by Texas law, thus limiting possible choices. Moreover, the informal pressure exerted by clients of agencies at times restricts the power of the governor in the selection process. (Both of these points will be discussed later in this chapter.)

Fourth, it is not easy for governors to remove people from administrative office. Until 1980, the chief executive could dismiss only members of his or her personal staff (some 350 people). The voters approved an amendment to the state constitution in 1981 that allows the governor to remove appointed administrators. The governor must show cause for termination and any recommendation for removal must be approved by two thirds of the Senate if this chamber originally confirmed the appointment. The governor cannot remove the appointees of his or her predecessor. The governor of Texas has yet to remove an administrator under these rules.

Even with these limitations, the governor's appointment power still allows the chief executive influence in shaping the executive branch of government. As shown in Table 6–1, Ann Richards, for instance, attempted to redress the gender and ethnic imbalance among administrators that existed in previous administrations, such as during Bill Clements's stint as chief executive, by appointing a substantial number of women (43 percent), African Americans (16 percent), and Hispanics (18 percent). In his first two years, the social backgrounds of Governor George Bush's 1,200 appointments have not been as diverse as those of the administrators chosen by his predecessor.

★ **TABLE 6-1**
Recent Gubernatorial Appointments by Ethnicity and Gender

	Bill Clements (1987–90 and 1979–82)	Ann Richards (1991–94)	George W. Bush (1995–96)
Ethnicity			
White (non-Hispanic)	89%	64%	79%
African American	3%	16%	8%
Hispanic	7%	18%	11%
Gender			
Male	82%	57%	66%
Female	18%	43%	44%

SOURCE: Dave McNeely, "Gov. Bush Appointees Becoming a Majority," *Austin American-Statesman*, January 28, 1997.

Budgetary Powers All state agencies and officials are required to submit detailed financial reports to the governor's Office of Budget and Planning twice a year. Further, this office has access to the accounts and financial records of all administrative units. The governor is fully involved in the work of the Office of Budget and Planning and, as the state's chief budget officer, is expected to formulate Texas fiscal policy. In reality, as we have mentioned in Chapter 5, the governor's role in budgetary matters is secondary to the part played by the Legislative Budget Board. Because of this imbalance, each administrative agency has a strong financial incentive to independently approach the legislature, forging political alliances that might improve its budgetary position regardless of the governor's preferences.

The governor's part in making fiscal policy was expanded in 1985 when a constitutional amendment was approved allowing the chief executive some financial discretion if an emergency arises during the legislative recess. During such emergencies, the Office of Budget and Planning is authorized to transfer funds from one administrative agency to another, to change the funding priorities of an agency, and to alter the timing of spending funds appropriated to an agency.

Military, Police, and Judicial Powers. The governor may unilaterally call out the Texas Rangers, the Department of Public Safety, and the state militia in times of natural disaster or civil unrest. In emergencies, the chief executive can declare martial law, and in so doing can suspend normal rights and freedoms. Moreover, the governor has a limited power of clemency (mercy). He or she may grant a thirty-day delay in the execution of any prisoner sitting on Death Row. Before 1936, the governor could issue pardons and reprieves and commute the sentences of prisoners. Much of this authority has now been transferred to the Board of Criminal Justice. The governor can still release prisoners from jails if they are overcrowded. In 1987, for instance, Governor Clements ordered the release of 750 prisoners per week. In executing this mandate, the Board of Pardons and Paroles let twenty Death Row inmates, including convicted killer Kenneth McDuff, out of prison.[6] McDuff subsequently was accused of going on a killing spree, terrorizing many people in Central Texas.

In short, the Texas governor occupies an ambiguous position in the state's political system. On the one hand, the governor's office is deliberately designed to be weak. Because his or her executive power is shared with other elected officials, and through checks and balances that operate in the other branches of government, especially the legislature, the governor's political autonomy is very limited. On the other hand, the governor's existing legislative, administrative, and military, police, and judicial powers are fairly substantial. Vetoes, appointments, fiscal responsibility, and emergency powers are resources that can be deployed to influence policy making. The governor's power is enhanced by public popularity, an aggressive style of leadership, and an ability to persuade others of the merits of his or her ideas. To gain some insight into variations in gubernatorial styles, let's look at four of Texas's most recent chief executives: Mark White, Bill Clements, Ann Richards, and George W. Bush.

Governor Mark White   Mark White served as governor between 1982 and 1986. Once in office, he tried to create a hierarchical structure in his administration. On the surface, White's executive organization appeared efficient and effective. However, in practice, it was marked by disorganization, lacking both direction and a clear chain of command. In the early stages of White's administration, his office had an "atmosphere . . . close to the chaos of a political boiler room."[7] Near the end of his term, it had become "weak on substance and strong—too strong—on appearance."[8] Part of the problem apparently stemmed from White's overall style of leadership, which was characterized by considerable indecisiveness. Moreover, he depended greatly on opinion polls to provide ideas and issues for him to promote. Consequently, "relying on polls . . . made White a follower, not a leader."[9] Over time, ironically, these polls revealed a growing loss of confidence among Texans in White's ability to do his job.

Governor Bill Clements   Bill Clements, the state's first Republican governor since Reconstruction, was initially elected governor in 1978. He was defeated in his bid for a second term by Mark White in 1982. In contrast to White's approach, the structure of Governor Clements's office during his first term "was more horizontal and diffuse."[10] Clements's office was run in a businesslike manner, more like a corporation than a political organization. By most accounts, he was judged an effective administrator and he appointed several capable people to administrative posts. Nonetheless, Clements's first administration was hampered by some poorly conceived ideas, and his abrasive, opinionated style of leadership provoked controversy, often interfering with the initiation and implementation of his programs.[11]

Clements was reelected in 1986, soundly defeating Mark White. He again installed a businesslike administration. However, the turmoil that afflicted Texas during this period of economic disequilibrium made it extremely difficult to establish a smooth, stable approach to problem solving. Faced with sluggish economic growth and declining revenue, Texas's lawmakers confronted the dilemma of either cutting state programs and services or raising taxes. Regardless of the direction the state took, leadership was crucial. Clements's brusque political style led to the debunking and obstruction of policy proposals, rather than the formulation of new ideas that might have alleviated the state's problems. Clements never could rally much public support. For instance, a year after his 1986 victory, only 2 percent of the public rated him an excellent governor; 21 percent thought he was doing a good job; 44 percent considered his performance "fair"; and 21 percent said he was doing poorly.[12] His approval score did improve to some extent in 1990—after he announced his plans to retire soon from state politics. Even then, a majority of Texans still evaluated his performance as governor as fair or poor; 3 percent rated him excellent; 33 percent, good.[13]

Governor Ann Richards   Ann Richards rose out of the rough-and-tumble of liberal politics in Austin. After gaining some notoriety by promoting liberal causes in the 1960s and 1970s, she sought and won a place on the Travis County Commissioners Court. During the 1980s, she was elected state treasurer, a post she held for two terms. She burst onto the national scene at the 1988 Democratic National Convention, when, during her keynote speech, she proclaimed that Republican George Bush was "born with a silver foot in his mouth." Richards entered the governor's race in 1990, defeating a strong field of candidates in the Democratic primary and, after trailing in the polls for most of the campaign, triumphing over her Republican opponent, Clayton Williams, on Election Day. Both her primary and general election campaigns were bruising, characterized not by debates on policy issues but by personal attacks and mudslinging.

As the state's chief executive, Richards displayed a flair for both leadership and pragmatism. Within the executive branch, she forced the resignations of several administrators with whom she had policy disagreements. As detailed in Table 6–1, she greatly expanded the number of women and minority members appointed to state positions. Working in partnership with the legislative leadership, she broke the gridlock that had nearly paralyzed state government in the late 1980s.

Throughout her career as governor, Richards was well aware of political realities. She was willing to ally herself with Republicans, liberals, and conservatives. She shied away from unpopular measures, such as raising taxes, and rarely directly confronted the state's powerful economic interests. Her pragmatic style inspired some criticism, most of which suggested that she would sacrifice substantive policy goals to her desire to be seen as someone who could get things done. Moreover, her reluctance to push for new taxes severely limited the ability of the state to move in new directions, thus, in effect, perpetuating the status quo.

Richards was a very popular leader. A strong majority of Texans gave high marks to her performance on the job and she was perceived as honest, an effective leader, hard-working, caring, and able to understand complex issues.[14] One evaluation concluded that "she . . . managed to serve . . . without accumulating any serious political liabilities or resolute enemies. She even appeals to many Republicans."[15] Perhaps her inability to appeal to a larger number of Democrats sowed the seeds of her electoral defeat in 1994.

Governor George W. Bush   George Bush entered the 1994 governor's race with excellent name recognition, as we have mentioned in Chapter 4, because of his famous father, and no political experience. He comes from a strong business background, having been an owner and managing general partner of the Texas Rangers baseball team and a major investor in various ventures. Bush reported a total of $610,722 in total income on his 1993 tax return.[16]

As Texas's third Republican governor, Bush, at least in his first three years, clearly, concretely, and concisely defined his legislative agenda. He also cultivated a pragmatic style in working with the legislature, whose leaders, as we have mentioned in Chapter 5, are Democrats. Indeed, his appeal to legislators was based more on a shared commitment to conservative principles than on party partisanship. Consequently, most of Bush's legislative proposals in the Seventy-Fourth Legislature were passed. More than two thirds of the public evaluated his performance after two years in office as good or excellent; only 4 percent rated him as poor.[17]

The Attorney General

The Office of the Attorney General provides legal counsel to the governor, the legislature, and a wide array of administrative boards, agencies, and commissions. The attorney general is the state's lawyer in legal matters. In civil cases, the office provides legal counsel whether the state is the plaintiff or the defendant, and no matter which governmental department is involved. In criminal proceedings, the attorney general can coordinate investigations, assist in the preparation of cases, and seek civil sanctions (fines, for example) against those who commit offenses, but the office cannot prosecute violators of the criminal law.

The attorney general can also issue advisory opinions to state and local officials throughout Texas and is authorized to answer questions about state law submitted by these officials. Although his or her opinion is not legally binding, in the absence of a court ruling the attorney general's view carries great weight and it is usually the final interpretation.

The Texas Constitution and state law authorize the attorney general to investigate activities of corporations and to guard against the rise of monopolies in Texas. This office has the power to search corporate records, gather any information that shows illegal corporate action, and submit it as evidence in a civil case against a company. This investigatory power is not much inhibited by the law: "The Attorney General has full, unlimited, and unrestricted right to examination of corporate books at any time and as often as deemed necessary."[18] A corporate executive who denies the governor's office access to company books can be fined or imprisoned. Yet, throughout the history of Texas, "there is a strong tradition of restrained use of these powers by the Attorney General."[19] A fairly recent evaluation, offered by a spokesperson for the state Chamber of Commerce, praised Attorney General Dan Morales—the highest-ranking, and first, Hispanic to hold state office in Texas—for "doing a good job . . . they're certainly not working against us."[20]

Finally, the office can be assigned various duties by the legislature. In recent years, the attorney general has been authorized to enforce state and federal laws requiring the payment of child support, to collect debts owed by students who have received state loans to attend college, to administer money to victims of criminal acts, to conduct investigations into Medicaid fraud, and to process claims made under the state's workers' compensation laws.

Dan Morales commands an office employing more than 3,800 people, 500 of whom are lawyers. Since taking office in 1990, Morales has dramatically increased the number of women and members of minority groups working in the attorney general's office.[21]

The Comptroller of Public Accounts

The comptroller of public accounts is the chief tax collector for the state. In this capacity, his or her office has the ultimate responsibility for the collection of the general sales tax, the severance tax on oil and natural gas produced in Texas, the motor fuels tax, the inheritance tax, and many occupational taxes and other minor taxes. Overall, this office collects 33 taxes, which account for 95 percent of all state revenue. As Texas's principal accountant, the comptroller keeps a complete record of all revenue received by the state and all its expenditures. Requests for payment of state funds must be made to this office; once approved, warrants (checks) are issued to the appropriate party.

In 1942, the comptroller was constitutionally authorized to certify that the appropriations bill passed by the legislature is in accordance with present or incoming revenue. If, in his or her judgment, funds are not or will not be sufficient to cover appropriated costs, the budget is void—unless four fifths of all legislators vote to override the comptroller's objections. Consequently, the comptroller is a major player in budget considerations. In recent years, Comptroller John Sharp has completed an extensive audit of state programs, in the course of which he has recommended billions of dollars in reductions of expenditures. Many of these suggestions have landed on the legislative agenda and have been incorporated into the state budget.

In 1996, the comptroller's office assumed the functions and responsibilities of the Treasury Department, the foremost of which is managing a large portion of the state's assets. As part of this task, state money is invested in various venues, including state banks. Thus, the comptroller's office now assumes all fiscal responsibility for the state's money, its investments, and its trust funds. The comptroller is also a member of other administrative agencies, the most important of which is the State Banking Board, whose responsibility includes the licensing of new banks in Texas.

The Commissioner of the General Land Office

Texas holds title to 20.6 million acres of land. Some of this land is suitable for agriculture, but the most profitable acreage contains petroleum products. Nearly 60 percent of this land is dedicated to the support of the public education system in Texas. The commissioner of the General Land Office administers the use of the state's land, including its veterans' land program. At times state land is sold outright, but most of it is leased. The commissioner is responsible for collecting money earned from the rental or sale of public land. In 1994, the commissioner deposited $270 million in the Permanent School Fund from revenue collected for state land.[22] Democrat Garry Mauro has been commissioner since 1982.

The Commissioner of Agriculture

The Department of Agriculture was established by the legislature in 1907. The commissioner enforces and promulgates regulations pertaining to the growth of plants; the marketing of fruits, vegetables, and eggs; the sale, use, and disposal of pesticides; and the accuracy of weights and measures such as meters, pumps, and scales. Therefore, its activities affect the wealth and well-being of growers, farm workers, and consumers. In addition, the Department promotes the sale of Texas agricultural products and disseminates information to farmers and ranchers through its market news service. Republican Rick Perry, who is a close friend of Governor George W. Bush, ousted Jim Hightower as commissioner of agriculture in 1990.

The State Board of Education

The State Board of Education consists of fifteen people, each of whom is elected from one school district. The board establishes policy for the state's primary, secondary, and vocational schools. Among other things, it prepares a budget for the public schools, approves textbooks for classroom use, sets general policy for all school districts, evaluates achievement of policy goals, reports to the legislature on progress toward meeting these objectives, and oversees the financial performance of local school districts. The governor (with the consent of the Senate) appoints the commissioner of education, who implements the board's policies and makes recommendations for its consideration. The commissioner is aided by the Department of Education (composed of professional and clerical staff appointed by the commissioner).

Together, the State Board of Education, the commissioner, and the Department of Education constitute the Texas Education Agency (TEA), the administrative unit responsible for public education below the college level in Texas. A special audit of the TEA, completed by the comptroller's office in 1993, concluded that the agency was an inefficient, bloated bureaucracy characterized by a workforce guaranteed tenure regardless of job performance. The report recommended 130 changes in the way the agency operates.

The Railroad Commission

The final major administrative agency whose members are elected statewide is the Texas Railroad Commission (TRC), which was created in 1891. Usually, however, the three commissioners are first appointed by the governor (with the confirmation of the Senate) to serve out the unexpired terms of commissioners who retire. The newly appointed commission member is subsequently elected to a full six-year term. The commission has jurisdiction over transportation and petroleum matters in Texas.

For many years, the TRC had regulatory control over railroads, buses, trucks, and energy firms doing business in Texas. In 1994, the legislature removed intrastate road transportation and high-speed rail travel from the commission's regulatory jurisdiction. The TRC's continuing jurisdiction over the petroleum business makes it extremely important, not only in Texas but also nationwide. It supervises many technical and substantive aspects of oil production, such as the spacing of wells and the amount of oil that can be removed from a field. Its regulatory powers not only promote conservation of petroleum, but also affect the market price of oil and the products derived from it. Rate hikes for natural gas also come under the jurisdiction of the commission. Moreover, it sets policy for the transportation and distribution of natural gas throughout the state and for the mining of coal, lignite, and uranium. Finally, the TRC is the state's watchdog over the environmental impact of exploration of Texas's mineral resources.

★ ★ ★ ★ ★ # APPOINTED ADMINISTRATORS

Officials appointed to their positions of administrative power abound in Texas. The functions of their offices, boards, and commissions cover a wide spectrum of activities. The Legislative Budget Board classifies these offices into several categories, including general government (for example, commissions on the arts, history, human rights, and veterans and the office of the secretary of state), health and human services, education, public safety and justice, natural resources, business and economic development (which includes commerce, the lottery, housing and community affairs, employment, and transportation), and regulation (of, for example, financial matters, insurance, real estate, racing, public utilities, and workers' compensation). Table 6–2 lists the most important of these administrative units. In addition, there are 24 boards responsible for licensing and certifying people to engage in certain occupations in Texas, including lawyers, doctors, nurses, accountants, architects, barbers, optometrists, pharmacists, chiropractors, dentists, psychologists, plumbers, and veterinarians.

The governor, ordinarily subject to Senate confirmation, appoints most of these administrators. Although terms of office may vary, the usual length of an appointment is six years. The administrative agencies are mutually independent. Within a common policy area, autonomy is frequently found. For instance, the ten boards of regents that supervise the senior colleges in Texas are distinct agencies. The Coordinating Board of Texas Colleges and Universities was established in 1965 to oversee the operations of the entire system and to prevent duplication in programs and curriculums. But the board has had some difficulty contending with the independence of various sets of regents, especially the regents of the University of Texas. Control over the administration of water policy is divided among numerous boards and commissions; for instance, the Public Utility Commission sets rates for water utilities, the Water Development Board establishes the general overall water policy of Texas, and river authorities, such as the Lower Colorado River Authority, regulate the development of major rivers in the state. Additional examples in which several agencies have jurisdiction in the same general administrative area are evident in other policy areas, such as the regulation of labor and of the environment.

In an interesting attempt to coordinate the state's role in environmental protection, the legislature created the Texas Natural Resource Conservation Commission in 1993. The commission consolidated several once-autonomous agencies, including the Texas Air Control Board, the Texas Water Commission, the Bureau of Solid Waste Management, and the Bureau of Environmental Health, under one administrative roof. Overall, it has primary responsibility for preventing degradation of the environment, although the elected Railroad Commission still maintains jurisdiction over environmental matters pertaining to the oil and gas industry.

Organizationally, most boards and commissions have similar structures. Many of the appointed members are nonsalaried, part-time administrators, meeting as a group to oversee the agency only on occasion. The heaviest burden of administrative duties is placed on the shoulders of a full-time, salaried commissioner or executive director appointed by the board or commission (with Senate confirmation in most cases). For instance, a board of regents for a college or university system appoints (in this case without Senate approval) a chancellor or president (the title varies with the

★ **TABLE 6–2**
Major Appointed Administrative Agencies in Texas

Administrative Units	Functions	Number of Members
General Government		
Secretary of State	Supervises the conduct of state elections	1
Education		
Board of Regents (10 in total)	Supervises senior-level universities	9 (on each board)[a]
Boards of Trustees (50 in total)	Supervises junior or community (two-year) colleges	varies[b]
Coordinating Board, Texas Colleges and Universities	Coordinates senior and junior college systems	18[a]
Business and Economic Development		
Transportation Commission (Heads Department of Transportation)	Oversees construction and maintenance of state roads and highways	3[a]
Board of the Department of Commerce	Promotes the economic development of the state	6[a]
Texas Employment Commission	Sets standards for receiving unemployment benefits	3[a]
Health and Human Services		
Board of Human Services	Supervises state participation in family assistance and medical assistance to the poor and elderly	6[a]
Board of Department of Health	Oversees a broad array of programs relating to disease prevention and provision of health services	18[a]
Board of Department of Mental Health and Mental Retardation	Supervises mental health and mental retardation services, including clinics, hospitals, and centers	9[a]
Health and Human Services Commission	Coordinates and plans the delivery of health and human services throughout the state; oversees state's Medicaid program	19[c]
Regulation		
Public Utility Commission	Regulates activities of (especially rates charged by) telephone and electric companies	3[a]
Finance Commission	Oversees activities of banks and savings and loan firms	12[d]

★ **TABLE 6-2 Continued**

Administrative Units	Functions	Number of Members
State Banking Board	Charters state banks, examines state bank records, and monitors state banks	3[e]
Public Insurance Counsel	Represents the interests of insurance consumers	1[f]
State Securities Board	Regulates the sale of stocks and bonds in state	3[a]
Credit Union Commission	Oversees operations of credit unions in state	9[a]
Workers' Compensation Commission	Determines compensation for injured workers	6[a]
Public Safety and Criminal Justice		
Public Safety Commission	Responsible for traffic and criminal law enforcement	3[a]
Commission on Jail Standards	Responsible for upgrading and standardizing jails in the state	9[a]
Board of Criminal Justice	Oversees operations of the state's prison facilities, grants pardons and paroles	9[a]
Natural Resources		
Natural Resource Conservation Commission	Implements air and water quality standards, monitors air and water pollution, issues water permits, settles water disputes, oversees waste management disposal	3[a]
Low-Level Radioactive Waste Disposal Authority	Oversees disposal of radioactive material in state	6[a]
Parks and Wildlife Commission	Oversees fish and wildlife in state	6[a]
Water Development Board	Promotes development of water resources and projects	6[a]

[a] All members are appointed by the governor (with Senate confirmation) for staggered six-year terms.

[b] Members of the Boards of Trustees are elected from the community college district; size and terms of office vary.

[c] Composed of the governor; lieutenant governor; Speaker of the House; two members of each legislative chamber; six members of state agencies, boards, and commissions; and six public members appointed by the governor, the lieutenant governor, or the Speaker of the House.

[d] Composed of six banking officials, three savings and loan executives, and three members of the public; each is appointed by the governor, with Senate confirmation.

[e] The State Banking Board is composed of the comptroller of public accounts, the commissioner of banking, and a third person appointed by the governor with Senate confirmation for a two-year term.

[f] Appointed to a two-year term.

system) to preside over that institution. The Coordinating Board of Colleges and Universities has a full-time commissioner of higher education. The Transportation Commission selects a state engineer to supervise its policies and programs. Similarly, a commissioner, executive director, or manager is appointed (with Senate confirmation) by the Department of Human Services, the Department of Health, the Department of Mental Health and Retardation, the Department of Commerce, the Natural Resources Conservation Commission, the Public Utility Commission, the Finance Commission, the Department of Insurance, State Securities, the Credit Union Commission, the Texas Employment Commission, the Workers' Compensation Commission, the Public Safety Commission, the Commission on Jail Standards, the Department of Criminal Justice, the Low-Level Radiation Waste Disposal Authority, and the Department of Parks and Wildlife.

Many of the administrative agencies listed in Table 6–2 are organized into divisions or sections (as are the departments headed by elected administrators or executives in Texas).

Subdivisions within a department are usually created to implement specific policies or to serve geographical areas of the state. The Public Utility Commission, for example, consists of seven units: hearings, telephones, electricity, operations, information and services, administration, and general counsel. The usual result is bureaucratic decentralization in the implementation of public policy, so that the actual responsibility of administration rests in the hands of a relatively obscure official or bureau within the agency.

The Texas Department of Transportation provides a good example of the decentralization process. A three-person commission appointed by the governor and the Senate establishes the general policy of the department. Its chief administrative officer is a state engineer, who is selected by the commission (with the consent of the Senate). Two assistant engineers work under the state engineer. One of these assistants supervises a division with eight component sections, while the other one supervises a division composed of seven separate administrative units. In addition, the department has offices and staff in twenty-five geographical areas of the state. A district engineer in charge of each office assumes most of the responsibilities for highway construction and maintenance in Texas. Specialization and decentralization leave day-to-day decision making in the hands of persons positioned deep within the structure of the transportation department.

In short, the executive branch in Texas is composed of units that are independent, autonomous, and decentralized. What results is duplication, fragmentation of services, hazy lines of authority, and confusion (especially on the part of the general public) as to who does what in the administration of policies. With decision making so far removed from large segments of the population, most people hardly know the name of the agency or its subdivision, let alone what it actually does. Without sufficient knowledge about the operation of an agency, it is difficult for the public to hold that agency accountable for its actions.

★★★★★ THE ECONOMIC ELITES AND THE EXECUTIVE BRANCH

Fragmentation, specialization, and decentralization in a multiagency executive branch of government facilitate a climate of mutual accommodation between the administration and special interests affected by it. Buried inside the maze of the administrative process (and hidden from the eyes of the general public), a close symbiotic relationship between administrators and private interests is often forged. In state governments that consist of a multitude of uncoordinated administrative units, "this accommodation has amounted to parceling out of public authority to private groups."[23]

Texas fits this pattern well. The interests of administrative agencies and their clientele—especially if their clients are from the corporate community—are tightly connected. McCleskey and his associates, for example, argue that the financial institutions of the state (i.e., banks, insurance companies, savings and loan firms, and stockbrokers) are affected by administrative agencies (such as the Finance Commission, the State Banking Board, and the State Securities Board) that have a "history of undue sensitivity to the wishes of the group being regulated."[24] Before it was abolished by the legislature in 1994, a confidential audit of the State Insurance Board revealed "just how cozy industry and some regulators [had] become."[25]

The Department of Transportation has a well-established and smooth working relationship with the highway lobby (primarily petroleum companies, automotive concerns, and road construction outfits): "In a real sense the interests of the highway bureaucracy and the highway lobby have become identical."[26] A detailed study of the Texas Railroad Commission and its primary client—the oil and natural gas industry—describes the connection between the two as follows:

> Railroad Commissioners and members of the industry engage in a series of mutual applications of influence that mute conflict and preserve harmony. Furthermore, members of the industry interact with one another in a manner that suppresses hostility and creates consensus. The Railroad Commission has to be thought of not as a discrete governmental body outside the industry but as an integral part of that industry. This means not that the commission is a "captive agency" but that (it) and . . . the industry have a reciprocally dependent relationship.[27]

A probe of the Department of Parks and Wildlife concluded that "from the beginning, the commission that rules the department has been oriented toward the firmly held belief that big men owning ranches are its principal constituency."[28] One way of providing services to wealthy landowners, as described in Highlight 6–1, is stocking their ranches with wildlife, some of which is very exotic. And so on throughout the labyrinth of the Texas administrative process, to the point that "interests that are regulated carry so much weight among so many agencies that they have, in effect, become their own regulators."[29]

An outlook that is shared by agency and regulated interests develops through the exchange of personnel. Some former executives land on the payrolls of major economic entities in Texas. For example, members of the Railroad Commission have left office and become high-ranking employees of companies regulated by the commission. Former state executives, including former governors, have taken positions with major corporations and banks. After departing the governor's office, Dolph Briscoe sat on the board of one of the state's largest banks, an insurance firm, and a major mortgage banking firm (Lomas Financial Corporation). Likewise, Alan Shivers was on the board of an influential bank. John Connally, chief executive of the state during most of the 1960s, was once a director at a leading bank and at an important oil and gas firm. After Bill Clements was defeated in 1982, he assumed the chair's position at SEDCO, the company he founded; he was also a director of a major bank and of Schlumberger, the Netherlands-based company that bought SEDCO in 1985. Ann Richards has sat on the board of J.C. Penney since her defeat in 1994.

Elected officials sometimes emerge directly from the ruling circles of the business community. Governor Briscoe (with extensive agricultural holdings), Governor Clements (SEDCO), and Governor Bush (the Texas Rangers baseball team and other investments) are prime examples.

★ ★ ★

Highlight 6–1: Parks and Wildlife and Wealthy Landowners

In 1987, oilman Louis Beecherl requested from the chair of the Parks and Wildlife Commission, fellow oilman Edwin Cox, Jr., a supply of antelopes for his Flat Top Ranch, located southwest of Fort Worth. Beecherl is the former owner of Texas Oil and Gas (now a part of USX) and ex-chair of the board of regents of the University of Texas. Although a staff member at the Parks and Wildlife Commission advised against stocking Beecherl's ranch with antelopes because of potential harm to the animals, thirty-nine pronghorns were placed on the land. Within a year, most of them had died of starvation. This incident "revealed the department's willingness to trade wildlife for political goodwill. In a practice known as 'political stocking,' Parks and Wildlife had been doling out animals to rich and powerful men, including members of the department's own commission and [former] Texas Speaker of the House Gib Lewis."[1]

Notes

1. Peter Elkind, "The Buck Stops Here," *Texas Monthly*, January 1990, p. 103 and passim.

Further, many of the people appointed to administrative office come from the world of business. Table 6–3 lists the business affiliations of a number of administrators who have recently been appointed to state agencies, boards, commissions, or departments.

Four reasons contribute to the pervasive practice of appointing business people to administrative posts in Texas. First, qualifications for appointment are at times written expressly to favor the selection of industry representatives. For instance, eight of the nine members of the Finance Commission (which has jurisdiction over banks and savings and loan institutions) must be active bankers, savings and loan executives, or investment house consultants. A governor's task force charged with studying the collapse of many savings and loan firms in Texas during the late 1980s found that the requirement of appointing to the state's Finance Commission people who worked full-time for these firms "insure[d] industry domination of the regulatory and administrative process."[30] Further, boards that examine and license people in certain occupations in Texas are mostly composed of members of the professions whose members are being certified. Usually, the chief administrative officers of these state boards double as executive directors of the professional associations of the groups that they regulate.

Second, the conditions of office often limit membership in administrative units to those who can afford to belong to them. Most of the boards, commissions, and agencies in Texas are composed of part-time, non-salaried officials. In effect, only those who have the money to engage in administrative service as an avocation, not a job, are eligible to do so. Members of the Parks and Wildlife Commission, for instance, spend between $50,000 and $75,000 of their own money each year to carry out their official duties. As noted by one of its former commissioners, "It's just a cold, hard fact of political life that people with money end up on these commissions."[31] As a consequence, according to Tom Smith, director of Public Citizen, "Texas has had a long tradition of having government of the wealthy, and often for the wealthy, by not paying its board appointees enough to live."[32]

Third, business groups intensely and quietly lobby the governor and the Senate to influence the appointment of key administrators. For example, over the last four decades, the Texas Good Roads and Transportation Association has sponsored virtually all appointments to the three-person commission that heads the Department of Transportation. In addition, about 87 percent of railroad commissioners have been appointed to their position by the governor. The oil and natural gas industry seldom nominates people for these posts, but it can always effectively veto the governor's recommendation.[33]

Fourth, in many instances campaign contributions may be key to securing or maintaining an appointed position. A former commissioner of the Parks and Wildlife Department has observed that securing a place on that board is highly dependent on money: "If a man is a big contributor, he can

★ **TABLE 6–3**
Corporate Affiliations of Some Recent Appointed Administrators in Texas*

Name	Corporate Affiliation	Administrative Position
Anne L. Armstrong	Director, American Express, Boise Cascade, General Motors, and Halliburton	Board of Regents, Texas A&M University
T. Louis Austin	President, Brown and Root; director, LTV	Chair, Board of Corrections
Lee Bass	Bass Enterprises	Parks and Wildlife Commission
Perry Bass	Bass Enterprises	Chair, Parks and Wildlife Commission
Robert Bass	Bass Enterprises	Transportation Commission
Louis Beecherl	Director, Texas Oil and Gas	Chair, Water Development Board; Chair, Board of Regents, University of Texas
Jack Blanton	Director, Texas Commerce, Southwestern Bell, Baker Hughes, Burlington Northern, and Ashland Oil	Board of Regents, University of Texas
J. Fred Bucy	Texas Instruments	Board of Regents, Texas Tech University
Charles Butt	Chair, H.E.B. Stores; director, Texas Commerce	Coordinating Board
John Cater	Director, Houston Industries	Board of Regents, University of Houston
Rita Clements	Director, Bank One and Dr Pepper	Board of Regents, University of Texas
Peter Coneway	Limited partner, Goldman Sachs	Board of Regents, University of Texas
Edwin Cox, Jr.	Owned Swift & Co.	Chair, Parks and Wildlife Commission
Harlan Crow	Trammell Crow, developers; director, Texas Commerce	Coordinating Board
Trammell Crow	Trammell Crow, developers	Board of Architectural Examiners
Hal Daugherty	Director, M Bank	Coordinating Board
Robert Dedman	Owner, ClubCorp; Chair, Franklin Savings	Transportation Commission
Charles Duncan	Director, Chemical Bank, PanEnergy, American Express, and Coca Cola	State Board of Education

be appointed. All of the commissioners I know of have been big contributors. . . . All have been big landowners with extensive ranches; their allegiance is with the landowners."[34] Echoing this sentiment, one observer has noted that the commission members are "almost always wealthy busi-

★ **TABLE 6-3 Continued**

Name	Corporate Affiliation	Administrative Position
J. S. Farrington	Director, Texas Utilities	Board of Regents, North Texas University
Lucien Flournoy	Director, Central Power and Light	Economic Development Commission
Gerald J. Ford	Chair, First Nationwide	Board of Regents, Texas A&M University
Tom Frost	Chair, Cullen-Frost Bank; director, Southwestern Bell	Board, Department of Commerce
Gerald Grinstein	Chair, Burlington Northern; director, Browning-Ferris	Board, Department of Commerce
Jess Hay	Chair, Lomas Financial Corp.; director, Exxon and Southwestern Bell	Board of Regents, University of Texas
Dennis R. Hendrix	Chair, PanEnergy	Board of Corrections
James Ketelsen	Chair, Tenneco	Board of Regents, University of Houston
Kenneth Lay	Chair, Enron; director, Baker Hughes and Lilly	Board of Regents, University of Houston
James R. Lesch	Director, Houston Industries	Board, Department of Commerce
Thomas McDade	Director, Texas Commerce and Houston Industries	Board of Corrections and State Securities Board
Mary Moody Northen	Director, American National Insurance Co.	Commission on the Arts
Erle Allen Nye	Chair, Texas Utilities	Board of Regents, Texas A&M University
James L. Powell	Director, Texas Commerce, Central and South West	Chair, Board of Regents, University of Texas
Martha Smiley	Director, Vought Aircraft	Board of Regents, University of Texas
Jack T. Trotter	Director, Houston Industries	Coordinating Board
Edward O. Vetter	Director, Champion International	Board, Department of Commerce
Edward E. Whitacre, Jr.	Chair, Southwestern Bell; director, May Department Stores, Anheuser Busch, and Emerson Electric	Board of Regents, Texas Tech University

*In some cases, the person named may no longer hold either the corporate affiliation or the administrative position.

nessmen—and major political contributors—[who] have sought the appointments because they love to hunt and fish."[35]

During the administration of Governor Mark White, it was not uncommon for appointed administrators also to be major contributors to his campaign. Almost 68 percent of White's 90 appointees to the top seventeen boards and commissions in Texas contributed to his campaign; all but three gave over $1,000 each.[36] In 1990, Governor Ann Richards received $1.4 million from people she subsequently appointed to administrative positions. Twenty-five of the thirty-four people selected for the six most important administrative agencies in the state, either directly or indirectly, contributed to her campaign; eleven gave more than $25,000 each. Her largest contributor, Beaumont lawyer Walter Umphrey, donated $405,709 and was appointed to the Parks and Wildlife Commission.[37] An examination of Governor Richards's twenty-five most generous donors between 1990 and mid-1994 revealed that more than one third of this "fat-cat" group were administrative appointees.[38] According to the former director of Texas Common Cause, "it's a time-honored tradition in Texas politics that if you expect to receive one of the plum appointed positions you should expect to be a hefty contributor."[39] On the other hand, in the words of Bill Cryer, press secretary to former Governor Richards: "Obviously, people who like you contribute to you, and people you like and trust get board and commission appointments. But there are also a lot of people on major boards and commissions who contributed absolutely nothing."[40]

With so much intermingling between the regulators and the regulated, it is not surprising that each identifies with the other. Mutual identification is furthered by the tangible rewards that can be gained through interdependence. The administrative agency, if it keeps its most valuable constituency satisfied, is assured of political support. Supportive clients can help the agency with such essential matters as enhancement of its budget or blocking of legislation threatening the agency. For private groups, favorable administration can bring about the receipt of state funds, the performance by the state of services essential to the well-being of these interests, the inhibiting of competition through administrative regulation, or the channeling of complaints raised about the actions of these groups into the peaceful confines of an administrative boardroom and out of the potentially violent realm of open confrontation. Hence, many important economic interests have found administrative regulation to be beneficial and have avidly sought it—public exhortations to the contrary.[41]

★ ★ ★ ★ ★ ## CONCLUSION

The executive branch of government in Texas is composed of hundreds of administrative offices. Some of the people holding these positions are elected, but most are appointed. Regardless of the selection process, administrative agencies are largely autonomous. Within an agency, operations are usually highly decentralized. Because of the organizational structure of executive offices, it is very difficult for people and groups not directly and immediately affected by the administrative system to evaluate decisions made within it.

Conversely, individuals and groups with a stake in the administrative process are keenly aware of the policies and procedures of administrators. Sometimes these interests play a major role in the selection of administrative personnel. On occasion, they have significantly assisted in the creation of these agencies and hold important positions on their boards and commissions. Through these connections, economic leaders in the state often have a substantial effect on the everyday business of the execution of public policy in Texas.

★★★★★ NOTES

1. *Guide to State Agencies,* 5th ed. (Austin: Lyndon Baines Johnson School of Public Affairs, 1978).

2. Texas Research League, *To Make Texas Government Modern, Viable, Responsive* (Austin: Texas Research League, 1975).

3. Officially, the position of lieutenant governor is listed in the Texas Constitution as an executive office. The importance of this position, however, lies in its legislative functions. Moreover, the state treasurer was elected statewide until voters approved an amendment to the constitution in 1995 incorporating functions of this agency among those of the comptroller's office and, in effect, abolishing the office of state treasurer.

4. Fred Gantt, Jr., *The Impact of the Texas Constitution on the Executive* (Houston: Institute of Urban Affairs, University of Houston, 1973), p. 1.

5. Virginia Gray, Herbert Jacob, and Kenneth N. Vines, eds., *Politics in the American States: A Comparative Analysis* (Boston: Little, Brown, 4th ed., 1983), p. 459.

6. Gary Cartwright, "A System Gone Bad," *Texas Monthly,* August 1992, p. 95.

7. Paul Burka, "Mark White's Coming Out Party," *Texas Monthly,* May 1982, p. 394.

8. Paul Burka, "The Strange Case of Mark White," *Texas Monthly,* October 1986, p. 213.

9. Ibid., p. 212.

10. Charles Wiggins, Keith E. Hamm, and Howard Balanoff, "The 1982 Gubernatorial Transition in Texas: Bolt Cutters, Late Trains, Lame Ducks, and Bullock's Bullets," in *Gubernatorial Transitions,* Thad Beyle, ed., (Durham, NC: Duke University Press, 1985), p. 392.

11. Paul Burka, "The Strange Case of Bill Clements," *Texas Monthly,* October 1986, pp. 136–137.

12. *Texas Poll,* Fall 1987.

13. *Texas Poll,* Winter 1990.

14. *Texas Poll,* November 1992 and May 1992, and Wayne Slater, "Richards Still Popular in Poll," *Dallas Morning News,* February 20, 1993, pp. A-33 and A-38.

15. Ibid. and *Texas Poll,* August 1991.

16. "Bush Income Tied to Reported Proponent of Gambling," *Austin American-Statesman,* August 1, 1994, p. B1.

17. "Texas Poll: Texans Rate Top Officials," *Austin American-Statesman,* September 28, 1996.

18. James G. Dickson, Jr., *Law and Politics: The Office of the Attorney General in Texas* (Manchaca, TX: Sterling Swift Publishers, 1976), p. 19.

19. Ibid.

20. Chris Shields, quoted in Bruce Hight, "Morales Trying to Move Out of Mattox's Shadow," *Austin American-Statesman,* January 31, 1993, p. A-7.

21. Ibid.

22. *Fiscal Size Up, 1996–97 Biennium State Texas Services* (Austin: Legislative Budget Board, n.d.), p. 9-7.

23. Grant McConnell, *Private Power and American Democracy* (New York: Knopf, 1967), p. 189.

24. Clifton McCleskey, Allan Butcher, Daniel E. Farlow, and J. Pat Stephens, *The Government and Politics of Texas,* 6th ed. (Boston: Little, Brown, 1978), p. 359.

25. Kate Thomas, "A Parable of What Ails U.S. Politics," *Houston Post,* June 16, 1991, p. D1.

26. Griffin Smith, Jr., "The Highway Establishment and How It Grew, and Grew, and Grew," reprinted in *Texas Monthly's Political Reader* (Austin: Texas Monthly Press and Sterling Swift Publishing, 1978), p. 157.

27. David F. Prindle, *Petroleum Politics and the Texas Railroad Commission* (Austin: University of Texas Press, 1981), pp. 144–145.

28. Richard Starnes, "The Texas Fat Cat Game," *Outdoor Life,* February 1980, p. 59.

29. William Earl Maxwell and Ernest Crain, *Texas Politics Today* (St. Paul: West Publishing Co., 1978), p. 430.

30. Governor's Task Force on the Savings and Loan Industry, *Savings and Loan Report* (Austin: Office of the Governor, 1988).

31. Walter Umphrey, quotation in Mike Leggett, "State Wildlife Board is a Preserve of the Rich," *Austin American-Statesman,* February 13, 1993, p. A-15.

32. Quotation, ibid.

33. David Prindle, *Petroleum Politics,* pp. 156–159.

34. Bob Burleson, quoted in Starnes, "The Texas Fat Cat Game," pp.134–135.

35. Peter Elkind, "The Bucks Stop Here," *Texas Monthly,* January 1990, p. 104.

36. See Geoffrey Rips, "Gov. White's Algebra," *Texas Observer,* October 25, 1985, pp. 4–5, and Wayne Slater and George Kuempel, "Key State Appointees Big Donors to White," *Dallas Morning News,* August 10, 1986.

37. Wayne Slater, "Money Donors a Majority of Richards Appointees," *Dallas Morning News,* March 28, 1993.

38. Wayne Slater, "Fuel for the Political Fires," *Dallas Morning News,* June 3, 1994.

39. John Hildreth, quoted in Wayne Slater and George Kuempel, "Key State Appointees Big Donors to White."

40. Quoted in Wayne Slater, "Money Donors a Majority of Richards Appointees," p. A-19.

41. For national examples, see Gabriel Kolko, *The Triumph of Conservatism* (New York: The Free Press, 1964).

CHAPTER 7

Justice and the Judiciary

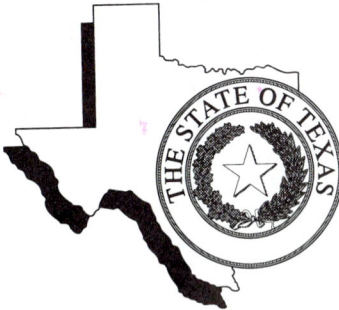

In societies where formal law regulates social conduct, courts are indispensable. Disputes among people, and between the government and various citizens, are frequently resolved in the thousands of state, local, and federal courthouses scattered across the United States. Courts can simply apply laws established by legislatures, administrative agencies, constitutions, or other courts, or they can modify, create, or, at times, nullify legal codes. Therefore, the judicial branch of government is an extremely important institution in the political system. This chapter outlines the structure of the Texas judicial system and discusses the major participants in the state's legal process. Throughout, the chapter focuses on how the operation of the state judiciary works to the benefit of economic leaders.

THE TEXAS COURT SYSTEM

The organizational structure of the court system in Texas is characterized by great diversity and complexity. These features are most evident when we examine the various types of courts in the state and their jurisdictions.

Texas Courts

The Texas judicial system includes three distinct yet overlapping types of courts: constitutional, statutory, and municipal. The Texas Constitution designates six different courts: the Supreme Court, the Court of Criminal Appeals, Courts of Appeals, District Courts, County Courts, and Justice of the Peace Courts. The legislature can enact statutes that create additional courts. Using this authority, it has established special courts at the county level (for example, county probate courts, county civil courts, and

147

county criminal courts) and at the district level (for example, domestic relations courts, juvenile courts, and criminal district courts). Finally, each incorporated city in the state can have its own municipal court, as well as a small claims court.

The result is a judicial system with a multitude of courts and judges. The highest courts in the state are the Supreme Court and the Court of Criminal Appeals; each is composed of nine justices. There are fourteen Courts of Appeals in Texas, each located in a distinct district. The number of judges sitting on a Court of Appeals varies: in Houston, for instance, there are nine, while there are six on the Austin court, thirteen in Dallas, and seven each on the Fort Worth and San Antonio courts. There are eighty justices on the Courts of Appeals and 396 District Courts; each has one presiding judge.

The Texas Constitution establishes a county court, with a county judge presiding, in each of the state's 254 counties. These courts are the principal governing units in the county and have limited judicial responsibilities over minor civil and criminal matters. To relieve county courts in more heavily populated areas of their judicial duties, the legislature has created other courts at the county level to hear more serious civil and criminal matters. By 1996, 18 probate courts and 171 county courts at law, each presided over by one judge, had been established by the legislature.

There is at least one justice of the peace (JP) court in each county; more heavily populated counties have more JP courts. In sum, in 1995, 842 of these courts, each with one presiding judge, existed in the state. Finally, there are 847 municipal courts functioning in Texas. More than 1,100 judges sit on municipal court benches across the state.[1] All told, with nearly 3,000 judges, "Texas reputedly has more judges than any geographic unit in the English-speaking world, including all of Great Britain."[2]

The Texas courts have a heavy workload.[3] Municipal courts handle more than six million cases a year, most of which involve traffic violations. The dockets of JP courts contain over two million cases annually, two thirds of which pertain to traffic cases. Each year almost 700,000 cases confront district court judges. Overall, the amount of work handled by district courts increased by about 40 percent between 1980 and 1995. In 1995, county-level courts examined more than 600,000 cases, 75 percent of which were criminal in nature. The workload for county courts also greatly expanded during the 1980s and 1990s.

The Supreme Court of Texas disposed of 3,025 cases—246 involving written opinions—in 1995. In the same year, the Court of Criminal Appeals resolved 6,345 cases, including 51 death penalty appeals. In any one year, it overturns lower court decisions less than 10 percent of the time. The fourteen Courts of Appeals decided almost 10,000 cases in 1995, more than half of which involved criminal issues. Still, at year's end, more than 9,000 cases were pending before the Courts of Appeals.

Jurisdiction

A court's jurisdiction is determined by the nature of the cases it hears and by the order in which it is asked to decide the matter. There are two types of cases: *criminal* and *civil* cases. Criminal cases involve alleged violations of laws considered by the government to be crucial for preserving harmonious social relations. Offenses falling into this category include murder, robbery, burglary, theft, arson, rape, assault, driving while under the influence of alcohol, public drunkenness, drug possession, manufacturing, or distribution, and illegal parking (among many, many possible examples).

Civil cases generally involve disputes in which one party accuses another of inflicting some harm and seeks financial compensation for it. In many civil matters, business practices (such as fraud, deception, making harmful products, maintaining dangerous workplaces, causing physical damage to the environment, fixing prices, and taking monopolistic actions) are at issue. Workers' compensation issues, tax problems, injuries sustained in automobile accidents, child support matters, divorces, annulments, adoptions, and mental health hearings are all covered by the civil law of Texas.

There are also two different time frames during which a case may reach a court. Some courts are the first to decide a case. When this occurs, the court has *original jurisdiction* over the dispute. At other times, courts try a case on appeal from another court. This is a situation of *appellate jurisdiction.*

Table 7–1 presents the actual jurisdictions of the state's courts in terms of types of cases heard (civil or criminal) and time of presentation (original or on appeal). There is very little symmetry in the jurisdictional pattern of the state's courts. It would be cumbersome (and probably would only increase the confusion) to attempt to sort out all the details of court jurisdiction in Texas. Instead, we will offer a few general points about this intricate network.

First, some of the state's courts (for example, several district courts, some county courts, and JP courts) have original jurisdiction in both criminal and civil disputes; other courts (i.e., municipal, small claims, some district and county courts) exercise original jurisdiction over one type of case or the other, but not over both.

Second, the first court to hear a case is usually determined by the severity of the crime (in criminal cases) or the amount of money sought as compensation (in civil cases); however, in many instances, more than one court has original jurisdiction over the same criminal or civil matter. For instance, municipal courts have original jurisdiction in misdemeanor criminal cases in which the potential fine for violating a city law is assessed at $2,000 or less; they share jurisdiction with JP courts within the city limits if the fine for committing a crime is under $500. District courts are the courts of first instance in cases involving felony criminal

★ **TABLE 7–1**
Jurisdictions of the Texas Courts

Court	Criminal Cases		Civil Cases	
	Original	Appellate	Original	Appellate
Supreme Court	None	None	Writs to remove political officials from office	Cases involving conflicting verdicts from Courts of Appeals; cases where a trial court or a Court of Appeals has declared a legislative act or an administrative decision unconstitutional; cases involving the Railroad Commission; cases in which a Court of Appeals makes an error in law; cases involving juveniles
Court of Criminal Appeals	None	All cases from Courts of Appeals in which a person is to be jailed or fined over $100	None	None
Courts of Appeals	None	Cases from district and county courts	None	Cases from county and district courts in which damages in excess of $100 were awarded
District Courts[a]	All felonies and, in some counties, misdemeanors	None	Cases involving over $200; cases involving $500 to $1,000, concurrent with county courts; cases involving $200 to $5,000, concurrent with JP courts; cases involving divorce, title to land, contested elections, and probate	Probate appeals from county courts and some special cases involving detention for alcoholism and mental illness

★ **TABLE 7–1   Continued**

Court	Criminal Cases		Civil Cases	
	Original	**Appellate**	**Original**	**Appellate**
County Courts[b]	Misdemeanors involving fines over $500 or jail	All cases from JP and municipal courts (de novo)[c]	Cases involving $200 to $5000—concurrent with JP courts; cases involving $500 to $1,000—concurrent with district courts	All cases from JP involving $20 to $200 (de novo)[c]
Justice of the Peace Courts	Misdemeanors not involving a jail term and a fine under $500—concurrent with municipal courts	None	Cases involving under $200; concurrent jurisdiction with county and district courts in cases involving $200 to $5,000	None
Municipal Courts	Violation of city ordinances where fine is less than $2,000 and misdemeanors involving a fine under $500—concurrent with JP courts	None	None (except in cases involving dangerous dogs)	None
Small Claims Courts	None	None	Claims under $2,500	None

[a]Most district courts are courts of general jurisdiction; that is, they handle both civil and criminal cases. However, the legislature has created district courts that specialize in criminal matters mostly, civil matters mostly, or family matters mostly.

[b]Most of the county courts are courts of general jurisdiction; that is, they handle civil and criminal cases. However, the legislature has created 185 special county courts with jurisdiction limited to civil cases, criminal cases, or probate cases.

[c]De novo means that the case must be tried again because the lower courts do not keep formal records of their proceedlngs.

charges. JP courts handle civil actions in which claims of damage do not exceed $200; county courts decide some civil cases with injury claims up to $100,000; and district courts settle claims starting at $200. JP courts and county and district courts have concurrent jurisdiction in civil matters involving sums between $200 and $5,000.

Third, the Supreme Court, the Court of Criminal Appeals, and the Courts of Appeals function basically as appellate courts. The Supreme Court hears only civil appeals. The Court of Criminal Appeals's specialty is criminal matters. The fourteen Courts of Appeals, owing to a 1980 amendment to the Texas Constitution, renders decisions on both criminal and civil disputes.

Fourth, constitutionally authorized county courts have both original and appellate jurisdiction over both criminal and civil cases, although in either case the matters in question are usually not very serious.

As a result of these patterns, in the words of the Citizens Commission on the Texas Judicial System, the state suffers from "a fragmented, decentralized system." The best word to describe the organization of the Texas court system is *complexity.* Mastering the system requires a full understanding of the nuances of the judiciary. Legal expertise is a purchasable commodity. Those with abundant financial resources are in the best position to buy the knowledge necessary to successfully traverse the intricate pathways of the Texas court system. The less fortunate, as we shall soon see, can find the journey tortuous and treacherous.

★★★★★ CHARACTERISTICS OF THE COURT SYSTEM

In addition to its complexity, the Texas court system has two outstanding features. First, judges are elected. Second, most of the key players in the judicial game come from the upper-middle or upper class.

Judicial Selection

Texas is one of thirty-two states that fill judicial positions by election. Only sixteen other states join Texas in allowing judges to run as partisans of a political party. The election of judges raises a couple of problems.

First, elections require determination of the geographical areas from which judges are to be chosen. Texas simplifies this task by creating omnibus districts from which several judges are elected simultaneously. For instance, district court judges are selected on a county-wide basis. Consequently, large urban counties have to select more than one district court judge. The nine most populous counties in Texas—Dallas, Harris, Bexar, Tarrant, Travis, Lubbock, Midland, Ector, and Jefferson—in fact elect more than half of the 396 district court judges chosen across the state.

This system of at-large election of state judges has drawn criticism. Minority groups, in particular, contend that at-large electoral districts favor the selection of officials who appeal to middle- to upper-class, mostly white, non-Hispanic Texans. Indeed, about 11 percent of all district court judges in Texas are African American or Hispanic, even though members of these groups make up about 40 percent of the state's population. It is further contended that if each judge, like each legislator, were elected from a geographically defined subdistrict in a county—rather than at large—more minority judges would be on the bench. A federal district court initially ruled in the case of *LULAC v. Mattox* that at-large court elections in Texas's nine most populous counties contravened the Voting Rights Act and ordered that judges be elected individually from subdistricts. However, the Fifth Circuit Court of Appeals overruled this decision and the U.S. Supreme Court subsequently refused to hear the case. Hence, state district court judges continue to be elected county-wide, regardless of the underrepresentation of minorities on the Texas bench.

Second, the election of judges opens the selection process to the influence that money, in the form of campaign contributions or in-kind services, can buy. This problem has been highlighted by a series of questionable practices that have dogged the court system. In 1982, wealthy rancher Clinton Manges poured a substantial amount of money—some $350,000—into judicial campaigns, usually those of challengers. Manges's intention was to assist in the election of judges who might be more sympathetic to the economic plight of landowners in their dealings with oil companies that held leases on their property. He apparently met with great success in his effort to elect the "right" court personnel.[5]

Also in the early 1980s, both Pennzoil of Houston and Texaco sought a merger with Getty Oil. Pennzoil apparently won the competition, but at the last minute, Getty chose Texaco. Pennzoil sued Texaco in a Texas court for unlawful interference and asked for billions of dollars in damages. As the case proceeded through the Texas judicial system, charges of influence-peddling were frequently aired—even on national television. Significant sums of money, in the form of campaign donations, were exchanged between litigants and judges deciding this case. For instance, Pennzoil's lawyer, Joe Jamail, gave the original district court judge a $10,000 contribution after he was assigned the case. The judge ruled in favor of Pennzoil. Texaco appealed to the Supreme Court, which at first refused to hear the appeal. However, after both Pennzoil and Texaco made substantial contributions to the 1986 campaigns of candidates seeking a position on the court, the Supreme Court changed its mind and eventually ruled in favor of Pennzoil (which had given the most money to the campaigns). Texaco was ordered to pay Pennzoil $11 billion.[6]

Since 1986, most judicial contests for the Supreme Court have been handsomely financed by contributors who can be divided into two opposing camps. One side is composed of trial lawyers; the other consists of large corporations, doctors, hospitals, and insurance companies. The first group supports candidates sympathizing with plaintiffs damaged by the malfeasance or negligence of companies or professionals, particularly physicians. The second group seeks a court staffed by justices who are on the side of the defendants in such actions. Between 1990 and mid-1994, candidates for the Supreme Court and other state courts collected $4 million in campaign contributions, mostly from members of these groups.[7]

As might be expected in this climate, the public's view of the Texas judiciary is not very positive. When, in 1985, Texans were asked whether "the courts in this state dispense justice fairly or do they favor the rich and influential," 32 percent answered "fairly" and 54 percent said that the judicial advantage went to the wealthy.[8] In both 1990 and 1997, 72 percent of the public said that "judges' decisions in some court cases are influenced by the political pressure of campaign contributors."[9] Moreover, the public is growing less supportive of the practice of electing district court judges.[10] The Chief Justice of the Texas Supreme Court recently told the legislature, "one thing can be said with confidence about our current system of judicial selection: No one likes it."[11]

In response, the Texas Legislature, in 1995, passed the Judicial Campaign Fairness Act, which imposes limits on the funds that candidates for state court positions can raise. Individuals are allowed to donate no more than $5,000 per election cycle. The primary, the primary runoff (if necessary), and the general election are considered distinct elections. Hence, a candidate could, if he or she ran in all three elections, accept $15,000 from an individual. PACs are restricted by a $30,000-per-election cap on contributions to statewide candidates and those seeking a judicial post in a county containing more than one million people. Candidates for statewide judicial elections cannot accept more than a total of $300,000 from PACs. The amount acceptable from PACs decreases as the population within the jurisdiction of the court decreases. Candidates in statewide races must restrict their total fundraising efforts to $2 million. These overall limits decrease in judicial races below the statewide level. It must be pointed out that *all provisions of this law are voluntary.* Hence, they only come into effect if a candidate agrees to the stipulations, as did all the candidates seeking the four open positions on the Texas Supreme Court in 1996.

Although all Texas judges must face the voters, in practice, many of them first gain their positions through appointment. It is not uncommon for the governor to appoint people to the bench as replacements for retiring judges. The appointments are often influenced by well-established interests, such as the state's leading law firms (for example, Fulbright and Jaworski, Baker and Botts, and Vinson Elkins). These "incumbent" judges usually have a distinct advantage in subsequent elections. In contested judicial races, the results of a poll conducted among members of the state bar frequently become the guide to media endorsements and, in many cases, to candidate selection. This pattern of appointment, then election, of judges appears to satisfy the corporate community in the state.[12]

Social Background

Three groups of people play starring roles in the Texas judicial drama: judges, lawyers, and, in some cases, jurors. People from a social and economic background similar to that of Texas's economic leaders predominate in most of these groups.

Lawyers   Most of the state's 55,000 lawyers are white, male, and largely from upper-middle to upper-class families. In 1992, 5.3 percent of the bar was Hispanic and only 2.4 percent was African American. The number of women practicing law in the state has grown, to 22 percent in 1992.[13] The class background of lawyers who represent firms with corporate clients is very close to that of their business customers.[14] Needless to say, the very opulence and success of corporations is responsible for the high-status position of many of the state's attorneys.

Jurors   Two types of juries operate in the state: grand juries and trial (petit) juries. The Texas Constitution guarantees that no person shall be charged with a serious (felony) criminal offense without first being indicted by a grand jury. An indictment is made if, in the opinion of nine of the twelve members of the grand jury, there is sufficient evidence to warrant a trial. In its proceedings, which generally last from three to six months, a grand jury can investigate any suspected criminal activity within its geographic jurisdiction (usually a county).

The twelve members of a grand jury are officially chosen by a district court judge, aided by a jury commission. The jury commission is composed of three to five citizens appointed by the district court judge. The commission compiles a list of fifteen to twenty residents of a county, from which the district judge selects the final twelve members of the grand jury. Available evidence shows that most of the jury commissioners in Texas "are upper-middle-class Anglo-Saxon males." Not unexpectedly, the jury commission selects people with similar social and economic backgrounds to be potential members of the grand jury. Hence, a district judge makes the final twelve choices from a panel of persons atypical of the general population.

Studies corroborate the fact that an overwhelming number of grand jurors in Texas are from high-status backgrounds.[16] Most of the grand jury members in Harris County, for instance, come from the upper-middle to the upper class. Even in one of Texas's poorest counties, Hidalgo, almost every grand juror is drawn from the ranks of the area's wealthy. Moreover, there is some indication that the social background of jurors influences the indictment process, with upper-middle to upper-class, male-oriented values guiding the deliberations of the grand jury.[17]

The fate of a person accused of a felony crime in Texas is usually decided by a trial jury. Juries in Texas are much more likely to convict than to acquit or dismiss charges in cases involving serious breaches of the law. Criminal offenses of a lesser nature and civil cases also can, based on the choice of the defendant, be adjudicated by trial juries. The size of the jury and the number needed to reach a verdict depends on the case.

On the surface, most Texans are eligible for jury service. A juror must be at least 18 years old, a citizen of the United States, a person of sound moral character, and able to read and write (unless an insufficient number of literate people is available). Several factors, however, have significantly reduced the population from which the jury is actually chosen.

Until recently, in most areas of the state, jurors were selected at random from voting registration lists; failure to register to vote excluded a person from jury duty. Most of the one third of voting-age Texans who do not register are young, poor, and members of racial minorities. Hence, jury selection tended to over-represent older, richer, white, non-Hispanic Texans. In 1991, the legislature enacted a law that enlarged the potential jury pool to include licensed drivers. The result has been to increase the number of eligible jurors and improve the chances that lower-income members of minority groups might be selected for jury duty. According to one defense lawyer, the new change is having an effect, at least in Houston, where "defendants are finally getting a jury of their peers rather than just a bunch of conservative Republicans who want to send everyone to the penitentiary."[18]

Still, people over 65, men or women who have custodial care of children under 10 years of age, and full-time students are automatically exempted from being jurors. Judges can excuse otherwise qualified persons for compelling reasons, for instance if economic hardship would result from missing work. Finally, lawyers have a number of peremptory challenges that they can use to prevent prospective jurors from serving.

Even with these constraints, research indicates that juries often contain people who are more representative of the wider community than are lawyers or judges. Indeed, there is some suggestion that juries will, at times, rule against wealthy persons and corporations in civil judgments simply because of the affluence of these parties.[19] Anecdotal evidence suggests that juries in civil suits, especially in trials held in Harris County, are more likely to side with plaintiffs seeking compensatory damages against businesses in cases of alleged negligence or the manufacture of faulty products.

Judges In Texas, judges on the Supreme Court, the Courts of Appeals, the Court of Criminal Appeals, and the district courts must be attorneys licensed to practice law in the state. All the judges sitting on the benches of legislatively created county courts are licensed attorneys. Judges of municipal courts and justices of the peace need not be lawyers. In fact, in 1995, just 39 percent of the municipal court judges, and only 6 percent of the justices of the peace, were licensed to practice law.[20]

Most of the lawyers who become judges in Texas, especially on the state's higher appellate courts (i.e., the Supreme Court, the Court of

Criminal Appeals, and the Courts of Appeals), come from wealthy backgrounds. Moreover, there is only one African American on the Court of Criminal Appeals, one on the Courts of Appeals, and ten on the state's district courts. Similarly, just one Hispanic sits on the Supreme Court, seven on the Courts of Appeals, and 35 on district courts. In sum, a mere 11 percent of judges sitting on the state's Supreme Court, Court of Criminal Appeals, Courts of Appeals, and district courts are African American or Hispanic.[21] Moreover, a significant minority of these judges come directly from the ranks of private law firms. Prior to his appointment, current Chief Justice of the Texas Supreme Court Tom Phillips, for example, was a member of the prestigious Houston law firm of Baker and Botts.

★★★★★ THE CRIMINAL JUSTICE SYSTEM

There are clear differences between the experiences of the wealthy and those of the poor in the Texas criminal justice system. Whereas the poor are unable to spend much money if they are confronted by the machinery of justice and are perceived to be of low status, the rich can afford to fight legal battles and are usually highly regarded.

Poor Texans and the Justice System

The lower one's economic standing, the greater one's likelihood of arrest, conviction, imprisonment, and execution by the state. The legal machinery begins with arrest; in Texas this has, at times, been a chilling experience, marked by undue abuse and harassment, beatings, and even death at the hands of the arresting officers. Several cases emerged in the 1970s and 1980s in which suspects, usually poor minority-group members, were killed by overzealous police.[22] In the early 1990s, Texas led the nation in the number of cases of police abuse. The U.S. Justice Department has conducted 2,015 investigations of allegations of violation of civil rights by Texas law enforcement officials.[23] In 1987–88 alone, the Department examined 634 such allegations, nearly 40 percent of which occurred in rural parts of the state (mostly in East Texas).[24] It was reported in 1993 that minority members were fifteen times more likely to be arrested and jailed for minor traffic offenses committed in Houston suburbs than were non-Hispanic whites.[25]

Police charged with using unnecessary force to arrest Texans, especially the impoverished, do not usually receive harsh punishment. In Houston, for instance, between 1974 and 1977, a grand jury investigated twenty-five cases involving police shootings of civilians and issued an indictment in only one instance.[26] Since 1987, more than 445 people have died in Texas either at the time of arrest or in jail, and "no criminal action has been taken in 99 percent of the deaths."[27] Commenting on the first Rodney King trial in Simi Valley, California, Curtis Stuckey, an African American lawyer in Nacogdoches, noted that "the remarkable thing about the . . . King case is not that the police officers were acquitted, but that they were indicted at all. Most of the time in East Texas a policeman who not only beats but shoots one of us is not indicted at all."[28] In sum, the federal government has prosecuted 125 police officers in Texas for violation of the civil rights of people accused of crimes.[29] When police have been convicted of misconduct by courts, their sentences have been relatively light.

The Constitution, as interpreted by the U.S. Supreme Court, guarantees a suspect an attorney, regardless of the magnitude of the crime. If an arrested person cannot afford an attorney, the court must appoint one. In Texas, in theory, the poor are represented by public defenders (attorneys who work for the government) or by private attorneys assigned by the court. The county and state pay the private attorney's fee, which is fixed by Texas law. In practice, poor defendants frequently are not provided with the best legal representation. The quality of the public defender system, for example, varies from locale to locale. In some areas it is quite good, providing indigents with conscientious attorneys who spend a great deal of time preparing a thorough defense. In many other instances, however, the public defenders are inexperienced and are not encouraged to become fully engaged in the trial of a poor client. Frequently, the public defender instructs his or her client to plead guilty and forego a trial. A study of the Travis County jail found that court-appointed attorneys did not even see their clients until ten to twenty-one days after the latter had been booked.[30]

Not surprisingly, the state jails and prisons are filled with impoverished Texans. As an indication of class background, 55 percent of the inmates in the state prison system have completed less than eight years of formal education. Only 16 percent went beyond the tenth grade. Their average I.Q. is 92 and their average age is 33. Forty-five percent are illiterate or can read at the sixth-grade level. Most (95.5 percent) are men. Seventy-two percent are African American or Hispanic, a 10 percent rise in the proportion of minority group members serving time over the last decade. In short, "inmates in Texas prisons are predominantly poor, young adult males with less than a high school education."[31]

Imprisonment strikes especially hard at the African American community. A study conducted by the Criminal Justice Policy Council of the seven largest counties in the state found that 46 percent of convicted felons are African American, 33 percent are Hispanic, and 21 percent are non-Hispanic whites. Among those convicted for felony offenses, African Americans are 8.5 times more likely than non-Hispanic whites and five times more likely than Hispanics to be sent to prison. According to the council, "some experts say that if this trend continues, at some point, as much as half of the African American population will be in prison or will have been in prison."[32] The average African American prisoner is a young male who has been jailed on a narcotics offense. Indeed, nearly 25 percent of all 58,266 Texans convicted of felonies in 1991 were imprisoned for drug possession, mostly cocaine and crack. Almost two thirds of those convicted of possessing cocaine had less than half a gram when they were arrested.

Theft and felony drunk driving were the crimes committed by most other prisoners; only 6 percent were in jail for sexual assault or homicide.[33]

Being behind bars in Texas is not a pleasant experience. Most poor people are forced to stay in jail while awaiting trial. Without sufficient funds to finance bail and with judges usually unwilling to release them on their own recognizance, the impoverished languish in confinement. Usually they are kept in county jails to await trial. A study completed in 1975 by the Texas Commission on Jail Standards discovered that only 6 of the state's 254 county jails met minimum criteria for facility management and living conditions.[34] By 1990, substantial improvements had been made.

Of the 244 counties operating jails, ten had closed their jails and contracted this service out to private firms, and 163 (67 percent) were in full compliance with minimum standards for construction, maintenance, and operation.[35]

The state penitentiary system has come under attack in recent years because of overcrowding. In the late 1970s, several state prisoners brought suit against prison authorities, basically claiming that the cramped and overcrowded penitentiary system violated their constitutional right, under the Eighth Amendment, not to be subjected to cruel and unusual punishment. After the longest prison trial in U.S. history, a federal district court agreed and ordered Texas to make sweeping changes in its prison system. In the words of the presiding judge,

> It is impossible for a written opinion to convey the pernicious conditions and the pain and degradation which ordinary inmates suffer within . . . prison walls—the gruesome experience of youthful first offenders forcibly raped; the cruel and justifiable fears of inmates wondering when they will be called upon to defend the next violent assault; the sheer misery, the discomfort, the wholesale loss of privacy for prisoners housed with one, two, or three others in a forty-five-foot cell or suffocatingly packed together in a crowded dormitory; the physical suffering and wretched psychological stress which must be endured by those sick or injured who cannot obtain adequate medical care; the sense of abject helplessness felt by inmates arbitrarily sent to solitary confinement or administrative segregation without proper opportunity to defend themselves or to argue their causes; the bitter frustration of inmates prevented from petitioning the courts and other government authorities for relief from perceived injustices.[36]

In its decision, the court imposed a cap on the number of inmates who could be housed in the state prisons and the conditions under which they would be imprisoned. The state was slow to develop a comprehensive, positive response to this verdict, and indeed only settled the case in 1991.

Consequently, overcrowding continued and threatened to get worse as an average of 185 Texans were sent to prison each day.[37] To cope with this problem, the state was forced to send prisoners to county jails. In the early 1990s, some 30,000 inmates were incarcerated in county facilities, waiting for space in a state prison. Moreover, officials began releasing prisoners early. The median time served in a state prison declined from 15.5 months in 1985 to 11.2 months in 1991. In 1987, Governor Clements ordered the release of 750 inmates per week. Some of these prisoners were high-risk. More than 200 criminals serving life sentences were freed in 1991; 45 of them were murderers. Over the years, at least 20 former residents of Death Row have been paroled. Included in this group was Kenneth McDuff, a convicted killer who spent 23 years in prison before his 1989 parole. It is alleged that after his release, McDuff committed nine murders. He was eventually convicted of killing two women and again sentenced to die.[38]

★ ★ ★

Highlight 7–1

It costs the state of Texas about $16,680 a year, excluding the cost of building new prisons, to provide accommodations and food for each inmate. If each prison guard contributed $1 a day to the purchase of his or her lunch, the state would save nearly $12.5 million a year.

Meanwhile, the state embarked on a major construction program to relieve the problem of overcrowding. In the early 1990s, voters approved the issuance of $2 billion in bonds to underwrite the cost of expanding the prison system. Construction that affected some 500 buildings at 75 job sites in 72 cities and towns across the state was started. By 1996, room for about 146,000 prisoners was available after what one writer has called "the greatest expansion of prison beds in the history of the free world."[39] Interestingly, there were only 129,000 prisoners in 1996, meaning that eight newly constructed jails remained closed for lack of occupants. The budget allocated to run the prison system mushroomed from $189 million in 1979 to more than $2.25 billion in 1997.[40] Accusations of improprieties in constructing buildings and contracting services on the part of officials in charge of the prison system have emerged.[41]

In the mid-1980s, Texas authorized the hiring of private companies to manage its prisons. Since that time, private firms, led by Wackenhut, Concept, Inc., and Corrections Corporation of America, have built 16 units for the state.[42] A report released in 1990 criticized some of these operators, claiming that they were not providing the educational and medical services to prisoners that had been promised in their contracts with the state and that, on occasion, their employees had used excessive force on inmates.[43]

Once the accused is in prison, especially if he or she is poor, nonwhite, and convicted of murdering a white person, the death penalty looms large. In early 1997, Texas held almost 400 prisoners, including four women, on death row. African Americans and Hispanics constitute a majority of the Death Row inmates.[44] After the reinstatement of the death penalty in 1982, Texas, by May 1997, had executed 112 people, the highest among all states. Considering that about 2,000 homicides occur in the state each year, more death penalty sentences and executions can be expected. Nearly 80 percent of Texans approve of capital punishment.[45]

In summary, the poor in Texas are more likely than any other group in the state to be arrested for a crime, convicted, imprisoned, and executed. Their treatment by police, courts, and jails often ranges from coldness and indifference to hostility and victimization. To those who might think that only the poor are disposed toward crime and therefore receive what any system of justice would deliver to its incorrigibles, consider the following.

★ ★ ★ ★ ★   # THE WEALTHY AND THE JUSTICE SYSTEM

The list of possible crimes that could be committed by wealthy corporations is extensive. It includes fixing prices, manipulating financial markets, bilking depositors of their savings, disseminating misleading advertising, issuing fraudulent securities, falsifying income tax returns, maintaining unsafe workplaces, manufacturing hazardous products, bribing officeholders, making illegal campaign contributions, discriminating in hiring and promoting employees on the basis of race and gender, and damaging the environment.

A look at corporate violations of the law during the first half of the twentieth century uncovered widespread offenses.[46] A more recent examination of corporate illegality shows a similar picture.[47] Between 1972 and 1982, 115 of the nation's top 500 companies were convicted of at least one major crime or paid fines for serious breaches of civil law.[48] Some of these violations are of great magnitude. A congressional subcommittee, for instance, estimates that monopolistic practices and the production of faulty goods cost consumers between $174 billion and $231 billion each year; by way of comparison, the 3 million burglaries that are committed annually cost Americans $2 billion.[49] According to one expert, "there is near universal consensus that all corporate crime and violence combined, both detected and undetected, prosecuted and unprosecuted, is more pervasive and more damaging than all street crime."[50]

Punishment, however, is usually light. In one year (1975–76), the federal government brought some 1,500 charges against companies. But, as noted by one expert in this area, "For the crimes committed by the large corporations the sole punishment often consists of warnings, consent orders or comparatively small fines."[51] Corporate executives accused of crimes are rarely imprisoned. During 1975–76, for example, sixty-one corporate officials were convicted of breaking the law, but in only 8 percent of these cases did the offenders serve time in jail.[52] Some convicted executives are sentenced to community service, even though "there is little evidence that these . . . orders have any deterrent effect, either against the individual convicted criminal or generally against those observing the sanctioning process."[53] When fines are assessed, they are relatively minor. The fine for a guilty corporate executive is, on the average, $18,250, a sum ordinarily paid by the offender's company.[54] Fines levied against companies are not excessive either. One study found that 80 percent of the penalties assessed against corporate violators were under $5,000; less than 1 percent involved fines of more than $1 million.[55] Law enforcement officials and corporations are well aware of these lenient outcomes. Consequently, there is an

> understanding between law enforcement and big business. Law enforcement won't be able to nail individuals and . . . come to accept that reality.

Corporations . . . recognize that if and when their employees are caught committing crimes, they have to plead guilty and pay a not too damaging fine."[56]

Underlying the kid-glove treatment often accorded corporations and their executives is the simple, but pervasive, belief among government officials that big business is beyond legal reproach. A leading expert in this area, Edwin Sutherland, explains this orientation well when he notes that there is

[a] cultural homogeneity of legislators, judges, and administrators with businessmen. Legislators admire and respect businessmen and cannot conceive of them as criminals: businessmen do not conform to the popular stereotype of the 'criminal.' . . . As a result of very mild pressures, . . . our most powerful group secures immunity by 'benefit of business,' or more generally 'high social status.'[57]

* * *

Highlight 7–2: Justice and T. Cullen Davis

T. Cullen Davis was once a very wealthy Fort Worth industrialist. His legal troubles began the night of August 2, 1976, when a man shot and killed his stepdaughter and a house guest, and seriously wounded his estranged wife and a family friend. Three eyewitnesses claimed that Davis was the gunman. Two years later, Davis was charged in another courtroom with attempting to hire a "hit man" to kill the judge who was presiding over his divorce trial. In this instance, the FBI had audio and videotapes in which Davis apparently discussed the assassination with the liaison for his contract killer.

Davis hired a first-class legal team, headed by celebrated criminal attorney Richard "Racehorse" Haynes, to defend him. All told, Davis was tried three times for his alleged offenses and spent over $12 million on his defense. The legal team used the money in instructive ways. Part of it paid for a detailed analysis of the background and character of every potential witness. Before the first trial, held in Amarillo, began, $30,000 was allocated to conduct a scientific study to identify the types of jurors who would be most sympathetic to Davis. All potential jurors were investigated thoroughly. A public relations expert was employed to court the press covering the Amarillo case. This expert was paid to have people write favorable letters about Davis to local newspapers, plant stories in the media, and provide inside information to reporters considered friendly to the defense.

The Amarillo trial dragged on for thirteen weeks. When the jury announced its verdict, Davis walked out of the courtroom a free man. The second trial, conducted in Houston, was for attempted murder of the judge hearing Davis's divorce case. It lasted eleven weeks. After deliberating for forty-four hours, the jury could not reach a decision. The judge declared a mistrial and Davis, after posting $30,000 in bond money, was again free. He was retried in late 1979, in Fort Worth, and a jury cleared him of trying to arrange to have the judge killed. Subsequently, Davis became a born-again Christian and his company, KenDavis, declared bankruptcy. After the verdict was announced at the first trial, the state prosecutor in the case—conservative former state legislator Joe Shannon—had this to say about justice: "I never thought I'd hear myself say this, but it appears that we do have two systems of law in this country. One for the rich and one for the poor."[1]

Notes

1. Quoted in Gary Cartwright, "How Cullen Davis Beat the Rap," *Texas Monthly*, May 1979, p. 220. Also see Gary Cartwright, *Blood Will Tell* (New York: Pocket Books, 1980).

If legal matters are brought into a Texas courtroom, the affluent, through their ability to hire legal help and to shape the court system (as discussed earlier), are better able to cope with judicial proceedings than are the less fortunate, as illustrated in the case of T. Cullen Davis (see Highlight 7–2).

★ ★ ★ ★ ★ ## CONCLUSION

The Texas judicial system is composed of a multitude of different courts. Knowledge of the court system is made difficult by its intricate and confusing lines of jurisdiction. Legal experts are necessary to successfully maneuver through the state's judicial maze, but the price of obtaining top-flight legal assistance is high. Consequently, wealthy individuals and corporations have a distinct advantage in legal disputes with ordinary citizens or with the government.

Moreover, the key figures in the state judicial process are similar in background to members of influential economic groups. Jurors—especially members of the grand jury—lawyers, and judges are socially akin to economic notables. The knot is tightened through campaign contributions to Texas's judges. Little wonder that, when asked if the defendants in the Watergate scandal during the 1970s would have fared better if their cases had been tried in Texas courts, Frank Erwin (former chair of the University of Texas Board of Regents) reportedly replied, "Hell, yes. We own the judges down here."[58]

★ ★ ★ ★ ★ ## NOTES

1. Figures from the Office of Court Administration, *Texas Judicial System, Annual Report for Fiscal Year 1995* (Austin: Office of Court Administration, 1996).
2. Allen E. Smith, *The Impact of the Texas Constitution on the Judiciary* (Houston: Institute for Urban Affairs, University of Houston, 1973), p. 19.
3. Office of Court Administration, *Texas Judicial System, Annual Report for Fiscal Year 1995.*
4. Commission chair Kenneth Pye, quoted in Bruce Hight, "Panel: Merge Supreme Court, Criminal Appeals," *Austin American-Statesman,* February 3, 1993, p. B3.
5. Paul Burka, "The Man in the Black Hat: Part I," *Texas Monthly,* June 1984, pp. 128–133, 212–223, and 230.
6. The amount awarded was eventually trimmed to $3 billion. For details, see James Shannon, *Texaco and the $10 Billion Jury* (Englewood Cliffs, NJ: Prentice-Hall, 1988).
7. Wayne Slater, "Lawyers' Donations Assailed," *Dallas Morning News,* September 14, 1994.
8. *Texas Poll,* July 1985.
9. *Texas Poll,* Winter 1990 and March 1997.
10. Ibid.
11. Justice Tom Phillips, quotation in "Phillips Proposes Judicial Overhaul," *Dallas Morning News,* February 24, 1993, A-21.
12. Paul Burka, "Heads, We Win, Tails, You Lose," *Texas Monthly,* May 1987, pp. 138–139 and 206.
13. Richard H. Kraemer and Charldean Newell, *Texas Politics* (St. Paul: West Publishing Co., 5th ed., 1993), p. 338.

14. See Griffin Smith, Jr., "Empires of Paper," in *Texas Monthly's Political Reader* (Austin: Texas Monthly Press and Stirling Swift Publishing Co., 1978), pp. 20–36.

15. Robert A. Carp, "The Behavior of Grand Juries: Acquiescence or Justice?," *Social Science Quarterly* 55 (March 1975):862.

16. Ibid. and David G. Hall, "Trial by Money, Power and Race," *Texas Observer,* February 25, 1977, p. 25.

17. Robert A. Carp, "The Behavior of Grand Juries," p. 865.

18. "Today's Juries Mirror Those They Judge," *Austin American-Statesman,* May 2, 1994, p. B3.

19. David W. Broder, "University of Chicago Jury Project," *Nebraska Law Review,* 38 (1959):750–51.

20. Office of Court Administration, *Texas Judicial System, Annual Report for Fiscal Year 1995.*

21. Libby Averyt, "Poll: 52 Percent of Texans Support Electing District Judges," *The Monitor,* March 12, 1997, p. 7C.

22. For details, see Glenn Garvin, "When Police Go Wild," *Inquiry,* January 8 and 22, 1979; Mark Vogler and Eric Hartman, "Inquest in Odessa," *Texas Observer,* March 17, 1978, p. 10; "Videotapes of Beatings Figure in Federal Inquiry of Police Force in Texas," *New York Times,* April 4, 1981, p. 7; *New York Times,* March 27, 1983, p. 38; "ExLawmen Guilty in Black Inmate's Death," *Austin American-Statesman,* May 4, 1990, A11; Howard Swindle, *Deliberate Indifference: A Story of Murder and Racial Injustice* (New York: Viking, 1992); Louis Dubose, "A Death in Cleveland," *Texas Observer,* April 8, 1988; and Jan Jarboe, "A Case of Black and White," *Texas Monthly,* January 1990, pp. 96–99 and 150–154.

23. Lorraine Adams and Dan Malone, "Texas Leads Nation in Police Abuse," *Dallas Morning News,* March 17, 1991, pp. A-1 and A-28.

24. James Cullen and Carol Countryman, "The Dividing Line," *Texas Observer,* June 19, 1992, pp. 6–9.

25. A *Houston Chronicle* investigation reported in the *Las Vegas Review Journal,* July 24, 1993, p. A-9.

26. Glenn Garvin, "When Police Go Wild," p. 14.

27. James Cullen and Carol Countryman, "The Dividing Line."

28. Quoted ibid., p. 9.

29. Lorraine Adams and Dan Malone, "Texas Leads Nation in Police Abuse."

30. Marianne Hopper and Cliff Robertson, "Jail Overcrowding: The Search for Solutions," *Texas Business Review* 56 (January–February 1982):19–20.

31. Raymond H.C. Teske, *Crime and Justice in Texas* (Huntsville: Sam Houston Press, 1995), p. 115; Texas Department of Criminal Justice, *1993 Fiscal Statistical Report;* and Robert Bryce, "Pay Now or Later: The Exploding Prison Budget," *Texas Observer,* October 16, 1992, pp. 8–9.

32. Mike Ward, "Crime Takes Toll on Black Community," *Austin American-Statesman,* February 14, 1993, pp. B1 and B2.

33. Christy Hoppe, "Drug Crackdown Fills Prisons, Hits Blacks Worst, Study Says," *Dallas Morning News,* February 11, 1993, pp. A-1 and A-6.

34. *Texas Observer,* December 24, 1976, pp. 14–15.

35. Legislative Budget Board, *Fiscal Size Up: 1990–91 Biennium, Texas State Services* (Austin: Legislative Budget Bureau, n.d.), p. 8-5.

36. From the opinion of Justice William Wayne Justice in the case of *Ruiz v. Estelle,* quoted in Betty Anne Duke, *The Ruiz Decision and Texas Prisons* (Austin: House Study Group, 1981), p. 3.

37. Mike Ward, "Prison Backlog Outpaces State's Expansion Plans," *Austin American-Statesman,* February 8, 1993, pp. A1 and A8.

38. See the *Texas Observer,* August 21, 1992, and Gary Cartwright, "A System Gone Bad," *Texas Monthly,* August 1992, p. 95.

39. Robert Draper, "The Great Texas Prison Mess," *Texas Monthly,* May 1996, p. 126.

40. See Mike Ward, "Prison Push," *Austin American-Statesman,* April 6, 1994, pp. A1, A4, and

A5; Stuart Eskenazi, "Are Texas Prisons Still Shackled?" *Austin American-Statesman,* February 20, 1994, pp. A1 and A19; "State Tries to Speed Building of Prisons," *Austin American-Statesman,* December 24, 1993, pp. B1–B2; and *Legislative Budget Board, Fiscal Size Up: 1996–97 Biennium Texas State Services* (Austin: Legislative Budget Board, n.d.), p. 8-5.

41. See Robert Draper, "The Great Texas Prison Mess."

42. These firms have also built jail facilities for local government and federal agencies operating in Texas. Bureau of Justice Statistics, *Sourcebook of Criminal Justice Statistics—1994* (Washington, D.C.: U.S. Department of Justice, 1995), p. 106.

43. Mike Ward, "Private Prisons Faulted on Services, Discipline," *Austin American-Statesman,* May 16, 1990, p. A1.

44. Michael Graczyk, "Killer on Hunger Strike," *Dallas Morning News,* April 1, 1993, p. A-24.

45. *Texas Poll,* February 1992.

46. Edwin Sutherland, *White Collar Crime* (New York: Holt, Rinehart and Winston, 1949).

47. From a study conducted by Professor Marshall Clinard. Findings reported to the Subcommittee on Crime, House Committee of the Judiciary, *LEAA Reauthorization* (Washington, DC: U.S. Government Printing Office, 1981), pp. 621–42.

48. Philip B. Heymann, "The Crime of Big Business," *Los Angeles Times,* June 16, 1985, Part IV, p. 3.

49. *Findings of the Subcommittee on Anti-Trust and Monopoly,* House Judiciary Committee, reported in Russell Mokhiber, *Corporate Crime and Violence* (San Francisco: Sierra Club Books, 1988), p. 15.

50. Ibid., p. 3.

51. Subcommittee on Crime, House Committee of the Judiciary, *LEAA Reauthorization,* p. 631.

52. Ibid., p. 631.

53. Russell Mokhiber, *Corporate Crime and Violence,* pp. 28–29.

54. Ibid, p. 28.

55. Philip B. Heymann, "The Crime of Big Business."

56. Ibid., p. 3.

57. Edwin Sutherland, *White Collar Crime: The Uncut Version* (New Haven: Yale University Press, updated ed., 1983), p. 56.

58. Quoted in the *Texas Observer,* June 18, 1976, p. 9.

PART IV

Public Policy in Texas

Part IV focuses on public policy in Texas and on those who benefit most from it. Chapter 8 discusses revenues and expenditures, reviewing in its course fiscal policy at the state level and major services—education, welfare, and transportation—provided by Texas government. Chapter 9 addresses regulation, focusing on the state government's impact on natural resources (oil, natural gas, coal, water, and air), electricity, financial institutions, consumer rights, and labor and working conditions in Texas. Throughout these chapters, the prime beneficiaries of state expenditures, revenue policy, and regulation are identified. In most cases, public policy either directly or indirectly benefits business. In other words, gaining access to the state's political institutions through campaign contributions and lobbying results in public policy favorable to Texas's wealthy individuals and corporations. In contrast, those who cannot exert much leverage over the state's decision makers do not fare as well at the hands of state government.

CHAPTER **8**

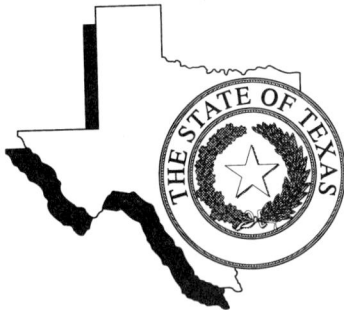

Revenues and Expenditures

The quantity and quality of goods and services provided by government largely depend on funds available to political decision makers. This chapter examines the interplay of revenue and expenditures at the state level, focusing on the major sources of funds and on how the money is allocated, identifying the beneficiaries of fiscal policy and government services.

★★★★★ REVENUES

Texas budgeted $79.85 billion to cover state government expenditures during the 1996–97 biennium, a 6.2 percent increase over what was spent during the 1994–95 period. Some 30 percent of this total, about $24 billion, came from the federal government to support programs principally in the areas of health and human services, business and economic development, and education. The remaining money, about $55 billion, was derived from a variety of sources, including taxes, fees, fines, penalties, lottery receipts, and income from investments, interest, and the sale and leasing of state land.[1]

State taxes alone accounted for $40 billion in revenue. As shown in Figure 8–1, the state imposes levies on a multitude of activities. About $22 billion was raised through the general sales tax, a 6.25 percent charge added to the price of many items purchased by consumers. The sale of motor vehicles and the products necessary to keep them on the road generated another $8.5 billion in taxes. Further reflecting Texas's reliance on petroleum for state revenue, the state collected nearly $1.7 billion from oil and natural gas companies, in the form of severance taxes, as compensation for the removal of nonrenewable natural resources from its land. "Sin taxes," levies imposed on the sale of alcohol and tobacco, raised another $2 billion. Corporations and limited-liability companies pay a franchise tax as the price of doing business in the state. A business must pay a 0.25 percent tax on its assets and 4.5 percent of earned surplus (which is fed-

⭐ **FIGURE 8–1**
Major Sources of State Revenues, 1996–1997*

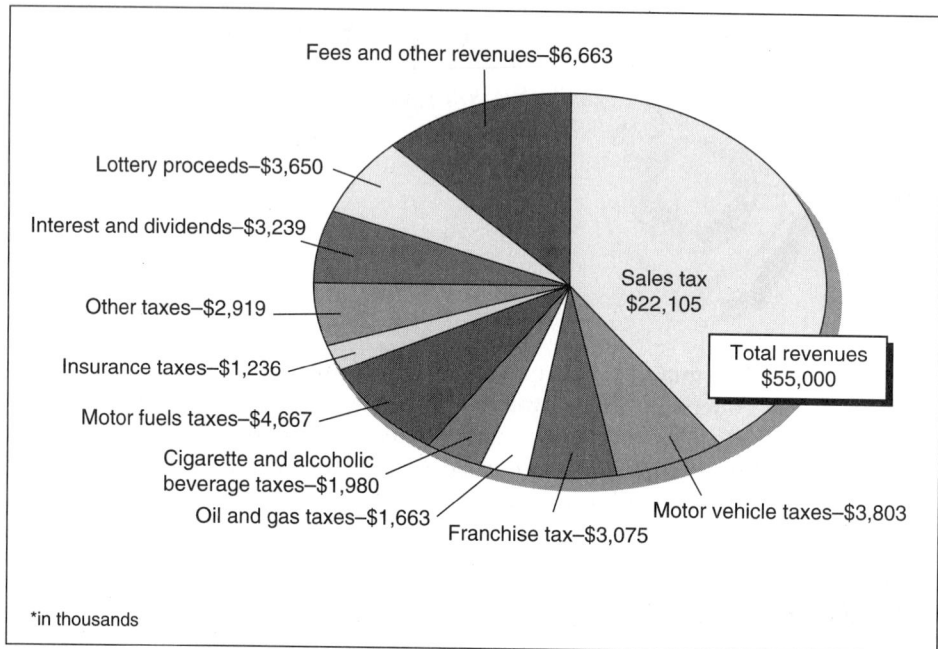

Fees and other revenues–$6,663

Lottery proceeds–$3,650

Interest and dividends–$3,239

Other taxes–$2,919

Insurance taxes–$1,236

Motor fuels taxes–$4,667

Cigarette and alcoholic
beverage taxes–$1,980

Oil and gas taxes–$1,663

Franchise tax–$3,075

Sales tax
$22,105

Total revenues
$55,000

Motor vehicle taxes–$3,803

*in thousands

SOURCE: Legislative Budget Bureau, Fiscal Size Up: 1996–97 Biennium Texas State Services.

erally taxable income, plus officer and director compensation) whichever is higher. In 1996–97, the corporate franchise tax amounted to $3.1 billion in revenue for the state. A tax on insurance premiums provided $1.2 billion; taxes assessed on hotels and utilities raised another $881 million. Finally, the inheritance tax brought in about $350 million.

In addition to collecting direct taxes, the state generates revenue through fees, fines, and penalties. All told, Texas gained $6.7 billion from these sources of revenue in 1996–97. The sale of lottery tickets produced another $6.8 billion, of which $3.1 billion went to the winners and to retail distributors and $3.7 billion was deposited in the state treasury. About $3.2 billion came from the state's investments, principally in the form of interest earned on money invested in the Permanent University Fund and the Permanent School Fund. Finally, the state gained almost $437 million from the sale and lease of state-owned land.

Beneficiaries of the Tax Structure

Texans pay less in state taxes than residents of most other states.[2] The tax burden in the state, however, is not evenly shared by all income groups.

Consumers, when they purchase goods and services, provide most of the revenue that funds state programs. It is estimated that nearly 80 percent of the taxes raised in Texas come from the sale of one item or another.[3] This heavy reliance on the sales tax means a *regressive* distribution of tax payments. That is, lower-income people pay a larger portion of their wages to tax authorities than do higher-income individuals. Indeed, Texas ranks third on a list of the ten states with the most regressive tax systems. Only 4 percent of the income earned by rich Texans goes to taxes, while almost 9 percent of the income of middle-class and 14 percent of the earnings of lower-class Texans is taken for taxes.[4] The very richest 1 percent of the state's population, who on the average make nearly $1 million per year, contribute 3.1 percent of their earnings to taxes.[5]

In sum, direct taxes, such as the franchise tax and severance taxes, on businesses account for about 16 percent of tax revenues collected in Texas.[6] Oil and gas companies can, however, pass the cost of their severance payments on to the purchasers of their products, thus transferring the tax burden to consumers, many of whom live outside of Texas. Utilities and insurance companies follow the same pattern. One source states that after the fiscal books have been balanced, "only about 7.8 percent of Texas' total tax collections come from corporations."[7]

Businesses and affluent individuals benefit, of course, from not having to pay certain taxes in Texas. Only about 15 percent of the 1.5 million businesses in Texas actually pay the franchise tax.[8] Moreover, owing to a 1978 amendment to the state constitution, the first $200,000 of a person's estate is exempt from any inheritance tax. It is estimated that this tax break directly benefits only about 3 percent of the state's population.[9] Texas is one of a small number of states that do not tax the personal incomes of their residents. A personal income tax, even with exemptions and deductions, tends to be a *progressive* tax. That is, the more money one makes, the greater the portion of one's income that is taxed.

Moreover, Texas does not directly tax the profits of corporations, although the structure of the corporate franchise tax allows the possibility of such a tax. Recall that a business can calculate its franchise tax on the basis of either the value of its capital worth or its profit, whichever is higher. Incidentally, a change in the franchise tax effected in 1991 reduced the amount of tax levied on assets, thus lessening the franchise tax burden on companies that pay on the basis of capital worth. Although most companies calculate their franchise tax as a function of their assets, the businesses that pay this tax on the basis of profit account for about 75 percent of the total amount raised by this tax.[10]

It has been estimated that the absence of a straightforward corporate profits tax means that at least $33 billion in net income earned annually by companies in Texas is left untouched by the state and is thus unavailable to help finance public services.[11] A corporate income tax might generate additional revenue of $641 million each year.[12] In 1993, an amendment that banned enactment of a personal income tax, unless it was first approved by the voters, was added to the state constitution. If an income tax measure were endorsed by the voters, at least two thirds of the revenue collected would have to be dedicated to achieving property tax relief; the remainder would have to be spent on education.

★ ★ ★ ★ ★   EXPENDITURES

As we have mentioned above, in the 1996–97 biennium, nearly $80 billion in revenue was available for state programs and services in Texas. Most of this money was authorized for education (42 percent), health and human services (33 percent), public safety and criminal justice (8.6 percent), and transportation (7.9 percent).[13] Combined, these four policy areas consumed 91.5 percent of all revenue spent by the state government.

Education

Providing education for the general public has traditionally been the responsibility of state and local governments in the United States. Economic factors have greatly influenced the degree to which states actually meet this obligation. In general, local educational systems have been very sensitive to the economic requirements—especially the employment needs—of their communities. The Texas economy requires a workforce with job skills at a variety of levels. Professionals, technical experts, corporate managers, scientists, and engineers are needed to command the top positions in the economy. People willing and available to fill less prestigious jobs are also required. The education system is geared to meet these requirements. Hence, some students receive an extremely sophisticated education, while others are prepared for semiskilled or unskilled work. Public schools are not designed to prepare all students equally, so that every student could potentially move to the top of the occupational hierarchy.

Public Schools   In 1996–97, about $34.6 billion was spent on the education of the state's 3.6 million primary and secondary students in its 6,343 public schools. The money came mostly from two sources. State government provided $16.4 billion (47 percent of the total) and local government—specifically, the 1,040 regular school districts across Texas—supplied $18.2 billion (53 percent of the total).[14]

Financing Schools   The current method of financing public education in Texas (as of 1997) is the result of a lengthy, controversial, and litigious process, the highlights of which are outlined in Highlight 8–1. The basic funding source for public schools is the Foundation School Program (FSP), a two-level method of financing education in the state.

★ ★ ★

Highlight 8–1: Public School Finance in Texas: A Tortuous History

For most of this century, local school districts in Texas could raise money to enhance their students' educational experiences by expanding the property tax beyond the minimum necessary for participation in tier one of the Foundation School Program (FSP). A school district with abundant valuable property could easily meet its basic FSP commitment and collect extra money for enrichment purposes. Property-poor school districts struggled to reach minimum standards and were unable to raise additional money for enrichment. This resulted in severe inequities in the financing of public schools in Texas.

In 1968, a group of parents in the Edgewood School District in San Antonio challenged the constitutionality of this method of financing education in federal court. Although the U.S. Supreme Court, in a close 5–4 decision, upheld the state's school funding program, this case prodded the legislature to address the inequity issue. In the late 1970s and the 1980s, laws were enacted to provide enrichment funds to schools in property-poor districts. Regardless of these attempts, inequality in school financing continued. For example, in 1986, the ten wealthiest school districts had property valued at between $2.4 million and $5.4 million per student, while the bottom ten districts had property valued from $21,979 to $42,089 per student. The statewide average was $220,000 per student.[1] Moreover, the 100 richest districts spent an average of $7,233 per student, while the poorest 100 averaged $2,978 per student. Consequently, as noted by one group of researchers, "wealthy districts can do anything they want: pay high salaries and attract the best teachers, adopt novel programs (such as computer-related courses), build new buildings, equip marvelous libraries and labs, and provide an array of special programs."[2] Furthermore, students in wealthier school districts performed significantly better on standardized tests administered in the 1980s.[3]

In 1984, another suit, again led by parents living in the Edgewood Independent School District, was brought against the state for its method of financing public education. Plaintiffs argued that locally based enrichment programs resulted in inequities that were in violation of the Texas Constitution. Ultimately, the state supreme court agreed and ordered the Texas Legislature to remedy this situation by May 1990. A flurry of activities culminated in a financial boost to both the basic and the enrichment levels of the Foundation School Program. Texas courts, however, rejected this plan and again mandated implementation of a new funding system by April 1991. In response, the legislature enacted a bill that required property taxes to be raised as part of a package designed to create financial equity among school districts in Texas. Again, the state supreme court invalidated this program on the grounds that it instituted a statewide property tax without voter approval, a clear violation of the Texas Constitution as amended in 1982. The legislature was given until June 30, 1993, to devise another school finance plan. It responded by proposing an amendment to the state constitution that essentially asked voters to establish a statewide property tax. On May 1, 1993, the voters overwhelmingly refused. That action left the legislature about 30 days to come up with a new method of financing schools before the courts took over the task of funding public education in Texas. The state responded with Senate Bill 7, which was approved by the supreme court in 1995 and imposes the current method, as described in this chapter, of funding public education in Texas.

Notes

1. These figures come from House Research Organization, *An Introduction to School Finance* (Austin, TX: House Research Organization, 1990), p. 16, and Select Committee on Tax Equity, *Rethinking Texas Taxes* (Austin: Select Committee on Tax Equity, 1989), pp. 350–351.

2. LBJ School of Public Affairs, *The Initial Effects of House Bill 72 in Texas Public Schools: The Challenges of Equity and Effectiveness* (Austin: LBJ School of Public Affairs, 1985), p. 1.

3. Texas Education Agency, *Statewide and Regional Results: Texas Educational Assessment of Minimum Skills* (Austin: Texas Education Agency, 1989).

The first tier of the FSP guarantees each school district enough money to cover basic costs, such as operating and maintenance expenses, transporting students to and from school, and the base salaries of teachers, administrators, and counselors. This money is allocated to districts in proportion to the number of students attending their schools on an average daily basis: the more students attending school, the more money the district gets from the state. In 1996, school districts received about $2,350 for each student in attendance.

Some of this level-one FSP money must be raised by each local school district. To meet this challenge, school districts tax property within their geographic boundaries at the rate of 86 cents for every $100 of its value. The state then provides money from its general revenue fund and from income earned by the Permanent School Fund, an endowment composed of state-owned land.

Level two of the Foundation School Program establishes the guaranteed yield program, which is designed to enrich schools beyond the minimum provided by level-one funding. For every cent that a local district adds to its basic 86-cents-per-$100 property tax rate, the state guarantees $20.55 for each student attending school in the district. Local districts can tack on a maximum of 64 cents per $100 of property to the tax rate. Districts can add another 50 cents to the property tax rate, with voter approval, to pay off debts incurred for educational purposes.

The legislature has set the "equalized wealth level" of school districts at $280,000 for each "weighted" student living within their areas. If a district's total taxable property exceeds this level, it is considered a wealthy district and must share its surplus with the districts that are farthest from this target. In the mid-1990s, more than 90 school districts were classified as property-rich. All told, about $350 million is redistributed annually from them to poor districts. There are five different ways in which the richer districts can share their wealth.[15]

First, a property-rich school district can merge with a poor one. Second, wealthy and impoverished districts can consolidate their property tax bases. As of 1996, no school district in Texas had chosen either of these two options. A third choice permits a school district to detach some of its property and transfer it to another district in order to bring each to the $280,000 equalized-wealth mark. By the mid-1990s, only one instance of selecting this detachment option had been recorded in Texas. Fourth, a wealthy district can decide, with voter approval, to contract with a poor district to educate some of the latter's school-age children. By 1996, eight wealthy school districts had chosen this method as their sole way of meeting the wealth equity target. Another 37 had combined contracting services with the fifth option, which is the purchase of attendance credits. About 52 wealthy districts have chosen to purchase attendance credits from the state as the only means of reducing their surplus. Under this plan, a district increases its reported student attendance (and thus

reduces its property wealth per student) by buying credits from the state. The state then redistributes this money to property-poor districts. No students from poor districts actually attend a wealthy-district school.

The current method of funding public schools in Texas relies heavily on the property tax. Consequently, many property holders, including homeowners, pay high taxes.

Educational Performance   The Texas Education Agency has surveyed the educational achievement of the state's school-children since 1978. In that year, Texas's youngsters fared worse than students in the rest of the country, specifically falling below par in vocabulary, reading comprehension, understanding mathematical concepts and their application, knowledge of the structures and functions of government, support for the political system, and writing that is expressive, persuasive, and explanatory.

By comparison to the national norm, Texans wrote sentences that were awkward and paragraphs that were incomplete, short, and composed of simple sentences.[16] Testing in 1982 revealed that students were "performing lower than desired in the more complex or higher order skills."[17]

In 1984, partially in response to these test results, the legislature instituted several sweeping changes in the state's educational system. The State Board of Education was authorized to keep close tabs on the academic (and financial) performance of schools. A school's inability to meet certain standards could lead to a loss of accreditation. In addition, teachers were given substantial pay raises and were required to pass a competency test or face dismissal. An aspiring teacher must also pass a competency exam in his or her principal area of competence before he or she can teach in the public schools. In the fall of 1996, pass rates for the 14 areas tested varied from 82 percent (comprehensive elementary-level test) to 39 percent (in industrial technology, at the secondary level); the average passing rate was 62 percent.[18] Moreover, students could not take part in extracurricular activities, including sports, unless they earned passing grades in their school courses. Finally, the legislature mandated that students were to be given a test that measured their skill levels in mathematics, reading, and writing. Currently, these tests are given at most grade levels in Texas. To graduate from high school, students must correctly answer 70 percent of the reading, writing, and math questions on the Texas Assessment of Academic Skills (TAAS) test; in 1993, about 89 percent of seniors passed this exit test, some only after taking the exam numerous times.[19]

Overall, only about half of Texas's students pass the TAAS tests. During the 1990s, there has been some improvement in the lower grades; 64 percent of fourth graders and 50 percent of eighth graders passed the test in spring 1995, as compared to 49 percent and 40 percent, respectively, two years earlier. However, success rates at the higher grade levels have stayed constant, hovering near the 50 percent mark. Economic status and racial and ethnic background are correlated with performance on these tests. As a rule, African American students are least likely to pass, followed by the economically disadvantaged in general, and then by Hispanics. Most (65 to 75 percent) non-Hispanic whites, on the other hand, handle the TAAS tests successfully. There have been some improvements in the pass rates of minority and poor students in recent years, but they still lag behind more affluent Anglos.[20]

Since 1993, the performance of each school, which is based on TAAS scores, attendance, and number of dropouts, has been measured in Texas. About two thirds of the state's 6,000-plus schools earn an acceptable evaluation. About 16 percent are a notch above, and are recognized for their effort. At the extremes, about 4 percent of the schools are rated exemplary and the same percentage are considered low-performing. Overall, the performance of the Texas public schools has been improving since they were first evaluated in 1993.[21]

Higher Education   There are 834,000 students attending public institutions of higher learning in Texas. About half enroll in one of the state's thirty-five general university units; the other half matriculate in the state's fifty two-year community or junior colleges. During the 1996–97 biennium, the state legislature authorized the expenditure of $9.3 billion on higher education in Texas, most of which went to the thirty-five general university institutions.[22]

The money provided to these senior-level units is not evenly distributed. Two systems—the University of Texas and Texas A&M—collect 63 percent of the funds. Moreover, within each of these systems, there is marked variation in the financing of individual campuses. To top the funding provided to the main campus at Austin, it takes the combined money allocated to the other eight branches of the University of Texas. Texas A&M, College Station, receives about $100 million more than the cumulated totals for the other eight universities in the A&M system.

Funding for each college or university in Texas is principally based on a formula devised by the Texas Higher Education Coordinating Board. The key element in the formula is enrollment: the larger the student body, the greater the amount allocated. However, the formula acknowledges that some types of students, for instance those in graduate schools, in health, engineering, business, and science, are expensive to educate, and therefore gives greater weight to these students. Hence, universities with large numbers of graduate students in these areas are given more funds than those composed predominantly of undergraduates, especially liberal arts majors.

Moreover, the University of Texas at Austin and the main campus of Texas A&M are financially assisted by the *Permanent University Fund (PUF)*. This fund began in 1876, when the state constitution set aside public land dedicated to raising money, through sales or leases, for the establishment of a first-rate university. Today, that land encompasses 2.1 million acres, spread across nineteen West Texas counties. Over the years, this property has raised an enormous amount of money, making PUF the second largest university endowment in the country (after Harvard University). This endowment, valued at $3.7 billion in 1993, cannot be spent; it must be invested. Income derived from these investments is accumulated into the *Available University Fund (AUF)*. The AUF, which contained $261 million in 1993, must be spent. About 20 percent is used to pay debts incurred by members of the Texas A&M and University of Texas systems, which may use the PUF as collateral in borrowing money for construction purposes. Two thirds of the remaining proceeds from the AUF goes to the University of Texas at Austin and one third to Texas A&M—mostly College Station and, to a much lesser degree, Prairie View A&M. Since 1927, the AUF has generated almost $4 billion for these universities.

The AUF clearly benefits relatively few institutions. To help level the playing field, voters in 1984 approved a constitutional amendment to establish the Higher Education Assistance Fund (HEAF), a pool of money available to non-AUF universities to build, maintain, or improve facilities and to buy equipment. Since 1996, the HEAF annual fund has been $175 million. Moreover, since 1996, the legislature has been committed to setting aside $50 million annually for the Higher Education Fund (HEF) until this pool of money reaches $2 billion. The HEF is designed to operate like the Permanent University Fund for non-PUF beneficiaries—virtually all general academic institutions other than the University of Texas at Austin, Texas A&M (College Station), and Prairie View A&M.

Finally, in the early 1990s, the League of United Latin American Citizens (LULAC) sued the state, charging that the methods employed to finance higher education in Texas were unconstitutional because, in effect, they discriminated against Hispanics, especially those residing in the forty-one counties that border Mexico. After a state court agreed, the Texas Legislature in 1993 authorized the expenditure of $315 million over a four-year period to improve the academic programs and physical infrastructures of thirteen campuses, most of which are members of either the University of Texas or the Texas A&M system, located on or near the border.

Corporate Ties   There are several links between the economically powerful and Texas's universities. First, it is not unusual for corporate executives and directors to serve on the boards, commissions, councils, and agencies that help govern these institutions. (Table 6–3 lists the names of some corporate officials who have held positions on the Coordinating Board and on various university boards of regents.) Since the determination of university policy often, in the words of a former chair of the University of Texas Board of Regents, "comes from the top,"[23] corporate leaders are in a position to play an important role in shaping critical decisions such as hiring, promoting, and firing administrators and faculty, curriculum development, admissions, construction priorities, and the investment of university funds.

Second, some key university officials have been appointed to the boards of directors of major companies. For example, William Cunningham, current chancellor of the University of Texas System, has been a director of Freeport McMoran and an Austin branch of Texas Commerce Bank. Diana Natalicio, president of the University of Texas at El Paso, is a board member of Lomas Financial and ENSERCH.

Third, some of the state's universities have a financial stake in the economic growth of corporations. The University of Texas, for example, is responsible for managing the investment portfolio of the Permanent University Fund and carries out part of this mission by purchasing large blocks of shares in corporations. One third of the PUF is invested in corporate stock. In the early 1990s, PUF funds were used to buy stock in more than 400 corporations; the book value of these investments was about $1.3 billion. In recent years, most of the stock has been from companies involved with health care, communications, electricity, and retail sales. Table 8–1 lists the twenty most valuable corporate investments. The advisory committee that makes stock purchase recommendations is usually composed of executives from financial institutions.

Fourth, through gifts and grants, corporations acquire some influence over university matters. About 9 percent of the total annual operating costs of the University of Texas system, for example, is funded through gifts and contracts, mostly from private sources. Hundreds of endowed professorial chairs have been established by corporations and wealthy individuals. In 1976, for example, the Chair in Free Enterprise was created at the University of Texas at Austin thanks to a generous gift from oilman Clint Murchison: "Its mandate was to instruct all students at the university, secondary, and elementary levels in the principles of private enterprise as it functions in an economic-political-culture of democratic capitalism."[24] In some cases, corporations that financially support the research activities of departments or centers in the state universities have some influence over the way their money is spent. In other words, in exchange for a donation, a company may shape the research agenda of a part of the university, perhaps even benefiting financially from the results of the research.[25]

★ **TABLE 8–1**
Top 20 PUF Investments, 1992

Name of Corporation	Book Value of Shares	Number of Shares Held
1. American Express	$22.1 million	957,392
2. Exxon	$21.9 million	427,600
3. IBM	$20.5 million	265,700
4. American International Group	$20.4 million	255,325
5. Merck	$19.1 million	633,800
6. Dow Chemical	$18.5 million	349,450
7. Archer/Daniels Midland	$18.3 million	800,648
8. AMP	$18.0 million	345,000
9. Philip Morris	$17.2 million	452,600
10. American Home Products	$16.5 million	398,200
11. AT&T	$16.4 million	432,200
12. Johnson & Johnson	$16.3 million	407,200
13. Becton Dickinson	$16.3 million	236,700
14. Toys "R" Us	$15.6 million	564,550
15. Anheuser Busch	$15.5 million	382,600
16. Shell Oil	$15.5 million	199,900
17. Eastman Kodak	$15.2 million	353,250
18. Glaxo	$15.1 million	662,100
19. General Electric	$14.9 million	402,700
20. Deere and Company	$14.4 million	288,900
TOTALS	$332.2 MILLION	8,815,815

SOURCE: The University of Texas System, *Permanent University Investments for the Fiscal Year Ending August 31, 1992.*

Welfare

Amid the corporate plenty of Texas there are large areas of poverty. As we have discussed in Chapter 1, about 17.5 percent of the population—3.2 million people—live below the poverty line. Poverty has an especially dire impact on housing, education, and health.

Few poor families, less than 15 percent, own homes in Texas. Those who are homeowners often reside in physically inadequate housing. A study of the quality of housing available to the poor in the forty-four largest metropolitan areas of the country revealed that Houston, Dallas, San Antonio, and Fort Worth/Arlington were the four worst places to live. Fifty-four percent of the poor homeowners in San Antonio, for instance, occupy substandard housing. In Fort Worth/Arlington, Dallas, and Houston, the figures are 38 percent, 33 percent, and 30 percent, respectively.[26]

Nearly 340,000 people live in *colonias* in Texas. About one third of Hidalgo County's 400,000 residents are *colonia* dwellers. Interestingly, more than 75 percent of these people own homes, despite the fact that they are by and large officially impoverished. A large number of these houses lack running water and sewage connections.[27]

The vast majority of the poor in Texas rent apartments or houses. Most renters live in tenements that are cramped, uncomfortable, and dangerous; many of these buildings are not in compliance with the structural specifications in housing codes. Thirty-nine percent of low-income renters in San Antonio occupy substandard quarters. The corresponding figures in Houston and Fort Worth/Arlington are 32 percent and 20 percent, respectively.[28]

The poor rank much lower in number of school years completed than more affluent Texans. Only about one third of the poor finish high school, a proportion that is about half the statewide figure. Another one third have not completed the fourth grade.[29] While poor children are in school, as we have indicated earlier in this chapter, the quality of the education they receive is often inferior to that offered to other Texans.

The federal government's definition of poverty is based on a family's ability to afford a nutritionally sound diet. A legislative investigation of hunger in Texas undertaken in the early 1980s found a relatively large number of people going without much food. Former Senator Hugh Parmer notes, "I assumed that there would be some people who were occasionally hungry, but I didn't really know whether there was chronic hunger in Texas. I'm convinced, absolutely, by listening to the testimony that there is."[30]

Insufficient nutrition and inadequate income often produce chronic health problems. For example, a high incidence of malnutrition exists among low-income pregnant women in Texas. The consequences are most clearly seen in their offspring: "[An] improper diet can prevent a child from reaching full height, delay bone development, cause skin ailments, increase susceptibility to disease and cause other problems."[31] Because of their housing conditions, many of the state's Hispanic poor who live in *colonias* along the Mexican border "have rates of illness much higher than the general population."[32]

Impoverishment also leads to substandard health care and, in turn, to poor health. Some 42 percent of the state's poor (over 70 percent of residents of *colonias*) are without any form of health insurance.[33] Four of every ten reside in counties that have neither a clearly defined health care policy for the poor nor public hospitals.[34]

Welfare Policy in Texas   During the Great Depression, in the 1930s, government assumed a greater role in attending to the economic hardships of its citizens. Public policy was enacted that provided assistance to the needy, the unemployed, the elderly, and the physically incapacitated. During the 1960s, federal assistance was expanded to include the hungry and some of the ill. Recently, the federal government has begun to cut back its commitment to these welfare programs.

From the onset, states have been encouraged to participate actively in welfare policy. They are enticed into some programs through the attraction of receiving matching grants from Washington, D.C. States and local communities are on the front line in program administration. Consequently, each state has traditionally maintained some control over welfare, and lately that influence has been expanded even more.

Texas was slow to join in welfare partnership with the federal government. By late 1940, for example, only eighty-five impoverished Texas families were receiving cash benefits from the federal and state governments.[35] Currently, the state government participates, with a varying degree of financial commitment, in three important federal assistance programs: Aid to Families with Dependent Children (AFDC), the food stamp program, and Medicaid.

AFDC is designed to provide income for the offspring of unemployed parents who are below the poverty line. Medicaid offers some medical assistance to the needy and the disabled. Food stamps are issued to the impoverished so that they can maintain an adequate diet. Funding for these programs is primarily distributed through two state agencies: the Department of Health and the Department of Human Services. In 1996–97, Medicaid-related expenditures consumed about $14 billion in tax money in Texas, most of which came from Washington, D.C. Food stamps cost about $5 billion, virtually all of which was covered by the federal government. AFDC, at $419 million, was the least expensive to fund in Texas.[36]

Welfare and the Poor   Many of the poor in Texas do not receive welfare benefits.[37] Out of the 3.2 million impoverished in the state, about 790,000 receive AFDC payments each month. Eligibility requirements limit AFDC to families with children under 19, whose principal caregiver is unemployed, whose annual income does not exceed 35 percent of the federal poverty level, and whose total assets, including a car but not a house, do not exceed $2,500 in value. Consequently, most AFDC recipients are children, half of whom are under age 6. AFDC pays, on the average, $58 per month to each eligible family member, the third lowest amount in the nation (after Alabama and Mississippi). Most recipients stay on the AFDC rolls for a relatively short period of time, usually less than twelve months. Fraud occurs in only about 1 percent of AFDC cases.

Food stamps reach more poor Texans. In 1997, about 2.8 million people received these coupons. All families receiving AFDC grants are eligible for food stamps. In addition, Texans whose gross incomes are below 130 percent of the federal poverty line and whose total countable assets (excluding a house and a car worth less than $4,500) cannot be valued at more than $2,000 may collect food stamps. Two thirds of the recipients are children, the elderly, or the disabled; the rest are adults who are unemployed or working in low-paying jobs. On average, each eligible Texan gets $71 in food stamps per month. Fraud is not widespread. Continuation in the food stamp and AFDC programs requires that adults register for work with the Texas Workforce Commission. If a person chooses not to accept available employment or quits a job, he or she automatically becomes ineligible for these benefits. In 1995, the Commission placed nearly 37,300 AFDC clients and 15,300 food stamp recipients in jobs.

Medical assistance programs for the needy have been expanded in Texas. Eligible participants include people receiving AFDC grants, pregnant women who would qualify for AFDC but as yet have no children, children from families that would qualify for AFDC but include two able-bodied parents, and some children whose family incomes are above the poverty line. In any one month, about 2.5 million Texans receive some government-sponsored medical assistance. Most of these are children (54 percent), the elderly (12 percent), and the disabled (10 percent). Even with expansion of medical assistance programs, it is estimated that 41 percent of the officially designated poor receive no support through Medicaid.

In short, while welfare programs provide some direct benefit to the poor in Texas, eligibility requirements and the restrictions on the amounts that are available limit the assistance provided to the impoverished. Each month, a poor family of three receives an average of $188 in AFDC grants and food stamps valued at $304. Over the course of a year, that family would receive government assistance worth $5,904, less than half the federal poverty level. In other words, even with welfare benefits, in Texas, the poor remain poor.

Welfare recipients often pay a great psychological price—and sometimes a great physical price as well—for participating in welfare programs. Many Americans view the recipients of these benefits as shiftless, lazy, promiscuous, and having no one but themselves to blame for their economic situation. These negative sentiments are reflected in the administration of these programs. Application forms are lengthy and probe into very personal areas. Refusals, especially in the past, have been capricious, fre-

★ ★ ★

Highlight 8–2: Constitutional Limits on Welfare Spending
In 1990, the Texas Constitution was amended to impose a cap on the amount the state can spend on assisting the needy, in particular the amount allocated to the AFDC program. The constitution limits assistance expenditures to no more than 1 percent of the total biennial budget. The 1996–97 state budget was $79.85 billion; hence, the state could allocate no more than $798.5 million to assistance for the poor. In actuality, the AFDC grant for that biennium was $419 million, some $379 million less than the amount that was allowed.

quently based simply on the whim of the administrator. Not all possible benefits have been explained to those who are eligible. Leaving the welfare rolls is encouraged. Hostility and suspicion about the morals, motives, and integrity of applicants and recipients pervade the administrative atmosphere of the programs. According to one observer of the officials administering welfare programs in Texas,

> The state has done just about everything it can do to make welfare demeaning for recipients. They call landlords to verify information, cancel appointments if the recipient is only minutes late, forcing them to wait another month for another, throw in delays through the system. . . . It really hurts [the] self-image [of the poor].[38]

Physical abuse of assistance recipients has also been recorded, especially in the state's nursing homes, which are financed through Medicaid to provide care for elderly Texans. A 1978 investigation of 113 randomly selected nursing homes, conducted by the Texas Attorney General's Office, revealed that 25 percent were inadequately maintained, 20 percent were below average in cleanliness, theft was a "serious problem," fiscal mismanagement was a "significant problem," neglect of patients was "serious," drug misuse existed in some, and, in a small number, physical abuse of residents occurred.[39] Three attempts were made in the early 1980s to indict the Autumn Hills Convalescence Home of Galveston County for the murder of eight residents through negligence and starvation. In its investigation, the Texas Department of Health found an inordinate number of deaths (thirty-five in a ninety-day period). A probe into one of these deaths "showed the staff to be totally negligent in observing visible signs of congestive heart failure." The home pleaded "no contest" to one charge of involuntary manslaughter and agreed to pay Galveston County $100,000, an offer that was later withdrawn.[40]

A House Research Organization report on nursing home conditions in the early 1990s states,

> Investigators found residents unbathed, lying in excrement, with matted, oily hair, feces caked under uncut fingernails and festering bed sores and rodent bites. In some facilities garbage and excrement were found on floors and linens,

a strong urine smell was noted and roaches seen crawling on food and night-stands. Residents were slapped, left unattended, overly restrained and found nude in public areas of a nursing home. Cold, unappetizing and undernourishing food and diets contrary to doctors' orders were served. Reports cited cases of poorly inserted catheters, inept resuscitation attempts, broken nurse-call systems, drugs administered without diagnosis or proper monitoring, . . . [and] unexplained deaths.[41]

In 1991, the Department of Health charged that 403 nursing homes, one-third of all nursing homes in Texas, had violated codes, laws, or procedures during the preceding three years.[42] In 1994, the state took over a nursing home in Llano after it was concluded that poor care had resulted in the deaths of five residents.[43] Several Texas juries have awarded the families of patients who died in Medicaid nursing homes million-dollar-plus payments for gross negligence in recent years.[44]

State agencies charged with the responsibility of regulating nursing-home care have been accused of neglect of duty. The Department of Health, in particular, has borne most of the brunt of this criticism. A report issued in 1991 by the Governor's Ombudsman Office discovered

Sargent © 1983 *Austin American-Statesman*. Reprinted with permission of UNIVERSAL PRESS SYNDICATE. All rights reserved.

eight major problems in the Department's regulation of the nursing-home industry and stated that as a result of administrative laxity, "the health and safety of many Texas nursing home residents [had] been jeopardized."[45] Former governor Ann Richards accused regulators of being "lazy, ineffective bureaucrats who have failed miserably in the job the people of this state pay them to do."[46]

In response, in 1993, the legislature transferred much of the oversight of nursing-home care to the Department of Human Services. Within its first year of regulation, the Department took over nearly a dozen homes, closed two others, and assessed derelict homes more than $1 million in fines.[47] Still, about one quarter of the Department's inspectors are not fully certified, delaying the process of investigating complaints against nursing homes.[48] Moreover, it is very rare for a nursing home administrator to be rebuked by the Texas Board of Nursing Facility Administrators, no matter what action has been taken against his or her establishment.[49]

Welfare and the Wealthy   Some well-established interests in Texas earn handsome profits from the state's welfare policies. This is most evident in the area of medical services. In the 1996–97 biennium, some $2.1 billion was distributed to the state's 1,100 nursing homes, most of which are privately owned, to provide care for about 66,000 people.[50] The typical resident of one of these nursing homes is a widowed woman over 80.[51] One third of the private nursing homes are owned by three corporations: Beverly Enterprises, the country's largest private nursing-home operator, has 128 facilities in Texas; ARA, a billion-dollar Northeast enterprise known more for its food-concession and vending-machine holdings than for its health services, owns 94 nursing homes and, through management contracts, operates another 5 percent of the state's nursing homes; Texas Health Enterprises runs 90 facilities.[52]

Texas is the only state that contracts with a private firm to channel medical assistance funds to health care providers. The company that processes recipients' claims is paid a substantial fee for service. Since 1981, National Heritage Insurance (once owned by H. Ross Perot and now a part of General Motors) has been the middleman between the health care establishment in Texas and government medical assistance funding agencies. In 1992, National Heritage (General Motors) processed $2.25 billion in Medicaid claims.[53]

One of the major results of the welfare system in Texas is the availability of a large pool of people who are willing to trade their welfare checks for paychecks, no matter how low the salary is. It has been a long-established component of Texas welfare policy to keep financial assistance to a minimum as an incentive to recipients to seek work. The state has instituted the Job Opportunities and Basic Skills (JOBS) program, which is designed to offer education, training, and assistance in finding work to AFDC recipients with children over 3. Between 1990 and 1992, about 87,000 Texans participated in the program; 28 percent actually found work during this period. Their starting pay, on the average, was $4.77 per hour, which would keep them well below the poverty line even if they worked full-time the entire year.[54]

Interestingly, most of Texas's poor work, often in full-time, year-round jobs. The working poor are usually employed in service occupations (for example, as maids, in fast-food outlets, as maintenance workers, and in heavy labor) and on the farms of the state, especially the larger ones. Their pay simply is not enough to elevate their incomes above the poverty line. One study concluded that "80 percent of ghettoites in our two most 'dynamic' and 'opportunity-rich' cities [Houston and Dallas] stay poor because of the jobs they have."[55]

Highways

In 1917, Texas established the State Highway Department and began to invest heavily in the construction of roads and highways. Over the last eight decades, the state's highway commitment has grown considerably. In the 1996–97 biennium, $7.4 billion was spent on transportation; 90 percent of this money was allocated for the construction and maintenance of roads and highways. Texas boasts one of the most extensive and expensive road systems in the world: 77,000 miles of state highway, 139,000 miles of county roads, and 78,500 miles of city streets.[56]

The state's commitment to highways is not the result of chance. Rather, it has been molded by groups with a vested, usually economic, interest in the development of a comprehensive road system. In 1946, the highway lobby, which includes motor vehicle manufacturers and petroleum companies, persuaded state legislators and voters to amend the state constitution and establish a permanent revenue source to finance highway construction. This revenue source is known as the *Dedicated Fund*, a pool of money composed of taxes from the sale of petroleum products and motor vehicles and fees paid to register cars, buses, and trucks in Texas. Seventy-five percent of the sales tax imposed on the purchase of gas and oil, 80 percent of vehicle registration fees, and 10 percent of tax paid to buy cars and trucks are dedicated to transportation purposes. The Dedicated Fund—officially referred to as Highway Fund No. 006—accounts for about 64 percent of the funds spent on highways; the federal government contributes most of the rest, and general revenue funds account for only a small fraction of highway expenditures.

Highways are welcomed by many people. Indeed, the widespread popularity of roads is a strong justification for continuing to define transportation policy as highway policy. Some interests benefit more than others, however. Industries (such as auto manufacturers, oil companies, and road construction firms) that supply the essential materials for highway travel reap handsome rewards from government subsidy of highway construction and maintenance. The 11.4 million licensed drivers in Texas ride a highway system second to none in engineering soundness and convenience. Yet drivers run some risk in highway safety. Each year, more than

⭐ **FIGURE 8–2**
Spending Priorities in Texas

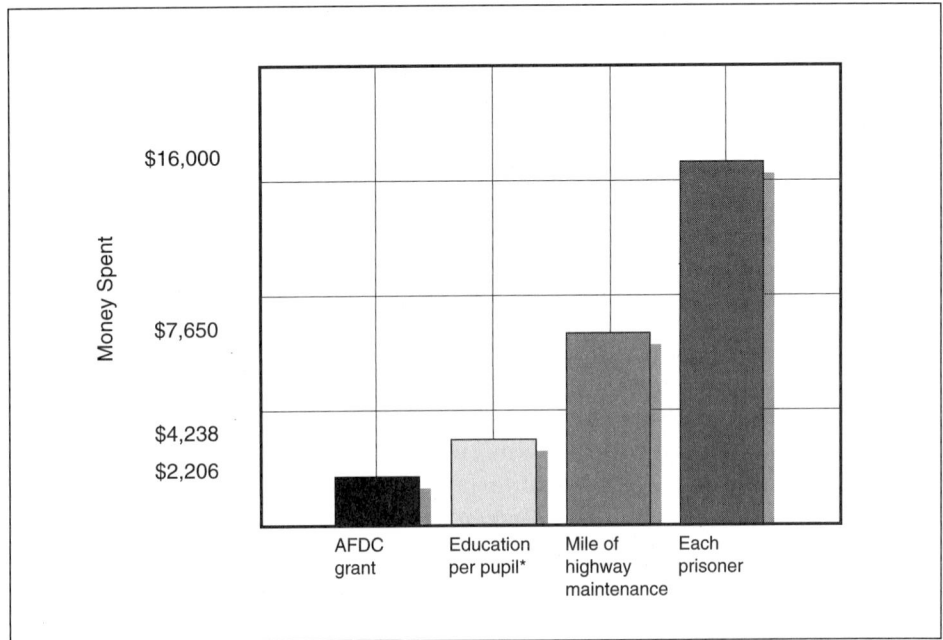

SOURCE: *Austin American-Statesman,* January 24, 1993, p. B-2.
*Includes state and local contributions to education.

3,000 Texans lose their lives in automobile accidents. An additional 298,000 are injured. More than $11.7 billion in property damage occurs annually through highway carnage.[57] The air Texans breathe becomes increasingly poisoned by exhaust fumes. Impoverished people find little comfort in a transportation policy dedicated to highway use rather than to the development of a comprehensive and sophisticated mass transportation system, which would probably be more useful to them.

The highway commitment reflects the overall spending priorities of Texas government. As shown in Figure 8–2, substantially more money is spent each year on highways than on either AFDC or public education (below the university level). Only incarceration of a prisoner (and most of these are from impoverished backgrounds) is allocated more money than the maintenance of a mile of highway in Texas.

★★★★★ ## CONCLUSION

Education, welfare, and highways together receive the largest portion of funds spent on public policy in Texas. In each case, there is a tilt in policy that favors the interests of wealthy individuals, families, and corporations in the state. The public school system of the state serves the overall economic needs of corporate Texas. Some students receive an exceptionally good education. They are well prepared to assume the lead positions in the state's corporate economy. Others leave school capable of only the most menial and mindless of tasks. The rest fall somewhere in between. The seeds of this disparity are planted in the early years of schooling. Historically, primary and secondary schools have best served youngsters residing in the state's more affluent school districts. Enough money has been available in these areas to employ excellent teachers, construct new buildings, and supply the most advanced equipment. Ironically, given their family backgrounds, many students in these affluent districts are probably already well advanced on the road to economic success. Districts in areas containing property of relatively little value have been hard pressed to provide quality education. The state government has recently attempted to close the educational gap, but there is still some distance to be traveled.

Texas colleges and universities also reflect the interests of the state's wealthy. State-supported universities train the future leaders of the corporate world, engage in research that is commercially useful for businesses, and infuse investment capital into the corporate sector. Many of these activities are directed by university governing boards consisting largely of people with connections to big business.

The billions of taxpayers' dollars spent each year on highways directly improve the economic status of companies involved in vehicular traffic. Conversely, mass transportation, which is probably more suitable to the transportation needs of the impoverished, is not fully developed. Indeed, policies ostensibly designed to upgrade the overall welfare of Texas's poor fall far short of the mark. The state provides little assistance to the destitute and the costs of participating in these programs are often high. However, welfare programs do benefit doctors, hospitals, nursing-home providers, and insurance companies. Additionally, the meagerness of the available benefits ensures a steady stream of labor hoping to get off welfare and into a paying job.

Finally, funding for these government programs mostly comes from taxes paid by lower- and middle-class Texans. Affluent individuals, families, and corporations are able to avoid certain taxes, such as state income and profit taxes. Companies can also pass some of their taxes on to consumers. Indeed, consumers pick up most of the tab for government expenditures when they pay taxes on the items they buy.

★★★★★ **NOTES**

1. Revenue figures come from the Legislative Budget Bureau, *Fiscal Size Up: 1996–97 Texas State Services* (Austin: Legislative Budget Bureau, n.d.), sec. 2.

2. Ibid., pp. 3–5.

3. Ibid.

4. "Regressing in Texas," *Austin American-Statesman,* June 29, 1996.

5. Lisbeth Lipari, "Income Taxes," *Texas Observer,* July 12, 1991, p. 4. Also see Kim Quaile Hill, "The Low-Tax Myth," *Texas Observer,* June 27, 1986, p. 7, and Norm Glickman, "Visions of Tax Reform," *Texas Observer,* March 20, 1987, p. 13.

6. House Research Organization, *Business Tax Alternatives* (Austin: House Research Organization, 1994), p. 2.

7. Fred Schmidt, retired member of the faculty of the UCLA Graduate School of Management, quoted in "Visions of Tax Reform," p. 14.

8. House Research Organization, *Business Tax Alternatives,* p. 7.

9. Jim Hightower, "Going Haywire over Tax Relief," *Texas Observer,* September 8, 1978, p. 5.

10. *Business Tax Alternatives,* p. 7.

11. Senfronia Thompson, "Taxing Corporate Profits: A Proposal," *Texas Observer,* December 10, 1982, p. 19.

12. Bob Eckhardt, "Time to Tax Corporate Income," *Texas Observer,* March 20, 1987, p. 9.

13. *Fiscal Size Up,* sec. 1.

14. Ibid., pp. 6–8.

15. As discussed in House Research Organization, *School Finance Issues Remain After Ruling* (Austin: Texas House of Representatives, May 1995); also see Terrence Stutz, "Education Funding on Agenda," *Dallas Morning News,* February 14, 1997.

16. Texas Education Agency, *Texas Assessment Project: Summary Report* (Austin: Texas Education Agency, 1978).

17. State Board of Education, *Texas Assessment of Basic Skills, Report for 1982* (Austin: Texas Education Agency, 1982), p. 2.

18. Figures from the State Board for Educator Certification.

19. A. Phillips Brooks and Jeff South, "Exam Slights Minorities, Critics Say," *Austin American-Statesman,* April 24, 1994, p. A13.

20. Legislative Budget Bureau, *Fiscal Size Up,* pp. 6–12.

21. Ibid., pp. 6–11.

22. Figures on higher education are from *Fiscal Size Up,* pp. 6-3–6-23.

23. Frank Erwin, quoted in Michael Parenti, *Power and the Powerless* (New York: St. Martin's Press, 1978), p. 135.

24. *Texas Observer,* August 26, 1978, p. 13.

25. For examples, see Jim Hightower, "Corporate Money in the Public Till," *Texas Observer,* January 28, 1977; "Public Work for Private Power," *Texas Observer,* April 26, 1974; and Scott Henson and Tom Philpott, "Our Invading University," *Texas Observer,* August 17, 1990.

26. Reviewed in the *Texas Observer,* December 25, 1992, p. 9.

27. Chad Richardson, *Batos, Bolillos, Pochos and Pelados: Class and Culture on the South-Texas Border* (Austin: University of Texas Press, forthcoming), Chapter 2.

28. *Texas Observer,* December 25, 1992.

29. Bureau of the Census, Department of Commerce, *Detailed Population Characteristics: Texas* (Washington, D.C.: Government Printing Office, 1983).

30. Quoted in Zy Weinberg, "Hunger in Texas," *Texas Observer,* August 17, 1984, p. 10.

31. Texas Department of Community Affairs, *Still the Darker Side of Childhood* (Austin: Department of Community Affairs, 1978), p. 61.

32. Chad Richardson, *Batos, Bolillos, Pochos, and Pelados,* p. 30 (manuscript).

33. Cited ibid., p. 30.

34. Task Force on Indigent Health Care, *Final Report, 1984* (Austin: Texas House of Representatives, 1984), p. 14.

35. Frances Fox Piven and Richard A. Cloward, *Regulating the Poor: The Functions of Public*

Welfare (New York: Pantheon, 1971), p. 117.

36. Legislative Budget Bureau, *Fiscal Size Up,* pp. 5–20.

37. Unless otherwise noted, all information presented in this section comes from ibid. and the Department of Human Services, *Annual Report, 1996* (Austin: Department of Human Resources, 1996).

38. Quotation from an anonymous legislative aide in Brett Campbell, "Gaining Ground," *Texas Observer,* March 24, 1989, p. 10.

39. Nursing Home Task Force, *Report on Texas Nursing Homes to John Hill, Attorney General* (Austin: Office of the Attorney General, n.d.).

40. Wayne King, "Nursing Home Deaths Raise Issue of Medicaid Pay System," *New York Times,* April 4, 1983, pp. 1, 16.

41. House Research Organization, *Nursing Homes in Texas* (Austin: House Research Organization, 1992), p. 41.

42. Discussed ibid., p. 23.

43. Dennis Gamino, "State Takes Over Llano Nursing Home After Five Deaths," *Austin American-Statesman,* May 27, 1994, p. B2.

44. Dennis Gamino, "2.4 Million Settles Nursing Home Suit," *Austin American-Statesman,* February 6, 1993, p. B5.

45. House Research Organization, *Nursing Homes in Texas,* p. 41.

46. Quoted ibid., p. 42.

47. "Progress is Evident on Nursing Homes," *Austin American-Statesman,* March 20, 1994, p. E2.

48. Dennis Gamino, "25% of Care Inspectors Uncertified," *Austin American-Statesman,* May 6, 1994, p. B1.

49. Dennis Gamino, "Officials Seek Nursing Home Board Changes," *Austin American-Statesman,* September 10, 1996.

50. Figures from *Fiscal Size Up,* pp. 5-20–5-27.

51. *Nursing Homes in Texas,* p. 6.

52. See ibid., pp. 10–11, and Nursing Home Task Force, *Texas Nursing Homes,* p. 19. The number of corporate owners of nursing homes in Texas may be underestimated, because not all subsidiaries report the name of their parent companies when registering with the state.

53. Department of Human Services, *1991 Annual Report* (Austin: Department of Human Services, 1992), p. 39.

54. House Research Organization, *The Welfare Debate* (Austin: House Research Organization, 1992), p. 21.

55. David Perry and Alfred Watkins, "The Working Poor," *Texas Observer,* May 26, 1978, p. 6.

56. *Fiscal Size Up,* p. 10-8.

57. *1996–97 Texas Almanac* (Dallas: Dallas Morning News, 1995), p. 573.

CHAPTER 9

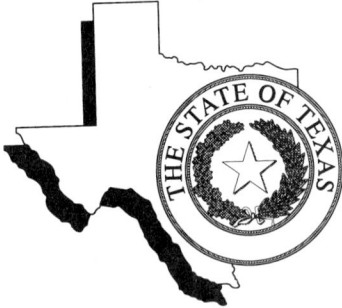

Government Regulation: Natural Resources, Financial Institutions, Consumer Protection, and Labor

State government shapes public policy through regulation. This is particularly true with regard to economic activities. Decisions made by legislators, administrators, and judges often have substantial effects on crucial economic matters such as the availability of goods, the prices paid for items in the marketplace, profits allowed on sales, and activities involving workers. This chapter examines government regulation of the following key components of the Texas economy: natural resources, financial institutions, consumer protection, and labor relations.

★★★★★ NATURAL RESOURCES

At various times during the twentieth century, the state government has entered into the regulation of mineral resources (oil, natural gas, coal, lignite, and uranium), electricity, water, and air. This section details state regulatory policy in each of these areas.

Oil and Natural Gas

Major producers of oil and natural gas, as outlined in Highlight 9–1, requested government intervention in their industry in the 1930s in order to reduce competition and stabilize prices. The legislature responded by extending the jurisdiction of the Railroad Commission to include regulation of oil and natural gas. The Railroad Commission establishes quotas on the amount of oil that may be produced from each field in the state. In so doing, the Commission generally follows the pricing needs of the big companies. If market prices for petroleum products are low, rigid production quotas are usually imposed. Since 1992, the Commission has per-

191

★ ★ ★

Highlight 9–1: Texas Government and the Regulation of Oil

The government became deeply involved in the petroleum business in the early 1930s. The largest oil discovery at the time was made on October 3, 1930, near Kilgore, in East Texas. The great East Texas field attracted thousands of independent wildcatters hoping to make quick fortunes. The lavish crude gushing from the field immediately created intense competition among producers and refiners, producing a substantial decrease in the price of petroleum products. By 1932, a barrel of oil was selling for about 10 cents. The profits of major oil companies plummeted.[1]

Oil producers, especially the largest firms, insisted that the state government intervene to halt the ruinous competition. Governor Ross Sterling, one of the original founders of Humble Oil (now Exxon), called for legislative action to regulate the immense quantities of oil being produced. Before the legislature could act, the Texas Railroad Commission imposed quotas on oil production. Many producers in the East Texas field, especially the independent operators, defied the proration orders. Governor Sterling declared martial law and ordered the National Guard and the Texas Rangers into the area to shut down production. Interestingly, the commander of the National Guard unit was also the chief legal counsel for the Texas Company (now known as Texaco).

By 1935, the Texas Legislature had given the Railroad Commission the power to regulate and limit production of oil in the state. Any proration order was intended to affect all producers equally; however, in effect, the decision was much more devastating to the small independents and wildcatters, because their production was limited to the East Texas field. The major oil companies, on the other hand, had holdings in other parts of the world and thus could afford to let their East Texas claims lie temporarily dormant. Many independents went out of business, usually selling their interests to the major companies. So many leases changed hands that "by 1938 the major oil companies had gained control over 80 percent of the production in the East Texas field."[2] Refineries were affected as well. Before regulation some 155 refineries were operating in the area; "by 1941, there were only three . . . , [all] owned by the major companies."[3] With the assistance of state government, by the late 1940s, the major petroleum companies controlled Texas oil.[4]

Notes

1. See Warner, Jr., E. Mills, *Martial Law in East Texas*, Inter-University Case Program, No. 53 (University, Alabama: University of Alabama Press, 1960).
2. William Earl Maxwell and Ernest Crain, *Texas Politics Today* (St. Paul: West Publishing Company, 1978), p. 25.
3. Hart Stillwell, "Texas: Owned by Oil and Interlocking Directorates," in *Our Sovereign State*, ed. Robert S. Allen (New York: Vanguard Press, 1949), p. 322.
4. Ibid.

---

mitted producers to decide the amount of natural gas to be recovered each month, thus giving them a major role in determining the supply and the price of natural gas.

Natural gas pipeline companies are allowed to set rates without any state regulation. This results in prices that are among the highest in the country and in healthy profits for the producers. Rates charged by companies distributing natural gas directly to Texas consumers are set by the Commission. Again, profit maximization has been its policy: "the natural sympathy of the Commissioners for the industry led them to grant rates that were by national standards almost confiscatory."[1]

The Commission also has jurisdiction over environmental problems arising from drilling for oil. In the past, it was criticized for displaying a "callous disregard for the environmental damage caused by oil companies operating in Texas."[2] In 1983, it was given the authority to regulate pollution precipitated by improperly plugged or abandoned oil wells. Since 1985, more than 600 wells have been plugged each year to prevent damage to the Texas environment.[3]

Although at times (see Highlight 9–2) the Commission has challenged the oil and gas industry, overall these companies have been very pleased with its regulatory performance. In 1970, for example, the companies were moved to publicly thank the Commission for having "served the oil industry . . . since 1891." (See the advertisement reprinted in this chapter.)

Coal, Lignite, and Uranium

Texas has a large supply of uranium and coal, especially lignite. Until the petroleum glut of the 1980s, declining reserves of oil and natural gas made lignite and uranium more attractive to producers and users of these energy sources. Indeed, in the late 1970s, the Texas Railroad Commission

━━━━━━━━━━━━━━━━━━━━━━━━━━ ★ ★ ★ ━━━━━━━━━━━━━━━━━━━━━━━━━━

Highlight 9–2: The Railroad Commission Takes on an Energy Company

For a brief period in the early 1970s, the Texas Railroad Commission challenged the practices of a large natural gas corporation, the Lo-Vaca Gas Gathering Company, then a subsidiary of the multi-billion-dollar Coastal Corporation.[1] Created in 1955, Lo-Vaca was initially a company that gathered gas and stored it for later distribution. It diligently searched for markets to sell its reserves. Several Texas cities were looking for a new gas supplier in the 1960s and Lo-Vaca successfully bid for their contracts, principally on the promise that the company would guarantee long-term delivery of cheap gas. A decade later, Lo-Vaca refused to meet its contractual obligations, probably hoping to sell its gas for a higher price.

This dispute came before the Railroad Commission. In 1973, the Commission agreed with Lo-Vaca and revoked the original contracts, permitting the company to charge whatever it cost to deliver gas plus some profit. The Commission reversed its ruling four years later and ordered Lo-Vaca to honor its original commitments (and deliver gas at the original low price) and also to refund $1.6 billion to its customers. With the company facing bankruptcy and consumers concerned about a stable supply of gas, new agreements were finally reached. The Commission rescinded its 1977 order and in 1979 wrote the final chapter of this story: Lo-Vaca was ordered to cease operations and a new gas utility, Valero, was created.

Although the punishment meted out to Lo-Vaca was the greatest ever dealt a large oil or natural gas company by the Railroad Commission, it was not severe. In effect, Lo-Vaca was allowed to break its contracts and increase its prices. The Coastal Corporation weathered the storm well. After initially faltering at the height of the controversy, it recovered quickly. Once Coastal was free of the many liabilities amassed by its Lo-Vaca subsidiary, its stock value shot up. Its assets are now worth more than $10 billion and its profits continue to rise. Customers who at one time paid very little to heat and light their homes, schools, and businesses now pay very high utility bills. Frank Erwin, once a lawyer for Lo-Vaca and chair of the Board of Regents at the University of Texas, was not pleased with Coastal/Lo-Vaca's fate. According to him, his former clients should have been "put in the penitentiary."[2]

Notes

1. An excellent account of this case is presented in Paul Burka, "Power Politics," *Texas Monthly*, May 1975, pp. 69–97.
2. Quoted ibid., p. 77.

---

instructed factories in the state to phase out the use of natural gas as a boiler fuel. The federal government also encouraged utilities to generate electricity from fuels other than conventional petroleum products.

Surface mining is the principal means of extracting lignite and uranium from the land of Texas. Strip mining is the process of digging large chunks of land (usually in 1,000-by-120-foot sections) with huge earth movers. This technique creates significant environmental problems. Destruction of agricultural land, release of damaging chemicals from the earth, and pollution of water and air are major worries. Farmers and ranchers near mining sites have complained bitterly about the effects of the digs. One farmer had this to say about strip mining by Conoco (owned by DuPont) in Karnes County:

It's already killed my daddy. He had a stroke. You know, they bought the land right across the road from us and right away stripped the topsoil off of about

This advertisement appeared in the *Texas Almanac and State Industrial Guide 1970–1971* (Dallas: A. H. Belo Corporation, 1969), p. 425, and is reproduced here with permission.

500 acres. Well, that stuff is real fine and when it blows into your house you can hardly breathe. There's footprints all over the house. Then you walk outside and you can't tell whether the whole world is on fire or if it's heavy, heavy fog just driftin'. They have those darned old lights and bulldozers running day and night—you don't have a moment's peace. It's not just a little old investment to us. It's our way of life—it's all we have.[4]

Government policy on strip mining emerged in the mid-1970s, when the Texas Legislature enacted the Surface Mining Control and Reclamation Act and the federal government passed similar legislation two years later. (The federal law pertains only to surface mining of coal and lignite and not to uranium.) Companies seeking to mine must apply for a permit from the Railroad Commission. Public hearings are usually conducted. Reclamation plans must be presented and carried out after the dig. The Commission is required to pay surprise visits to the mining sites and, after inspection, issue orders to correct any faults uncovered. Failure to follow regulations can lead to a fine or a prison term.[5]

Although both laws require mine operators to restore excavated land to its original state, the federal law is more stringent. For instance, it requires strip miners to improve the use of the land through reclamation, whereas approximating the status quo ante is all that is required by the state law. Federal policy also designates some 70 to 80 percent of the farmland that covers Texas's lignite reserves as "prime farmland," to be carefully restored on completion of any strip-mining operation. The Texas Railroad Commission has exclusive jurisdiction over reclamation matters and has exempted lignite miners (most of which have been major corporations such as Texas Utilities, Shell Oil, Phillips Petroleum, and ALCOA) from having to systematically and comprehensively restore land—including agricultural land—to its original condition. Contrary to the federal viewpoint, the Commission has argued that much of the lignite is under farmland of such poor quality that perfect reclamation is a waste of time and money. However, critics have contended that "most of the lignite is under good farm and grazing land. . . . [T]he lignite belt runs through several counties in Texas' blackland prairie, the richest farmland in the state."[6] Moreover, some strip mine operators have been allowed to carry out their digs without a permit. For instance, Chevron extracted uranium from its Panna Maria site throughout the 1980s, even though its permit lapsed in 1981.[7]

Electricity

In 1975, the Texas Legislature created a statewide regulatory body, the Public Utility Commission (PUC), to oversee service and to set rates for all telephone providers and for all nonmunicipal electric utilities—including investor-owned companies, electric cooperatives, and river authorities—

operating in rural areas. Cities have original jurisdiction (unless they vote to give the PUC this jurisdiction) in setting the rates of investor-owned and municipally owned electric utilities. Most cities have retained the right to regulate these utilities. Companies displeased with a city's rate decision may appeal to the PUC for an adjustment. In 1983, the legislature established the Office of Public Utility Counsel to assist utility consumers in proceedings before the PUC. During 1994, the PUC had original jurisdiction over 157 utilities, twelve of which involved the Office of Public Utility Counsel.[8]

Since 1976, the PUC has decided about 4,000 cases, mostly involving electric companies. In its earlier years, the Commission tended to decide cases very quickly, to rely on the utility companies for its information, and to trust companies to implement its rulings without much oversight.[9] Currently, the PUC takes longer to reach decisions and now has 215 full-time positions for staff who can gather data and monitor implementation of decisions. However, the PUC has acted contrary to staff recommendations. For instance, the staff recommended that the Commission hold a hearing into Houston Lighting and Power's management of the South Texas Nuclear Power Project, since construction was behind schedule, costing much more than originally budgeted, and the subject of a federal investigation into safety violations. The commissioners refused to address the issue.

Overall, the PUC does not give the utilities all that they seek. The pattern of decisions shows a sharp reduction in rate increases that are requested by the companies. However, especially in the past, the PUC has sought to guarantee that utility companies earned a high yearly rate of return, usually hovering around the 16 percent mark (a rate some 4 percentage points higher than the national norm).[10] As noted by a former chair of the Commission, "The things about which we are concerned are rate stability, system reliability and the financial health of the [utility] companies."[11] In setting rates, the PUC has permitted rate increases, which are passed on to customers, to cover the costs of building new electric generating plants (thus obligating utility customers to pay for electricity that would be produced in the future), advertising, and, until recently, charitable contributions and potential (not actual) taxes to be paid to the federal government.

In recent years, the PUC has been tackling the difficult problems of facilitating the advancement of technology in telecommunications and of introducing more competition into the utilities arena. The legislature ordered that the Commission begin creating a competitive environment in telephone service and in the delivery of electricity. Some progress has been made along this front. For instance, the media giant Time-Warner has gained access to the Austin telecommunications market by contracting to provide phone service to the University of Texas, much to the chagrin of long-term provider Southwestern Bell.

Water

The availability of water is critical to the economy of Texas. The state government, mostly through the activities of the Texas Water Development Board, plays a major role in the delivery of water. Three fourths of all the water in Texas is underground, stored in seven aquifers located throughout the state. Until fairly recently, Texas contained enough water to meet its residential, agricultural, and business needs. But the explosive growth of population and of industry, coupled with the depletion of some key aquifers, has raised doubt about the future availability of an adequate water supply. One study estimates that by the early 2000s, almost three fourths of the state's forty-three zones and coastal basins will be well below adequate water levels.[12]

The hardest hit will be farmers and ranchers living in the High Plains (Panhandle) region of the state. The water source (the Ogallala Aquifer) that has served this area well in the past is rapidly running dry. By the year 2030, only about 37 percent of the current water supply is expected to be available for softening the hard, dry High Plains soil. Most of the state's irrigated farming is done here. One fourth of the nation's cotton, 20 percent of its sorghum, and 5 percent of its wheat are grown on the High Plains. In addition, Panhandle water irrigates the land that produces the grain that fattens many of the cattle raised in Texas.

Urban areas of the state are also endangered by the growing water crisis. San Antonio, for instance, is rapidly depleting the Edwards Aquifer, an underground water source that lies under five counties encompassing a large area in the state's Hill Country. More than 300 pumps operating in Bexar County draw 100 billion gallons of water per year, fully 60 percent of the total taken from the aquifer.[13] Some parts of Houston are sinking because of overuse of underground water sources. The drought of 1996–97 exacerbated the situation. By mid-1996, the Texas Water Development Board declared that seven of the state's ten climatic regions were experiencing severe drought.[14]

One of the most perplexing problems facing water policy makers is the "rule of capture," which allows landowners in most of the state to pump water on their property freely, without concern for any effect on their neighbors' water supply or the flow of water downstream. The Texas Supreme Court in 1904 approved the rule of capture, granting almost unlimited pumping rights to farmers and ranchers.

For about four decades, the state has been grappling with the problem of formulating a comprehensive and sensible water plan. The latest attempt is Senate Bill 1, which was passed by the legislature in 1997. The bill requires local, regional, and state water districts to establish water conservation plans, authorizes interbasin transfers of water (after environmental and economic impact reviews), and, while adhering to the rule of capture, allows the establishment of conservation districts that can regulate pumping.

The delivery of water amounts to a subsidy for big business, because 75 percent of the state's water is used by agribusiness, 15 percent is consumed by business and industry, and the remaining 10 percent flows into municipalities for home and business purposes.[15] Without government aid, businesses in some of the most lucrative economic arenas of the state would have great difficulty surviving.

Pollution

Texas began regulating the quality of its water in 1961 and that of its air in 1965. These early efforts were marked by claims that the state was lax in its efforts. In the area of water pollution, critics claimed that state administrators condoned pollution by issuing permits to discharge, rather than orders to control, pollutants flowing into the state's waterways, established ineffective quality standards, allowed polluters the right to monitor their own activities, rarely prosecuted violators, and assessed lenient penalties.[16] Likewise, with regard to air pollution, state government was charged with being lenient with polluters (1) by almost always giving them variances allowing the emission of harmful substances (see Highlight 9–3 for an example), (2) by not prosecuting them to the fullest extent allowed by law, and (3) by openly fighting against the federal government's Environmental Protection Agency (EPA) developing an air pollution plan for Texas.[17]

Progress in cleaning the water and air has been made since the early days of reluctant government regulation. By the late 1970s, a major transformation in the state's water had occurred: much of the pollution had been eliminated. Between 1971 and 1976, for example, private industries in Texas reduced the amount of suspended solids discharged into the state's waterways by 85 percent. The owners of cattle feedlots in the state had virtually no pollution facilities in 1969. Five years later, there was not a feedlot in the state without such facilities.[18] By the early 1980s, according to the Department of Water Resources, "of the more than 16,000 stream miles subject to quality standards, over 87 percent currently meet the . . . fishable and swimmable goals of federal clean water legislation, with another 4.5 percent to 5.0 percent projected to be in compliance by 1983."[19] Fifteen years ago, the Colorado River was filled with raw sewage and noxious plants; today, for the most part, it is a safer, cleaner place.[20]

What about the quality of the air in Texas? Before government regulation began, polluters emitted hundreds of thousands of tons of damaging materials daily into the atmosphere. By the late 1970s, this amount had been substantially reduced. Lead emissions from automobiles, for instance, have been reduced some 50 percent, from 55,000 tons in 1980 to 27,000 tons in 1988.[21]

The impetus for more government regulation of water and air pollution came from several sources. The federal government began to take a more direct role in pollution cases in Texas. For example, ARMCO Steel

★ ★ ★

Highlight 9–3: Regulation of Air Pollution: The Early Days

During the formative years of government air quality regulation, polluters were rarely denied permission to continue polluting Texas's air. In 1969, for instance, the American Smelting and Refining Company (ASARCO) was granted a variance by the Texas Air Control Board (TACB), the agency then in charge of regulating air pollution, to continue releasing cadmium from its Amarillo plant even though a TACB staff member warned that "the magnitude of the polluting generated by ASARCO was absolutely unsanctionable by any enforcement agency."[1] Staff also discovered a link between ASARCO's pollutants and the high level of cadmium in the bodies of children living close to the plant. Cadmium is associated with hypertension and arteriosclerosis; indeed, Potter County, which was home to the plant, led the state in the number of annual deaths stemming from these diseases. On four different occasions, ASARCO was granted a variance by the TACB, contrary to staff recommendations. The last extension to continue polluting lapsed on the day in 1975 when ASARCO closed its Amarillo plant, an event that had been fully anticipated by the TACB. Prosecution of polluters was also unusual. The TACB preferred persuasion over legal coercion. The deaths of nine Texans in 1975, caused by emission of harmful fumes at the ARCO plant near Denver City, prompted former TACB member Joe Bridgefarmer to comment, "I realize that they [ARCO] were probably in violation of some regulations . . . , but I fail to see how the State of Texas had been damaged."[2]

Notes

1. Quoted in Gary Keith, *Air Pollution Control in Texas* (Austin: House Study Group, 1981), p. 46, and Paul Stone, "TACB Won't Close Amarillo Smelter," *Texas Observer*, September 8, 1972, p. 10.
2. Quoted ibid., p. 45.

Corporation, which owns and operates a mill on the Houston Ship Channel, was successfully prosecuted by the federal government for dumping cyanide, phenols, ammonia, and sulfides on "a significant and substantial scale with results, actual and potential, deleterious and even deadly to the existence and survival of organic and marine life in the Channel."[22] Similarly, variances granted to air polluters at the state level ceased after the EPA began to systematically review every extension granted. Next, financial inducements, in the form of grants and tax breaks by the federal government, made the installation of water treatment facilities and air pollution abatement equipment more attractive to business. Finally, in 1993, Texas consolidated its regulation of water and air pollution into one agency, the Texas Natural Resources Conservation Commission (TNRCC), and, in so doing, increased its efforts to control pollution by adding staff, increasing penalties for polluters, and becoming more vigilant in the prosecution of violators.

Some areas of concern remain, however. Pollution continues to plague the state. In many parts of Texas, the air is heavy with odor, haze, and eye irritants. The EPA has identified seven pollutants that foul the air: carbon monoxide, sulfur dioxide and sulfates, nitrogen dioxide and nitrates, hydrocarbons, oxidants (ozone), particulates, and lead. Each can have a harmful impact on health. For instance, a steady intake of carbon monoxide and sulfur dioxide may lead to respiratory problems. The EPA has designated standards that may not be exceeded for each pollutant. For example, ambient (moving) air is considered legally polluted if the amount of photochemical oxidants (ozone) is in excess of 0.12 parts per million, using an hourly average, on three days during any three-year period.

In 1990, four metropolitan areas—Beaumont/Port Arthur/Orange, Dallas/Fort Worth, El Paso, and Houston/Galveston—failed to meet the federal standards for acceptably clean air. The amount of volatile organic compounds (VOCs), the core of smog, that are released into the Houston/Galveston air annually is nearly 800 million pounds.[23] In Dallas/Fort Worth it is almost 400 pounds, while in Beaumont/Port Arthur/Orange and El Paso, the total releases are 242 pounds and 54 pounds, respectively. Large companies are the primary sources of these compounds in the Houston and Beaumont areas. Indeed, among industrial polluters, the leading culprits are electricity companies whose plants "spew more than 200 million tons of carbon dioxide, sulfur dioxide, particulate matter, nitrogen oxides, and other pollutants into the air every year."[24] Motor vehicles are mostly responsible for the smog in Dallas/Fort Worth and El Paso. The federal government has ordered that the release of these compounds be reduced by 60 percent in Houston/Galveston (by 2007), by 33 percent in Beaumont/Port Arthur/Orange (by 1999), by 30 percent in Dallas/Fort Worth (by 1996), and by 25 percent in El Paso (by 1996). Failure to meet these reductions could mean a loss of federal highway funds and the imposition of expensive pollution controls on new businesses.

A recent report released by a congressional subcommittee notes that Texas contains 20 percent of the nation's 205 industrial sources emitting "air toxics with very high cancer risks."[25] Fourteen of the forty named companies are facilities releasing toxics that pose an "estimated maximum individual lifetime risk" of cancer "greater than or equal to 1 in 100 but less than 1 in 10." Indeed, the only plant in the nation that was listed with a risk factor of 1 in 10 was the Texaco operation in Port Neches, which emits butadiene.[26] The refinery section of Corpus Christi is being investigated by the EPA for possibly releasing chemicals harmful to health, mostly poor African Americans and Hispanics who live near these plants.[27] Finally, the air in the Big Bend area is becoming polluted by compounds being released from coal-driven electricity plants in Piedras Negras, Mexico, 135 miles southeast of the National Park.[28]

Along the waterfront, cities continue to lower the quality of water, primarily through the discharge of sewage. A political problem inhibits cities from stemming the tide of pollution. They are reluctant to anger voters by raising taxes to build water treatment facilities. Recently the state and federal governments have provided some financial incentives for metropolitan areas to construct new waste treatment facilities.

In addition, companies continue, sometimes with the permission of the TNRCC, to dump hazardous waste material into the state's waterways. In 1990, 419 million tons of hazardous waste were released into streams, rivers, and lakes. Texas was second only to Louisiana, which led the nation, in toxins flowing into the water supply. More than half the total came from the factories of eight companies: Monsanto, DuPont, BP Chemicals, Sterling Chemicals, Amoco, Dow Chemical, Union Carbide, and 3M, in that order.[29] The TNRCC's enforcement unit has difficulty monitoring contamination and prosecuting companies that illegally dump into the waterways. Most of its information about these practices is supplied by waste handlers. Complaints are slow to be acted upon. A voluntary approach to regulation is preferred to invoking penalties, although recently fines have been levied against several major corporations.[30] A substantial amount of this dumping occurs in neighborhoods containing poor African Americans and Hispanics.[31]

Business has input into the TNRCC through membership on its 19-person advisory committee. Executives from leading companies such as Exxon, Tenneco, Radian, Dow Chemical, State Farm Insurance, Diamond Shamrock, Texas Utilities, USX-Marathon, Cooper Industries, Chevron, Phillips Petroleum, ALCOA, and Champion International sit on this committee.[32]

★★★★★ FINANCIAL INSTITUTIONS

The state government of Texas has the authority to oversee many of the activities of the financial institutions located within its boundaries. This section explores state regulation of the banking business, insurance practices, and savings and loan associations.

Banks

In the past, Texans were very distrustful of banks. As we have discussed in Chapter 1, the framers of the Texas Constitution prohibited the granting of state charters for commercial banks. The ban on banking was lifted in 1904. However, to prevent dependency on a few dominant financial institutions, a bank could operate in only one geographic location; that is, branch banking was forbidden. Without branches, it was difficult for any one bank to amass a large asset portfolio. To strengthen their position, in the early 1970s the larger Texas banks began to form bank holding companies that purchased other banks. The bank holding company movement successfully circumvented the state's prohibition of branch banking. Most key government officials in Texas acquiesced in this subterfuge. Finally, the legislature and voters, in 1986, approved a bank-sponsored amendment to the Texas Constitution that legalized branch banking in the state.

The regulation of banks in Texas encompasses the power to grant charters for new banks, to review the fiscal integrity of banks, and to deposit state funds in banks. At times, the state has been criticized for the manner in which it carries out these functions. Charters, it has been contended, have been granted more on the basis of cronyism than for sound economic reasons. Campaign contributions, the inclusion of politicians among the prospective shareholders of a bank, and outstanding loans to political figures are only some of the forces that appear to sway charter decisions. "The results of all this are obvious: banks that should not necessarily exist, controlled by people who are not necessarily fit to operate them."[33]

Administrative oversight and review of established banks are hampered by the fact that staff charged with these responsibilities are few in number, poorly paid, and, because of a rapid turnover in personnel, relatively inexperienced. Between 1987 and 1989, more than 200 state-chartered banks closed in Texas. Another 146 institutions were classified as "problem" banks in 1989; 26 of them were placed under supervisory control.[34] Four years later, Texas still had 79 troubled banks, more than any other state in the nation.[35] In sum, 516 national and state banks ceased operations in Texas between 1985 and 1993—fully half of the nation's bank closures. Federal bailouts for these insolvent institutions cost the U.S. taxpayers more than $13.3 billion.[36] Insolvent state-chartered banks have been characterized by rapid changes in ownership and excessive lending to owners and their friends, relatives, and associates. State regulatory agencies ordinarily did not catch up with these indiscretions until the deposits were gone and the banks were unable to meet their financial obligations.

State officials deposit substantial sums of the government's money in select financial institutions. For example, when she was state treasurer, Kay Bailey Hutchison chose the investment banker Goldman Sachs and Company as the exclusive broker to sell $300 million of short-term notes on behalf of the state. Goldman Sachs had contributed $29,000 to Hutchison's campaign. Moreover, her campaign finance chair worked for the company. Goldman Sachs faced no competitors for the contract and earned more than $100,000 in fees.[37]

Between 1989 and 1996, the state treasurer's office managed TexPool, a multi-billion-dollar investment pool composed of local property taxes and other funds. The results were not impressive: TexPool lost money and eventually had to be bailed out (for $497 million) by Texas taxpayers. In 1997, the state comptroller's office, which had absorbed the state treasurer's office, assigned the task of managing the $6.2 billion TexPool to Texas Commerce Bank, which is owned by the Chase Manhattan Corporation of New York.[38]

Insurance

The Texas Department of Insurance regulates, charters, and sets rates for the insurance companies of Texas. Before the mid-1950s, a company could issue insurance in the state with a minimal financial foundation and not worry about stringent government regulation. After a large number of failures among insurance companies and widespread scandals in the industry, the state tightened its rules and regulations. Still, regulation has not been disadvantageous to insurance companies.

Insurance rates have been determined largely by the profit requirements of the insurance companies.[39] The Department of Insurance allows flexibility in setting insurance rates by setting a benchmark figure to be charged for insurance, then allowing companies to charge up to 30 percent above or below this figure without its approval.

During the 1980s, many of the state's insurance companies overextended their investments and were unable to pay claims. By 1991, 283 insurance firms were experiencing financial troubles.[40] Investigations into problem companies revealed that some of their difficulties resulted from inadequate regulation of the industry. In one case involving National County Mutual of Dallas, the owner managed to doctor the company's books to show a $350,000 profit, when in actuality the firm was $20 million in debt. The owner fled and the company collapsed. This occurred even though various state regulators suspected that the company was in trouble and had initiated examination of its books. A lack of coordination among regulatory agencies, poorly trained administrative personnel, and a general sympathy among key administrators for the industry were cited as reasons for inadequate supervision.[41]

After these events, the legislature abolished the State Board of Insurance and created the Department of Insurance, headed by a Commissioner of Insurance. The legislature also established the Office of Public Insurance Counsel in 1991 to represent the consumer's interest in rate hearings held by the Department of Insurance. In general, the insurance companies oppose this office and have worked to curtail its influence.[42]

Savings and Loan Associations

Texas created the Savings and Loan Department in 1961 to charter state-based savings and loan institutions, to examine and monitor their performance, and to prosecute violators of the law. The fundamental weakness of this agency was fully revealed in the 1980s as the state's savings and loan institutions sank ever farther into a quagmire of financial disaster. More than 700 of the country's 3,300 savings and loan firms failed; Texas, according to one federal administrator, was "60 percent of our problem."[43] In sum, this collapse cost the federal government nearly $500 billion, of which $321 billion was for interest on money borrowed to finance the government's bailout of the savings and loan industry, $88 billion was provided to the Resolution Trust Corporation, established by the government to sell the assets of insolvent savings and loan firms, and $65 billion was to reimburse investors who had saved with an association in the federal government's depositor insurance program. It is estimated that 41 percent of the taxpayer money used to directly fund the bailout has gone to Texas.[44] What led to this fiasco?

First the federal government, in 1982, eased regulations on savings and loan firms in an attempt to make them more competitive with other financial institutions. These firms were allowed to lend money at competitive rates to a wide variety of borrowers. Encouraged by the building boom spurred by rising petroleum prices in the late 1970s, Texas's savings and loan firms invested heavily in the development of condominiums, apartment houses, shopping malls, and commercial buildings. To maximize fees and profits, some of these institutions engaged in activities that systematically increased the value of property and the loans necessary to build on it. One such practice was the so-called land flip, which involved selling and reselling the same piece of property in a short period of time—sometimes one day—to drive up its price. For instance, the day the savings and loan industry was deregulated in 1982, "a group of speculators associated with Bell Savings and Loan Association in Belton, Texas, sat around the table and bought and sold three parcels of land over and over again; they changed hands five times, netted the developers paper profits of $12m[illion,] and left the S&L with $14.4m[illion] in bad loans. Such loan auctions became standard."[45]

It is estimated that about $5 billion in losses in the savings and loan business were the result of outright fraud, half of which occurred in Texas (see Highlight 9–4 for an example).[46] A governor's task force on the savings and loan industry concluded that 95 percent of Texas's troubled savings and loan associations were chartered by the state. Blame was quickly fixed: "The Task Force finds that the State system of supervision and examination of State Associations is inadequate."[47] It specifically faulted the lack of resources available to the Savings and Loan Department to do its job properly. It also cited the requirement that two of three members of the state's Finance Commission be full-time savings and loan employees, noting that "this . . . insur[es] industry domination of the regulatory and administrative process."[48] Indicative of the close relationship between the Department and the industry it was meant to regulate is the fact that the former director of supervision for the Savings and Loan Department, Patrick King, left his office to become president of the troubled Vernon Savings (Highlight 9–4). In his position at this institution, he used money "to pay women escorts, including topless dancers, for Vernon officials and for Linton Bowman III, head of the Texas Savings and Loan Department."[49] For this and for other activities, King was convicted of misappropriating funds and sent to prison for five years.

In general, however, penalties against savings and loan failures, even if such failures have been caused by criminal activities, have been mild. Relatively little of the money that was lost has been recovered. Very few officials suspected of bilking their depositors have had their records subpoenaed, or have been forced to make restitution, or have been indicted for crimes, let alone imprisoned.[50]

★ ★ ★

Highlight 9–4: The Vernon Savings and Loan Disaster

Vernon Savings had the reputation of being a staid, conservatively run thrift until Don Dixon, using other people's money, bought it in 1981. Within two years, its assets nearly tripled, to $440 million. Most of these assets, however, were estimated based on the values of speculative loans made in the commercial real estate market. By 1985, Vernon was showing an asset worth of $1 billion. A year later, the federal government, concerned about the number of high-risk loans underwritten by Vernon Savings, imposed a cease-and-desist order on the institution, requiring it to exercise strict controls on its future lending practices. Federal regulators also began to sift through Vernon's financial records. By March 1987, it was declared insolvent. Vernon was sold at auction in late 1987.

Although the financial base of Vernon was shaky during its growth years, the asset base of Don Dixon was very solid. Using the thrift's money, he amassed a fortune. His tastes ran to extravagant holidays, art collecting, and a lavish lifestyle. Among other items purchased by Dixon were luxury cars, houses, yachts, and jet planes. Investigators claimed that he possessed a $60,000 Ferrari, shotguns valued at $25,000 each, gold chains and jewelry worth more than $100,000, $31,000 worth of French wines, a $1.7 million Lear jet, a $2.6 million yacht, a $1.9 million house in Beaver Creek, Colorado, $900,000 worth of art, and several other valuable cars. By the time it was closed, 96 percent of Vernon Savings's loans were delinquent. The government charged Dixon and his fellow officers with "systematic looting . . . The defendants misappropriated at least $40 million."[1] Dixon eventually pleaded guilty to several charges of fraud. He was sentenced to prison for 10 years and ordered to pay restitution to the government.

Note

1. Quoted in Ronnie Dugger, "Blitzing the American Dream," *Texas Observer,* December 15, 1989, p.12. Also see Byron Harris, "Break the Bank," *Texas Monthly,* January 1988, pp. 88 and 134–143.

★ ★ ★ ★ ★ CONSUMER PROTECTION

During the 1970s, Texas became a leader in protecting consumers from defective goods and deceptive sales practices. For consumers victimized by an unscrupulous salesperson or a faulty product, the state's laws, especially the Consumer Protection Act of 1973, provided a host of legal remedies. Individuals were encouraged to sue businesses for fraudulent trade practices or for making defective products. The attorney general of the state was authorized to seek civil penalties against the violators of these consumer protection laws.

Since that time, many business interests have expressed their displeasure with Texas consumer protection laws. Businesses, it is claimed, have suffered great financial losses in consumer suits, the compensation awarded to customers by generous juries and judges, and the increasing cost of product liability insurance for some enterprises and individuals, including doctors, hospitals, day care centers, newspapers, and small businesses.[51] Conversely, it has been argued that in reality, consumers win only a small portion of suits brought against businesses and that the financial awards granted by juries are not very high.[52]

In the past twenty years, businesses and insurance companies, contrary to the wishes of trial lawyers, have whittled away at the consumer protection laws of Texas. In the 1993 legislative session, a product liability bill was enacted that made businesses manufacturing a product known by the public to be dangerous immune from being sued for damages and required that for a litigant to receive damages in cases involving a flaw in a product, that litigant must prove that a safer alternative design existed when the product was manufactured. Consumer advocate Ralph Nader called this product liability law "a surrender of the health and safety rights of the people of Texas."[53]

Governor George W. Bush made legal reform a top priority in 1995 and the legislature responded by enacting laws that limited the award of punitive damages to an injured party to twice his or her economic actual harm (such as wages lost, hospital bills, etc.), plus no more than $750,000. Before any damages can be collected, the injured party must present proof that the defendant acted fraudulently or with malice. Consumers harmed through deceptive trade practices can now collect compensation equal to no more than three times the actual economic harm of the deception; previously, no cap was imposed on financial awards. The amount owed by a defendant with deep pockets if a codefendant has relatively little or no money has been limited. The cost of filing a "frivolous" lawsuit has been increased. Finally, lawsuits against a company must now, in most cases, be filed in the county where the business's principal office is located and not where the injury took place or where the plaintiff lives.[54]

★ ★ ★ ★ ★   # LABOR

In the wake of industrialization, workers found themselves toiling long hours in unsafe jobs for little pay. Unemployment and work-related accidents were as common as they were unpredictable. There was no financial compensation during periods of unemployment, no matter what the reason for losing one's job. Pressure soon mounted to alter the vulnerability of employees. Workers organized into unions and demanded higher pay, greater job security, safer working conditions, and compensation for unemployment and injury. For the most part, corporations balked at these demands for change. An intense economic conflict ensued, featuring wildcat strikes, work slowdowns and stoppages, and deadly violence. Government at the federal and state levels ordinarily allied with employers in these disputes, although on occasion laws improving the lot of workers were enacted. The balance tipped in favor of labor during the New Deal period of the 1930s.

Surprisingly, much of the pressure for government intervention in labor matters came from corporate sources. As early as 1900, executives of large corporations and banks expressed great concern over labor unrest in the United States. Strikes, slowdowns, stoppages, and lengthy litigation over industrial accidents, as well as growing dissatisfaction among more and more workers, cut into profits and stimulated big business to seek remedies.[55] Business-sponsored groups played a major role in drafting and enacting many labor laws, including compensation for both unemployment and injury and the recognition of a labor union as the workers' agent for bargaining with employers.

Federal law allows states to regulate many labor activities. Workers in jobs that produce goods used only within the state, for instance, are under the jurisdiction of the state. Labor activities not covered by federal laws also remain open to state control. Finally, some federal labor statutes invite state participation in the regulation of the workforce. Texas has responded by enacting legislation that regulates working conditions, wages, union activities, and farm workers.

Working Conditions and Wages

Throughout this century, the Texas Legislature has enacted a variety of laws affecting the status of workers in the state. This section probes into four areas of legislative concern: the protection of laborers against work-

WORKERS! Demonstrate
on
INTERNATIONAL FIGHTING DAY—FEB. 25th. 1931
at the
STATE CAPITOL at 12 NOON
Demand Unemployment Insurance and Inmmediate Relief for the Unemployed

NEGRO, MEXICAN, WHITE WORKERS; WOMEN and YOUNG WORKERS:

Come to the demonstration before the State Capitol Building, on Feb. 25th at 12 noon to demand of the Governor and the State of Texas and the City of Austin the right to work, demand work or wages.

Demand unemployment insurance for all workers and poor farmers of Texas.

Demand inmmediate relief in the form of cash for all unemployed.

10.000.000 workers are without a job in United States, over 1000 a day die from starvation, 40 000.000 are hungry and sick from lack of food, clothing and shelter in the richest country in the world.

Women, young workers and children of the working class join your fathers and mothers, your brothers and sisters and husbands in the fight against this deplorable condition of the working class.

Negro workers, join the demonstration and fight for full social, political and economic equality for the Negro workers.

Governor Sterling turned down our demands on Feb. 10th.

Demonstrate on Feb. 25th with the workers of the entire world and again tell the Governor or Texas, the workers and farmers of Texas will not starve.

Auspices: Trade Union Unity League and Unemployed Councils Add of Texas.

For information of these organizations write:
T. U. U. L. 404½ Nebraska St. San Antonio, Texas

Courtesy of the Archives Division, Texas State Library.

related accidents, compensation available to unemployed Texans, regulation of the employment of women and children, and the minimum wage.

Workers' Compensation   In 1913, Texas enacted the Workman's Compensation Act, which established procedures for paying compensation to workers injured on the job. Employers were required to contribute money to an accident insurance fund; insurance companies issued policies covering work-related injuries. For compensation payments, injured workers applied to the State Industrial Accident Board, a three-person panel appointed by the governor. If they were dissatisfied with the board's decisions, the workers could appeal to a state district court.

The workers' compensation program ensured quick decisions on an employee's claims and offered workers a good chance of receiving at least some compensation for injuries sustained in the workplace. Before the passage of accident compensation laws, workers found it extremely difficult to secure payment for injuries, even though, in many instances, company practices had caused their injuries.

Employers also benefited from the law. Businesses participating in the Texas compensation program could argue to the Industrial Accident Board that the worker was partially responsible for his or her injury, or that a fellow employee had contributed to the cause of injury, or that the worker was plainly aware that his or her job was risky from the beginning of employment. If accepted, any of these common-law defenses would free the company from at least some liability. Furthermore, a limit was placed on the amount of compensation that a worker could receive. Instead of facing the possibility of a financially ruinous settlement in an liability case, a company was assured that no matter what the administrative decision, it would not be financially drained. Finally, having state administrators decide compensation matters saved companies the expense of a lengthy court battle.

For many years the compensation system worked smoothly in Texas. Things began to change in the late 1970s. Insurance companies found themselves paying out more in compensation than they were receiving in premiums. In 1989, for instance, insurance companies earned $3.41 billion in premiums, but paid $3.5 billion in compensation to injured workers. In response, these companies substantially raised the prices of their policies to employers. By 1991, insurers were again profiting from the workers' compensation program.[56] However, many of the 376,000 employers enrolled in the scheme complained loudly about these price hikes and some exercised their option to withdraw from the program.

Accusations flew in many directions. Insurance companies, and many employers, blamed workers and lawyers. Spurred by the incentive of receiving hefty contingency fees for judicial awards, lawyers, according to their detractors, were encouraging injured workers to appeal their administrative decisions to state judges. Indeed, in 1987, 93 percent of the 12,100 board decisions were appealed to district courts.[57] The medical profession, which receives nearly 50 percent of the benefits disbursed, came under attack for driving the awards higher. According to a former member of the Industrial Accident Board, "the board found an increasing number of attorneys working with doctors to milk the system by giving questionable medical findings."[58] Insurance companies were accused of raising their rates capriciously and arbitrarily.

The Texas Legislature rewrote the workers' compensation law in 1989. Now companies can avoid the state program and establish their own workers' compensation schemes. Procedures for receiving compensation are more clearly delineated and greater emphasis has been placed on the administrative system as the final arbitrator of awards. Workers' benefits have been increased to a maximum of the average weekly salary paid in the state. Injured workers are limited to consulting two doctors unless the insurance carrier is willing to waive this requirement. Lawyers' fees cannot exceed 25 percent of the total award granted. Finally, the three-person Industrial Accident Board has been replaced by the six-member Texas Workers' Compensation Board; employees and employers are equally represented on the board. The common-law defenses that protect any employer who joins the program against injury claims remain unchanged.

Workplace Safety   Workers' compensation applies only after a worker suffers an accident. Legislation to prevent industrial accidents was put in place in 1967, when the Texas Legislature passed an occupational safety measure; the federal government followed suit in 1970. These laws do not contain stringent safety codes, nor are they comprehensively or rigorously enforced. With penalties set at a maximum of $1,000 for the first safety violation found and $20,000 for death, it is tempting for employers to risk fines rather than to install expensive safety equipment. Moreover, it is difficult to prove a causal link between conditions in the workplace and injuries sustained by employees. For instance, workers in Texas's petrochemical plants appear to contract illnesses, such as brain cancer, that might be attributable to the chemicals that are present in the factories. Yet, since some illnesses are invisible in their formative stages, or take their toll outside of the workplace, or may be related to factors elsewhere than at work, to prove beyond a shadow of a doubt that a firm is responsible for an injury is almost impossible.

In recent years, agencies such as the federal government's Occupational Safety and Health Agency (OSHA), responsible for keeping workplaces safe, have suffered budgetary cutbacks and staff reductions, resulting in even less enforcement of occupational safety codes. In the late 1980s there were, for example, only 82 OSHA inspectors available to monitor the workplace safety of 8.3 million employed Texans.[59] One source noted that "the Occupational Safety and Health Administration is so understaffed that work sites in Texas can expect an OSHA inspector every 70 years—based on the ratio of inspectors to work sites."[60]

A study commissioned by the legislature estimates that more than 500 Texans are killed at work each year. An additional 500,000 are injured. Work-related injuries involve 24,000 more Texans, and result in 4,000 deaths, each year. On-the-job deaths and injuries cost the Texas economy at least $3.8 billion annually.[61]

In recent years, workers sustaining injuries on the job have been turning more to state courts for compensatory damages. Lawyers offer their services in such cases for a contingency fee, usually set at 30 percent of the financial damages won. State court judges have been inclined to grant financial awards to workers injured during the course of their employment. However, as we have mentioned, new restrictions on this type of suit have been enacted recently. In 1993, for example, the legislature prohibited workers injured at job sites in countries outside the United States from suing their employers in the Texas courts after the Texas Supreme Court ruled, three years earlier (in the case of *Dow Chemical v. Alfaro*), that a Costa Rican worker employed on a banana plantation could sue Shell and Dow Chemical for damages in the Lone Star State. These companies manufactured a pesticide, which is banned in the United States, that was handled by Alfaro and, according to his suit, caused him personal injuries including sterility. He brought his claims to a Texas court because both Shell and Dow Chemical have extensive business activities in the state.

Unemployment Compensation   Since the mid-1930s, Texas has provided a compensation program for workers who lose their jobs. Unemployment compensation is available to most out-of-work persons who have held a steady job, who did not quit voluntarily or to attend school, who were not fired for misconduct, and who actively seek work during the period in which they receive benefits. Through a fairly complicated formula, most employers pay fees into an unemployment compensation fund. Employer costs are usually added to the price that consumers pay for products or services. Those eligible to receive unemployment compensation are provided with an amount in accordance with their prior earnings, although the maximum obtainable amount is $245 per week (about half the average weekly salary in Texas) for 26 weeks.[62]

Protection for Women and Children   Since 1915, Texas has regulated the hours that women and children may work. Children under 15 are barred from working in heavy industry, in laundries, or as messengers. Youngsters may work in other occupations, but for no more than forty-eight hours each week. Special dispensation from these restrictions may be granted by the state. Until 1971, women could work no more than nine hours per day and fifty-four hours per week. The "nine-and-fifty-four" law was amended in 1971 to allow women who are professionals, executives, administrators, or salespersons, or who simply wish to work longer, to do so. This change was enacted to end state-authorized sex discrimination in employment.

State Minimum Wage Finally, Texas passed a minimum wage act in 1970. It was one of the last states to enact such legislation. The Texas hourly wage has always been far below the federal standard. Currently, it is $3.35, which is $1.80 less than the federal minimum. Persons working for firms whose market lies entirely in Texas are generally paid the state's minimum hourly wage. Some employers, such as dairy farmers, nonprofit organizations, religious orders, and prisons, are exempt from paying the minimum wage.

Labor Unions With the passage of the Wagner Act in 1937, the federal government recognized the right of unions to mobilize and represent workers in disputes with management. Some of the most influential backers of this act were from the corporate world; they saw the advantages of having unions to create "greater efficiency and productivity from labor, less labor turnover, the disciplining of the labor force by labor unions, the possibility of planning labor costs over the long run, and the dampening of radical doctrines."[63]

The federal government grants states the power to control many activities of labor unions. Texas has traditionally enacted legislation that restricts, regulates, and monitors union efforts. In 1943, the legislature established a set of rules to guide the internal activities of labor unions in the state, requiring every union to file an annual report with the Texas Secretary of State. This report is to include the union's affiliations, its property, its constitution, its by-laws, and its finances. Union records must be open for inspection at any time by any member. A union cannot expel a member without just cause and a formal hearing. Reinstatement may be ordered by a state judge. Union fees may not be automatically deducted from employee paychecks without prior written authorization. A state union organizer must register with the state and obtain a card to solicit funds or recruit new members. A union cannot contribute money to political candidates or parties, although it may establish a political action committee for this purpose.

Other laws prohibit certain workers from joining unions. For instance, domestic servants are not only denied the benefits of unemployment, workers' compensation, and, in some cases, the minimum wage; they cannot bargain collectively. Since 1973, all state and local government employees may form unions, but their right to collective bargaining with their employers is limited. Police and fire department personnel can enter into collective bargaining only if a majority of local voters approve this action. Many elections have been conducted to establish such collective bargaining, but in most cases voters have rejected unionization. Some cities repealed, through election, the authorization of collective bargaining after initially endorsing it.

The tactics a union can use in dealing with employers are greatly circumscribed by state law in Texas. Under Section 14(b) of the Taft-Hartley Act of 1947, states can decide whether employers must hire only union members as employees or may hire workers regardless of their union status. Texas has chosen the latter option, joining nineteen other states with this "right-to-work" rule.

During disputes with management, unions may not do any of the following: threaten or actually use violence; insult, slander, libel, or obscenely speak against a business; harass workers; block entrances to the workplace; engage in mass picketing (defined as two or more pickets, within fifty feet of either the entrance to the firm or each other); or involve parties not primarily relevant to the labor dispute, such as another company doing business with the original target. Union actions that result in a breach of contract with an employer are in violation of the state's antitrust acts. Strikes aimed at forcing business management to recognize a union must cease if a majority of workers vote not to join the union. (If a majority of workers approve the union, it is thereafter certified as their bargaining agent.) Finally, union strikers and sympathizers are denied unemployment compensation benefits.

Overall, union efforts in Texas are severely curtailed by these legal obstacles. Only about 5 percent of the state's workforce is unionized. This is approximately one third of the estimated national average.[64] For the last three decades, the state has ranked near the bottom in percentage of unionized employees; among industrialized states, it is last. Union membership is mostly concentrated among workers in the industrial plants located in the southeastern portion of the state, near the Gulf Coast. As more major companies move their manufacturing plants across the Mexican border to take advantage of NAFTA (see Chapter 2), unions become weaker. Workers at these factories are mostly Mexican and are paid much less than American workers, especially unionized ones.

Given the overall weakness of labor unions in Texas, it should come as no surprise that they have relatively little influence in state politics. Lacking a large membership base, unions do not have much say in the selection of candidates for elected office. Nor are they as effective as are business groups in lobbying policy makers. Very few appointed officials come from the ranks of unions. Consequently, unions do not serve as much of a political counterweight to big business in Texas.

Farmworkers

Texas is home to 443,000 farm laborers, 282,000 of whom participate in the migratory stream that flows from Texas throughout the rest of the country each year. Most of them live within the four-county area (Hidalgo, Cameron, Starr, and Willacy) that makes up the Rio Grande Valley in Texas.[65] The average yearly wage for the migrant farm worker in the 1980s was $3,500. Most work less than half the year.[66] When they are unemployed, farmworkers receive few benefits from the state. Many refuse to apply for AFDC benefits out of a strong sense of self-respect: "People willing to travel thousands of miles a year, suffer great indignities, and do backbreaking work for very low pay are not the sort eager to take government handouts."[67]

Until recently, farmworkers were not covered by many of Texas's labor laws. They were not eligible to receive workers' compensation or unemployment benefits, for instance. After some prodding from state district courts, the legislature finally extended these benefits to farm laborers. They also must now be paid $3.35 per hour and not according to the number of items they harvest, as they often were in the past. Thanks to some sweeping reforms initiated by the Department of Agriculture, current regulation of the use of pesticides protects farm workers from indiscriminate exposure to dangerous chemicals. It is illegal to require farm laborers to use short hoes in their work, a physically harmful practice that was common before 1989. Nonetheless, "farm work is still America's most dangerous occupation."[68]

These successes came only after a long, tortuous, and often bitter struggle by organizations dedicated to improving the plight of Texas's farmworkers. A taste of that struggle is evident in the early efforts to unionize farm laborers. The first major attempt to organize them occurred in 1966, when the Independent Workers' Association moved into Starr County.[69] At the time, farm laborers were paid about 25 cents per hour. The union mobilized some 700 workers and called for a strike against the large agribusiness firms in the area. In response, local authorities requested the presence of the Texas Rangers. During their eight-month stay, the Rangers implemented the state's labor union regulations so strongly that many union supporters, including members of the clergy, claimed that they had used excessive force, denied people their constitutional rights, and used trumped-up charges to arrest union sympathizers. Critics asserted that the actual motive behind the Rangers' actions was to protect the economic interests of the growers of Starr County by destroying the union through breaking the strike, which they did in June 1967. In 1974, the United States Supreme Court scolded the Rangers for engaging in "a persistent pattern of policy misconduct" and pointed out that "because of the intimidation by state authorities, [the union's] lawful effort was crushed."[70]

Undocumented Immigrants

Undocumented immigrants, the vast majority of whom are from Mexico, occupy jobs that are among the lowest paying in Texas. It is extremely difficult to gauge accurately the number of undocumented workers in the state because they constitute a transitory population whose residency is illegal. Statewide estimates place their number at between 300,000 and nearly one million; 552,000 is accepted in state government circles as a good ballpark figure.[71]

Undocumented workers from Mexico tend to be very poor, uneducated, young, predominantly married men who speak little if any English and, especially if they have migrated from deep in Mexico, strongly desire to return to their homeland. Compared to nonmigratory Mexicans, the immigrants are more work-oriented, more disposed to think about and plan for the future, less fatalistic about their lives, less submissive to authority, and more likely to condone the practice of birth control (although just as likely not to use it because of their poverty).[72]

One study of a sample of undocumented immigrants found that they stayed in the state an average of 4.3 years: "This suggests that a large proportion of the sample population has established permanent residence in the U.S."[73] Nearly two thirds came to Texas in search of jobs: 40 percent worked in service positions, 22 percent were employed on construction sites, 12 percent were domestics, 12 percent worked in factories, and 6 percent were farm laborers. In the mid-1980s, they earned about $4.13 per hour, working 39 hours per week. Their yearly income was about $8,500.[74] Describing the jobs available to the undocumented worker, one observer notes that "they involve dirty, often physically arduous tasks, . . . low social status, low job security (often due to the short-term or seasonal nature of the work), and little chance for advancement."[75] These are not jobs coveted by most United States citizens, and there is evidence that undocumented workers do not take jobs away from Americans.[76]

For employers, the undocumented worker is usually a cheap source of labor. As noted by one student of this subject, "the hiring of the illegal alien is generally a profitable business which contributes to the widening of [employers'] profit maximization margins."[77] This pattern is especially evident on the farms and ranches owned by large agribusiness outfits in South Texas, where "wage exploitation of Mexican workers seems to be practiced on a far wider scale . . . than in any other sector of the U.S. economy where large numbers of Mexican illegals are still employed."[78]

Furthermore, undocumented laborers raise few complaints, require negligible discipline from their employers (although historical examples of undocumented workers' rebelling against their employment status have been recorded), and can be used to replace striking workers. Until recently, the undocumented were at the mercy of their employers, who sometimes handed them over to immigration officials instead of paying them. This unsavory practice has been declining since immigration law now compels employers to compensate the undocumented even if the latter are turned in. Since 1986, federal law makes it illegal for employers to knowingly hire undocumented workers.

Measuring the costs of undocumented immigration is difficult and controversial; researchers fail to agree in their conclusions. One estimate suggests that the undocumented cost Texas $1 billion annually for the government services they use, far more than they contribute in taxes. Others dispute this account, arguing that undocumented workers cost the state about $456 million annually, of which $419 million is required to school their children (estimated to number about 94,000), $23 million is spent on the imprisonment of some of them, and $12 million subsidizes their medical expenses.[79] Very few of them receive welfare, food stamps, rent or utility supplements, unemployment or workers' compensation, or senior citizen services: "The use of social services by the undocumented sample was quite low given the generally low income status of this population."[80] Around half received legal aid and used public transportation systems.[81]

The undocumented do pay taxes. Federal taxes, such as Social Security and personal income tax, are ordinarily deducted from their wages. The state receives revenue through the sales tax, which does not discriminate on the basis of the buyer's citizenship. Property taxes are included in rent charged for lodging. It is estimated that in sum they pay about $290 million in taxes, some $166 million short of the amount the state spends on services used by them.[82] Recently, however, the federal government has agreed to reimburse states for some services provided to the undocumented.[83] Moreover, a fair share of the earnings of the undocumented worker ultimately boosts the U.S. economy. About two thirds of their money stays in this country to cover their housing, food, transportation, and other amenities.[84]

★★★★★ CONCLUSION

The regulatory policies of the state government of Texas generally benefit business. Financial institutions, electric companies, and petroleum firms find a favorable regulatory environment in the state. Legislative, administrative, and judicial decisions mainly permit these enterprises to go about the business of making profits without much interference from state government. Recent legislation has granted additional legal protection for the manufacturers of products that can be dangerous to people.

Many of Texas's labor laws have improved working conditions and wages. These advances, however, have not undermined the position of large businesses in the state's economy. Indeed, state regulation of labor fosters a more stable environment in which corporations can plan rationally for future profit. Further, the cost of these programs is not fully borne by companies. Instead, the costs of higher wages and unemployment and accident compensation insurance are passed along to consumers in the form of higher prices for products. Laws regulating labor unions are restrictive. The plight of the farmworker has improved in the state and undocumented workers make up a hidden economy, accepted without much public concern.

★★★★★ NOTES

1. David F. Prindle, *Petroleum Politics and the Texas Railroad Commission* (Austin: University of Texas Press, 1981), p. 113.

2. Joint Report of the Interim Committee on Pipeline Study and Beaches, *Pollution vs. the People,* 62nd Legislature of the State of Texas, 1971, p. 1.

3. Legislative Budget Board, *Fiscal Size Up: 1990–1991 Biennium* (Austin: Legislative Budget Bureau, 1990), pp. 10–12.

4. Quoted in House Study Group, *Strip Mining in Texas* (Austin: House Study Group, 1978), p. 18.

5. The act is discussed ibid, pp. 38–40.

6. Betty Anne Duke, "Texas Lignite: Stripping Away Illusions," *Texas Observer,* August 11, 1978, p. 11 and *passim.*

7. Louis Dubose, "Let Them Eat Cake," *Texas Observer,* May 19, 1989, pp. 6–7.

8. Legislative Budget Board, *Fiscal Size Up: 1996–97 Biennium Texas State Services* (Austin: Legislative Budget Board, n.d.), pp. 11–13.

9. Jack Hopper and Eric Hartman, "Rating the PUC," *Texas Observer,* July 19, 1979, p. 6.

10. Rick Piltz, *The Public Utility Commission* (Austin: House Study Group, 1982), p. 50.

11. Quoted in Jack Hopper and Eric Hartman, "Rating the PUC," p. 5.

12. Texas Water Development Board, *Continuing Water Resources Planning and Development for Texas* (Austin: Texas Water Development Board, 1977), vol. 1, pp. 111–138.

13. Al Reinert, "This Water Is My Water," *Texas Monthly,* November 1988, p. 168.

14. Ken Herman and Rebecca Thatcher, "Bush Calls for Statewide Water Saving," *Austin American-Statesman,* May 31, 1996.

15. Clint Winters, "Texas Water Problems: Work Begins on a New Plan," *Fi$cal Note$,* September 1982, p. 2.

16. See, for documentation, Joint Report of the Interim Committee on Pipeline Study and Beaches, *Pollution vs. The People,* 62nd Legislature of the State of Texas, 1971, pp. 10–11; Kaye Northcott, "Hugh Yantis is a Scare Word," *Texas Observer,* February 28, 1975, pp. 6–7; and Subcommittee on Environmental Pollution of the Committee on Environment and Public Works, 95th Congress, 1st Session, U.S. Senate (Washington, DC: Government Printing Office, 1977), p. 28.

17. For documentation, see G. Todd Norvell and Alexander W. Bell, "Air Pollution Control in Texas," *Texas Law Review,* 47 (June 1969): 1086–1123; Gary Keith, *Air Pollution Control in Texas* (Austin: House Study Group, 1981), p. 43; and Legislative Budget Board, *Fiscal Size Up: 1990–91,* pp. 9–12.

18. Presented in the testimony of Dick Whittington, acting deputy director of Texas Department of Water Resources, before the Committee on Public Works and Transportation, Federal Water Pollution Control Act Amendments, 95th Congress, 1st Session, House of Representatives (Washington, DC: Government Printing Office, 1978), p. 95.

19. Texas Department of Water Resources, *Water for Texas: Planning for the Future* (Austin: Department of Water Resources, February 1983), pp. 1–2.

20. *Dallas Morning News,* April 28, 1993, p. A-28.

21. Texas Air Control Board, *Biennial Report: 1986–88* (Austin: Texas Air Control Board, 1988).

22. *U.S. vs. ARMCO Steel Corporation,* reprinted in Hearings Before the Subcommittee on Public Buildings and Grounds of the Committee on Public Works, 92nd Congress, 1st Session, House of Representatives (Washington, D.C: Government Printing Office, 1971), p. 466.

23. Information from a special advertising section sponsored by Texas Air Care in the *Texas Monthly,* January 1995.

24. Peter Altman, "Texans Want Deregulated Electric Industry to Reduce Pollution, Too," *Austin American-Statesman,* December 18, 1996.

25. Quotation in "Toxic Texas Top Forty," *Texas Observer,* September 29, 1989, pp. 5–6.

26. Ibid. The subcommittee's report contained a disclaimer noting that "the facility-specific risk estimates are not accurate determinants of local public health hazards." Also see "Texas Research Group to Study Link Between Cancer, Petrochemicals," *Lubbock Avalanche-Journal,* March 22, 1993, p. A-8.

27. Michael King, "The Way the Wind Blows," *Texas Observer,* May 17, 1996, pp. 8–9, and "Refinery Woe," *Texas Monthly,* May 1995, pp. 98–102.

28. Joe Nick Patoski, "Big Bend, R.I.P.?" *Texas Monthly,* March 1996, pp. 20–22.

29. "Texas Second in Releases of Toxic Chemicals, EPA Reports," *Houston Post,* May 28, 1992, p. A-6.

30. See Office of the State Auditor, *Report on the Hazardous Waste Program of the Texas Water Commission* (Austin: Office of the State Auditor, 1990); Texas Water Commission, *Annual Report of the Hazardous and Solid Waste Program* (Austin: Texas Water Commission, 1987); David Armstrong, "Plastic Peril," *Texas Observer,* May 17, 1991, pp. 4–7; and the *Texas Observer,* May 7, 1993, p. 23, and February 11, 1994, p. 11.

31. See Randy Lee Loftis and Craig Flourney, "More than 10 years of Pollution Unheeded," *Dallas Morning News,* May 9, 1993, p. A-29; Mike Ward, "Citizens Use Voice for Change," *Austin American-Statesman,* February 14, 1993, pp. A-1 and A-18–A-19; and Carol Countryman, "Arsenic and Old Lakes," *Texas Observer,* February 24, 1995, pp. 6–12.

32. Texas Research League, "Texas New Environmental Superagency," January 1994, p. 6.

33. Harvey Katz, *Shadow on the Alamo* (Garden City, NY: Doubleday, 1972), p. 181.

34. Legislative Budget Board, *Fiscal Size Up: 1990–91,* p. 11–13.

35. *Austin American-Statesman,* January 23, 1993, p. B-5.

36. *Austin American-Statesman,* February 1, 1993, p. F-4.

37. Wayne Slater, "State Treasurer Picked Aide's Firm to Sell Notes," *Austin American-Statesman,* February 27, 1993, pp. A-1 and A-12.

38. *The Monitor,* February 16, 1997, p. 10B.

39. Elizabeth Travis Roberts, "Unhealthy Profits," *Texas Observer,* February 22, 1991, pp. 12–13, 19.

40. *Texas Observer,* March 8, 1991.

41. "Mutually Insured Destruction," *Texas Observer,* February 10, 1988.

42. Terrence Stutz, "State Insurance Counsel May Lose Her Job," *Dallas Morning News,* March 21, 1993, pp. A-47 and A-54.

43. M. Danny Wall, quoted in Ronnie Dugger, "Blitzing the American Dream," *Texas Observer,* December 15, 1989, p. 6.

44. See Richard W. Stevenson, "Minimum Sentences, Maximum Costs," *Austin American-Statesman,* July 13, 1996; Joel Bleifuss, "Texas S&L Absolution," *Texas Observer,* August 5, 1994, pp. 13–14; and Michelle Mittelstadt, "Bailout Helps Texas Most," *Austin American-Statesman,* May 7, 1993, pp. E-1 and E-2.

45. Ibid.

46. Michele Kay, "RTC Report Sparks Senators' Criticism," *Austin American-Statesman,* April 16, 1994, p. F1.

47. Governor's Task Force on the Savings and Loan Industry, *Savings and Loan Report,* 1988, p. 28.

48. Ibid.

49. Ronnie Dugger, "Blitzing the American Dream," p. 15.

50. Joel Bleifuss, "Texas S&L Absolution"; Michele Kay, "RTC Report Sparks Senators' Criticism;" Richard Kell, "RTC Fails to Recoup S&L Losses in Texas," *Austin American-Statesman,* January 1, 1994, p. F1; and "Texas S&L Monetary Recovery is Unlikely," *Austin American-Statesman,* April 21, 1994, p. F2.

51. For a summary of business complaints about consumer protection laws, see the statement of Gerald Dorsey, staff attorney of the Texas Association of Business, presented to the Select Committee on Small Business, *Impact on Product Liability,* 94th Congress, 2nd Session, U.S. Senate (Washington, DC: U.S. Printing Office, 1976), pp. 1430–35, and Tani Adams, "The Lawsuit 'Crisis' and the Justice Issue," *Texas Observer,* May 16, 1986, pp. 9–12.

52. See Tina Lam, "Making the State Safe for Unsafe Products," *Texas Observer,* April 13, 1979, pp. 2–7; Tani Adams, "The Lawsuit 'Crisis' and the Justice Issue"; and Bruce Hight, "Questioning Tort Reform," *Austin American-Statesman,* January 8, 1995.

53. Quoted in "Product Liability Bill Assailed," *Dallas Morning News,* January 29, 1993, p. A-29.

54. Steve Wisch, "Tort Reform's Bad Cop," *Texas Observer,* June 16, 1995, pp. 25–26.

55. See G. William Domhoff, *The Higher Circles* (New York: Vintage, 1970), Chapter 6.

56. State Board of Insurance, *Annual Report, 1990* (Austin: State Board of Insurance, 1991), pp. 10 and 124.

57. House Research Organization, *An Introduction to Workers' Compensation in Texas* (Austin: House Research Organization, 1989) and "The Smoking Gun," *Texas Monthly,* April 1988, pp. 7–10.

58. Jim Kaster, quoted in House Research Organization, *An Introduction to Workers' Compensation in Texas,* p. 23.

59. Ibid, p. 16.

60. *Texas Observer,* September 4, 1992, p. 24.

61. See Michael Graczyk, "Worker Injuries, Deaths Cost Texas $3.8 Billion a Year," *Dallas Morning News,* March 5, 1993, p. A-27; the *Texas Observer,* September 4, 1992, p. 24; and *An Introduction to Workers' Compensation,* p. 16.

62. Figures from the Texas Employment Commission, *1994 Annual Report* (Austin: Texas Employment Commission, 1993), p. 30.

63. G. William Domhoff, *The Higher Circles,* p. 225 and *passim.*

64. *Houston Post,* September 2, 1991, p. A-19.

65. Chad Richardson, *Batos, Bolillos, Pochos, and Pelados* (Austin: University of Texas Press, forthcoming), Chapter 1.

66. These figures are from Geoffrey Rips, "The Battle for Farmworker Compensation," *Texas Observer,* January 13, 1984, pp. 7–15.

67. John Davidson, "A Harvest of Poverty," *Texas Observer,* February 3, 1978, p. 5.

68. Chad Richardson, *Batos, Bolillos, Pochos, and Pelados,* p. 2 (manuscript page).

69. Drawn from Julian Samora, Joe Bernal, and Albert Pena, *Gunpowder Justice: An Assessment of the Texas Rangers* (Notre Dame, IN: University of Notre Dame Press, 1979), Chapter 8.

70. *Alee v. Medrano,* 416 U.S. 815 and 814 (1974).

71. James E. Garcia, "Border Equation Defies Easy Answers," *Austin American-Statesman,* February 20, 1994, pp. B1 and B6.

72. Wayne A. Cornelius, *Mexican Migration to the United States: Causes, Consequence, and U.S. Resources* (Cambridge, MA: Center of International Studies, Massachusetts Institute of Technology, 1978), pp. 19–20 and 82.

73. LBJ School of Public Affairs, *The Use of Public Services by Undocumented Aliens in Texas: A Study of State Costs and Revenues* (Austin: LBJ School of Public Affairs, 1984), p. 9.

74. Ibid.

75. Wayne A. Cornelius, *Mexican Migration to the United States,* p. 56.

76. Michelle Mittelstadt, "Immigrants Don't Take Jobs from Americans, Study Says," *Austin American-Statesman,* May 25, 1994, p. D1.

77. Gilbert Cardenas, *Manpower Impact and Problems of Mexican Illegal Aliens in an Urban Labor Market* (Ph.D. diss., University of Illinois at Champaign-Urbana), p. 195.

78. Wayne Cornelius, *Mexican Migration to the United States,* p. 60.

79. Figures presented in Gregory Curtis, "The Gate-Crashers," *Texas Monthly,* January 1995, p. 5.

80. LBJ School of Public Affairs, *The Use of Public Services by Undocumented Aliens,* p. 32.

81. Ibid.

82. James E. Garcia, "Border Equation Defies Easy Answers."

83. "States Will Get Funds for Aliens," *Las Vegas Review-Journal,* October 7, 1994, p. 8A.

84. Wayne Cornelius, *Mexican Migration to the United States,* p. 75.

PART V

Local Politics and the Economically Powerful in Texas

To this point, we have developed the theme that big business and wealthy individuals prosper from the politics of the state of Texas. State funds allocated for welfare, transportation, and public education have improved the economic climate for business in Texas. State policy regarding the use of natural resources, the activities of financial institutions, and labor unions and working conditions in general has also benefited business. Texas's major economic entities have effectively shaped the process of state politics through candidate selection, campaign contributions, and lobbying. Does this same pattern of influence exist at the local level? Part V addresses this question by describing local government and examining the impact of the economically influential at this level.

CHAPTER 10

Local Politics

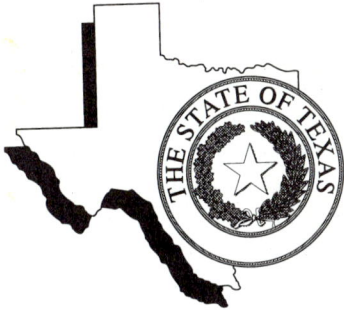

Citizens have more contact with local government officials than with any other officeholders in America. One reason for this intimacy is the large number of local government entities throughout the country. It is virtually impossible to avoid public school teachers, police, tax appraisers, sanitation workers, and thousands of other kinds of municipal and county employees. In Texas, there are more than 4,000 distinct local political bodies, which can be classified into three different types: municipal government, county government, and special governing districts (such as hospital districts, water districts, school districts, and sanitation districts). By far, the largest category comprises the special districts, which, when school districts are included, add up to nearly 2,800 distinct governing entities. Each of Texas's 1,179 incorporated cities has its own municipal government. Finally, a separate government operates in every one of the state's 254 counties. In this chapter, we describe the organizational pattern, the political authority, and the funding of local governments, examine citizen participation at the local level, explore the political power wielded by business in various communities, and discuss changes in local politics in Texas.

★★★★★ LOCAL GOVERNMENT: ORGANIZATION, AUTHORITY, AND FUNDING

Governments at the municipal, county, and special-district level in Texas vary along four dimensions: their legal basis, their structure, their political authority, and their funding.

Legal Basis of Local Government

The state government of Texas legally establishes municipal, county, and special district governments. Cities with fewer than 5,000 people are regulated by the general laws of the state. These *general law* cities are legally limited in the types of governmental structures that they may establish. Voters in cities with more than 5,000 people have the right to choose their structure of government; these municipalities are called *home rule* cities. Altogether, Texas has 284 home rule cities and 895 general law cities.[1]

County governments are created by the Texas Constitution to administer general state policies within their boundaries. Everyday implementation of state laws and formulation of more specific county-wide policies are primarily controlled by the county government. After the county government is given a set of general guidelines, it receives little assistance or interference from Austin in county business.

A special district is a governing unit established by state law to make decisions in a specific policy area affecting matters such as sanitation, water, education, or hospitals. The number of special districts has grown tremendously in Texas: the total has more than doubled over the last quarter century.

Structure of Local Government

Local government in Texas is organized into a multitude of political structures.

Municipal Government   City governments are organized around the offices of the mayor, the council, the commission, and the manager. Cities that choose to have a mayor differ in terms of the power they give to this office. Some cities have a strong mayor; that is, the mayor is authorized to participate in city council deliberations, to veto council proposals, to formulate a budget for the city, and to control the heads of administrative departments through powers of appointment and removal. Other cities have weak mayors. In these municipalities, the mayor participates in the business of the city council, but the council has more power than the mayor in most matters. It can, for instance, override the mayor's veto. Furthermore, the council, not the mayor, assumes responsibility for oversight of the operations of the city's administrative departments.

Cities with a commission form of government are governed by an elected board of commissioners. The board collectively legislates policy for the city. Each commissioner individually heads a specific administrative office in the city.

Many council and commission governments appoint a manager to be the chief administrative officer of the municipality. Preparing the budget, directing administrative offices, and implementing city policies are all part of the manager's job. The manager serves at the pleasure of the council or commission.

Each of Texas's 284 home rule cities can select its form of government. Most (some 249, or 88 percent) have some form (council, commission, or mayor) of manager government. The remainder are governed by mayor-council governments.[2] General law cities must become either council-manager or council-mayor (with a strong or weak mayor) municipalities. Most fall into the latter category.

Elections in almost all of Texas's cities are *nonpartisan;* that is, candidates do not run for local office under the banner of any political party. In addition, candidates for most local elections run *at large;* that is, they are chosen by the entire electorate, regardless of the office. In 1992, fully 88 percent of the 6,409 elected officials in cities and towns across Texas were elected at large, even though the federal government, through the efforts of the Justice Department, has put pressure on municipalities to select council and commission members from geographically distinct districts.[3] Larger cities, such as Dallas, El Paso, Fort Worth, and San Antonio, have instituted district representation.

County Government   The government of every county in Texas is organized in the same way. Each county is run by a commissioners' court, which is composed of four commissioners and a county judge. The four commissioners are elected from separate districts, equal in population. The county judge is elected county-wide. County voters also choose a sheriff, a county attorney, the county tax collector–assessor, the county clerk, the county treasurer, justices of the peace, and constables. The state requires the commissioners' court to appoint a health officer. In counties whose populations exceed 35,000, the commissioners must also appoint an auditor to attend to the financial books of the county government. Most counties also have an agricultural extension agent and a home demonstration agent, each of whom is appointed by the commissioners' court to assist residents in farming and homemaking.

Special Districts   The governing structures of special districts vary widely. About three fourths of these districts, including school districts, are governed by boards or commissions elected by people who reside within the district. Since 1983, each school board's members must be elected from a distinct geographical area within the district. The remaining special districts are headed by personnel appointed by the governor, other state officials, mayors of cities, city councils, or county commissioners, depending on the district in question. The size of the board or commission differs from district to district, although every school board is composed of seven elected members. The chaotic nature of special districts in Texas has prompted one observer to comment that generalizations about them "are certain to be misleading, if not totally false."[4]

Functions and Powers of Local Government

Municipal governments in Texas have authority over a wide range of policy matters. First, they provide citizens with numerous social services, including police and fire protection, health care, parks and recreational facilities, libraries, streets, jails, and sanitation services. Second, cities are responsible for planning the growth of their communities. They may annex new land. Under Texas law, each home rule city has extraterritorial jurisdiction, ranging from half a mile to five miles (depending on the city's population), over land outside its immediate boundaries. A municipality is permitted to annex up to 10 percent of this area each year. If property owners in adjacent areas request incorporation into a city, it may grow even larger. Third, a city can decide on how land within its boundaries is to be used through its zoning powers. Fourth, municipal governments regulate a good deal of human behavior. City housing codes, for instance, establish minimum requirements that residences must meet before citizens are permitted to live in them.

County government in Texas must carry out functions delegated to it by the state. For instance, county officials administer welfare programs, build and maintain roads and bridges, construct and repair jails and courthouses, provide health care and police and fire protection, oversee elections, and keep the vital statistics of residents (birth, death, marriage, and so forth). State law authorizes, but does not require, counties to operate public libraries, hospitals, welfare programs, and parks. The most populous counties provide all these services.

Special districts are authorized to govern in a specific policy area. School districts constitute the single largest category of special districts (see Chapter 8). Districts involved in some form of water policy—such as delivery, conservation, navigation, and flood control—total almost 1,000 and form the second largest group of special districts. Housing and redevelopment authorities (some 400), soil conservation districts (about 200), and hospital districts (123) make up most of the remaining special districts in Texas.[5]

Funding Local Government

Revenue to support local government comes from several sources, the most important of which are the sales tax, user fees, miscellaneous taxes, borrowed money, intergovernmental transfers, and the property tax.

Local Sales Tax The state allows local bodies to add as much as 2 percent to the existing 6.25 percent state sales tax. By the early 1990s, more than 1,000 cities, several special districts, and 91 counties had imposed taxes on the sale of items within their boundaries.[6] In 1994, the local portion of the sales tax generated nearly $2.5 billion, 5 percent of all revenues raised, for the funding of local programs and services.[7]

User Fees Local governments have increasingly been charging the users of their services, such as garbage collection. About 15 percent of all local funds are derived from this source; cities are a bit more dependent upon user fees than are counties.[8]

Miscellaneous Income   Local governments have created a wide array of income-producing programs, including issuing building permits, collecting fines for the violation of traffic and parking laws, and earning interest from investments. This miscellaneous income accounts for about 13 percent of all revenue available to local governing entities in Texas.[9]

Borrowing Local governments borrow money to fund the construction of major capital projects such as bridges, wastewater treatment plants, and water delivery systems. Borrowing is accomplished by the issuing of two types of bonds. One is the *general obligation* bond, which requires the local unit to commit tax revenue as security for the loan. The second is the *revenue* bond, which requires that money collected from the project being financed be dedicated to repayment of the debt. The issuance of a general obligation bond must be approved by voters; this is not the case for a revenue obligation bond. By the late 1980s, local governments had borrowed about $41 billion.[10]

municipal bonds

Intergovernmental Transfers About 30 percent of the funding for local governmental programs comes from other government sources, principally the federal government and the state government. The state assists in the financing of roads, health care facilities, public schools, and the administration of federal and state programs. The federal government provides money for schools (for example, financing special reading programs, services for migrant children, and health care for students), construction of capital projects (for example, highways, airports, and waterways), and the administration of federally mandated programs (for example, environmental protection, welfare services, and public housing).

Property Tax More than one third of the revenue possessed by local governing bodies is collected through the property tax, making "property taxes the most important source of local revenue in the state."[11] Moreover, in recent years the amount raised by the property tax has increased dramatically, almost doubling between 1984 and 1993. In the latter year, $14.6 billion was collected by taxing property. Fully 59 percent of this money ($8.7 billion) was generated by school districts to pay for public education. Cities accounted for about 16 percent of the total, about $2.4 billion. County governments received about $2.1 billion, or 14 percent of the total, through levies on property, while special districts (excluding schools) received $1.5 billion (10 percent).[12]

All real and personal property in Texas is subject to the property tax, unless the legislature or the constitution provides an exemption. Property in the state is appraised on the basis of true market value. It is estimated that as of 1996, $660.5 billion worth of property was taxable in Texas.[13] Property is assessed at 100 percent of its appraised value. The actual tax rate must be established. In some cases, such as taxes for public education, the tax rate, say $1.50 for every $100 of the appraised value of the property, is set by the state legislature or by other governing units. In other cases, the voters decide the exact tax rate. Each county has a five-person board, whose members are chosen by all the taxing units in the area, which is responsible for all property tax administration, including appraising property, setting the tax rate, collecting taxes, and handling appeals. If in any given year property taxes within the county rise more than 8 percent, the voters may roll back the increase. A rollback occurs if 10 percent of eligible voters petition for an election and if a majority of the voters approve the rollback. For the election to be valid, 25 percent of the registered voters in the area must vote. In most instances, these elections have been successful.[14]

★ ★ ★ ★ ★ CITIZEN PARTICIPATION

Although local government in Texas touches the daily lives of virtually every person residing in the state, most Texans have little say in the formulation of local policy. Participation in local politics is extremely low. The number of voters who actually cast ballots in the elections of the state's major cities, such as Houston, Dallas, San Antonio, Austin, and El Paso, rarely exceeds 25 percent of the number of people registered to vote.[15] Considering that many more Texans are eligible to vote than bother to register, the actual turnout for local elections is truly dismal. The very structure of local government discourages widespread participation.

Local government is fragmented. Government services are performed by a variety of distinct local units. Within the same geographic area, residents are usually caught in a web of governmental jurisdictions. A person living in the Houston area in the 1980s, for example, could count 622 separate governing authorities in his or her environs.[16] This complexity makes it difficult to learn about local decision making, thus preventing citizens from knowing which local governing body exercises what political authority. This public unawareness in turn produces extensive apathy. Organized interest groups with a clear stake in local politics, however, ordinarily gravitate to the correct governing unit and monopolize its time.

Moreover, a managerial form of government has been established in many Texas cities expressly to put distance between the day-to-day running of government and the pressure of citizen influence. For example, after Dallas experienced widespread political activism, led by socialists and populists, at the turn of the century, the city's civic leaders successfully led a campaign to install a council-manager system of government to distance policy making and implementation from the pressure of voters.[17]

The method of electing officeholders to local positions in Texas further dampens mass attention and participation. Nonpartisan elections, which are the norm in electing municipal and special-district officials, make it unnecessary to develop mass-based political parties in order to win office. Instead, candidates solicit the support of smaller, more narrowly focused interest groups. The prevalence of at-large elections allows people and organizations with robust financial resources to support candidates for all offices in local government. This form of election in effect gives "disproportionately larger shares of representation to white, upper-middle-class areas."[18]

In cities where district elections are institutionalized, minority community leaders believe "that the change in electoral systems improves the responsiveness of city government to their needs."[19] In addition, a district system increases community participation (but not voting turnout per se), the diversity of candidates seeking local office, the length of local government meetings, the level of conflict in local political bodies, and the workloads of local officials.[20]

Finally, most local officials in Texas work part-time and are not well paid. With the clear exception of chief administrators (city managers and heads of city departments in large municipalities, for example), local governments are generally run by amateurs.

Managerial government, nonpartisan elections, at-large representation, and amateurism in politics are usually features associated with progressive "good government," a form of government that is preferred by the business community. Indeed, the "good government" movement was originally advocated by corporate interests during the early part of the twentieth century. In Dallas, for instance, business leaders "believed that a professional city manager, removed from immediate political accountability, and an at-large, 'non-partisan' city council could more fully and easily implement the elite's vision of urban growth."[21] Assessing the overall impact of the "good government" movement, sociologist G. William Domhoff concludes that "the actual goal of these reforms was to reduce working-class influence on city government."[22] Although some changes have occurred recently, the political infrastructure advanced by the movement is still well entrenched in Texas.

★★★★★ ECONOMIC INFLUENCE AT THE LOCAL LEVEL

This section examines the impact of big business on local government. Local government is important to corporations because, through its actions, it can promote or hinder business interests. The basic amenities that companies seek from local governing bodies are public services (fire and police protection, water, sewage plants, sanitation, and storm drainage, among others) and favorable local regulation (such as tax breaks). Indeed, in recent years, cities have recruited industry with promises of low taxes (sometimes no taxes), fast-track clearance of building plans, and a wealth of basic services at an attractive cost. Austin's pursuit of MCC and Sematech and Dallas's wooing of American Airlines, Exxon, and J.C. Penney featured concerted efforts by large Texas cities to encourage corporate movement into the state.

Strong economic power structures are found at the local level in Texas. Houston's economy is based on agriculture, real estate and land development, some heavy manufacturing, aerospace technology, and, most emphatically, the petrochemical industry and financial institutions. Some of the country's biggest energy companies (such as Shell) are headquartered there. Exxon is one of Harris County's largest landowners.[23] Texas Commerce (owned by Chase Manhattan Corporation) links big business representatives in Houston through interlocking directorates (see Chapter 2). The three big law firms located in the city—Fulbright and Jaworski, Baker and Botts, and Vinson Elkins—also forge common bonds among major corporations. These three law firms have traditionally had close ties with Houston's major banks.

The origins of Houston's power structure are grounded in the Suite 8F Crowd. As we discussed in Chapter 3, some of the most important economic figures in Texas regularly met in Suite 8F of Houston's Lamar Hotel. In addition to the important role that this group played in state politics, it has been noted that "Houston's business community from the late 1930s to the 1960s was primarily centered in the Suite 8F Crowd, a loose coalition of business leaders who called themselves the 'builders' of modern Houston."[24] This suite of rooms was permanently leased to George and Herman Brown, founders of Brown and Root (now a part of Halliburton) and Texas Eastern (now PanEnergy). The inner circle of the group included Jesse H. Jones, once known as "Mr. Houston," who served as Secretary of Commerce and chair of the Redevelopment Finance Corporation during the presidency of Franklin Roosevelt and helped begin several businesses in Houston, including Texas Commerce. Another member of the 8F Crowd was Gus Wortham, founder of American General, the largest insurance company to emerge from Texas. Also among the charter 8F members were James Elkins, Sr. (of Vinson Elkins), and James Abercrombie, who founded Cameron Iron Works (now Cooper Industries). With the dissolution of the 8F Crowd, its role of coordinating the business community in Houston was transferred to that city's chamber of commerce. As noted by sociologist Joe Feagin, "since the 1970s the chamber's governing board of top corporate executives, although much larger than the old Suite 8F Crowd, has pursued similar goals: to protect, enhance, and expand business investments in the city."[25]

The economy of Dallas is very diversified; the principal sectors revolve around the manufacture of aerospace, military, electronics, and oil equipment; the retailing of goods; the generation of electricity; the processing and distribution of food; real estate development; and insurance and banking. The largest employers in the area are American Airlines, Texas Instruments, General Motors, PepsiCo, Sears Roebuck, Tom Thumb Food and Drugs, Southwestern Bell, and Kroger.

Business interests in Dallas have long been linked through interlocking directorates and civic organizations, the foremost of which is the Dallas Citizens Council, which began in 1937. Most of its 200 to 250 members are board chairs and company presidents. The purpose of the Council is "to study, confer, and act upon any matter, civic or economic in character, which may be deemed to affect the welfare of the city of Dallas, or the state of Texas."[26] Its goal is "to promote unified thinking on a problem or issue" facing Dallas.[27] Its success has been unparalleled in the city's history: "Dallas' influential bankers and corporate heads joined together to control virtually all major political and economic developments in Dallas from 1937 to the present."[28]

The Good Government League (GGL) of San Antonio has been described as "a power structure's power structure."[29] The GGL was formed in 1955 and held together for two decades. At its peak, some 2,000 San Antonians were members of the League. The thirty-six-member executive committee, composed of business leaders, guided its activities. According to one observer, "the GGL served as a highly effective instrument of elite integration in San Antonio, bringing together leading bankers, developers, manufacturers, and other businessmen with a scattering of other community leaders on its board of directors, finance committee, and especially its crucial nominating committee."[30]

El Paso also had a Good Government League composed of a group of business executives. Before its inception some forty years ago, officials from businesses situated in this border city came together in the Committee of Fifty. Fort Worth's economic elite coalesced through "Seventh Street," a loose confederation of business leaders in the city. Over the years, the major figure behind Seventh Street was H. B. "Babe" Fuqua, a former executive of Gulf Oil (now Chevron), founder of a Fort Worth energy firm, and the prime developer of what was once Fort Worth's leading financial institution.

Corporate Links to Local Politics

The mere presence of an economic power center in a geographical area sometimes gives it political power there. The sheer size and economic importance of major companies cannot be ignored by local officials. Corporate decisions to enter or leave an area can have a profound impact on a community. The effect reaches beyond economic ramifications (such as jobs gained or lost) to include political and economic effects (such as local taxes gained or lost).

For this reason, many local taxing units are reluctant to confront a large corporation, probably out of fear of the power of the company, over items such as the appraised worth of its property. Instead, tax officials often rely on the "honor system," which allows companies to calculate the value of their own property. For example, Shell Oil built its corporate headquarters in Houston at an announced cost of $35 million, yet the tax rolls of Harris County showed the appraised value of the structure to be only $12 million. Shell had provided the lower figure to the tax board. When quizzed about the large difference between stated values, a tax collector replied, "We just have to take [Shell's] word for it."[31] The fifty-story Trammell Crow center, located in Dallas, was valued on the tax rolls at $124 million, substantially less than the $170 million owed on the property.[32] Indeed, most corporate property in Dallas appears to be undervalued. One Dallas tax official, when criticized for blindly accepting corporate estimates of business property value, snapped, "I don't feel like I should call a man a liar and I'm not going to."[33]

Big business also employs direct means to influence political decision makers, the foremost of which are elections and lobbying. We shall discuss each of these.

Elections As we mentioned earlier, local elections in Texas are nonpartisan. That is, candidates do not align themselves with political parties. One of the major consequences of this type of electoral system is that political parties hardly exist in local politics. In their absence, economic organizations have assumed electoral functions, such as recruiting candidates and financing campaigns, that are usually performed by parties.

In Texas's most populous cities, each of the above-mentioned economic groups has been deeply involved in local electoral politics. Fort Worth's Seventh Street "orchestrated campaign financing to elect conservative city council candidates who would keep taxes low and downtown healthy."[34] During the 1950s and 1960s, El Paso's Committee of Fifty, according to its most influential member, "would urge people to run and finance their campaigns."[35] That city's Good Government League continued the tradition into the 1980s. League member Judson Williams (former Texas Tech University regent and Southern Union Gas board member) describes the screening process as follows:

> Somebody says "Let's get together and encourage people to run." They'd sit down and have a brainstorming session, "Here's an area"—a name would be discussed. If the feeling was they should be encouraged they'd be talked to and asked [to seek office].[36]

The Good Government League of San Antonio, over the course of its twenty-one-year existence, had a clear political goal: "Candidates for the [city] council, including the mayor's position, [were] carefully screened, selected, and 'nominated' by the . . . GGL."[37] The City Charter Association (CCA) of Dallas, the political arm of the Citizens Council, "persuade[d] 'qualified' men to run for office, and then backed their campaigns financially."[38] Electoral politics in Houston "has long been dominated by a pro-growth establishment consisting of developers, realtors, architects, engineers, the construction industry, and downtown banks and law firms that service these other industries."[39] In the past, the Suite 8F Crowd handled candidate selection and recruitment; today, the city's chamber of commerce serves business interests by screening prospective officeholders in the Bayou City.

At their peak, the success rate of these organizations was quite impressive. In Dallas, between 1937 and the mid-1970s, only two mayors and a handful of candidates won seats on the city council without the support of the City Charter Association.[40] Throughout its existence, the Good Government League of El Paso "seldom failed to get its favorite into the mayor's post."[41] Between 1954 and 1973, the mayor's office and seventy-eight of eighty-one local council seats in San Antonio were occupied by candidates recruited and supported by that city's Good Government League.[42] According to political scientist Robert Lineberry, even "the most hard-headed pluralist could not ignore the potent electoral influence of the Good Government League. The electoral success of the organization would rival that of the strongest old-style urban machine."[43] In Houston, the Suite 8F Crowd obtained its electoral goals: "From 1947 to the early 1970s Houston had only four mayors . . . , all of whom more or less depended on the Suite 8F Crowd. Generally speaking the core of the business elite controlled the composition and major activities of the mayor's office."[44] Finally, the clout of Fort Worth's Seventh Street was so overwhelming that "no politician could [have] endure[d] without its imprimatur."[45]

Over the years, economic groups have succeeded at the expense of representation of those from other backgrounds in local political decision-making units in Texas. In the past, very few women, African Americans, Hispanics, or lower-income people sought, let alone won, political office in the large cities. In the two decades before 1979, only nineteen blacks or Mexican Americans, for instance, ran for a place on the Houston city council; only one of these candidates won.[46] As we shall soon discuss, installation of district electoral systems in many of these cities has altered this exclusionary pattern.

Lobbying Organizations also exert pressure on local governments to effect political decisions. In many instances, lobbying begins with the group's advocating new plans and ideas to the government. This phase of lobbying has been most clearly evident in Dallas, where the Citizens Council has been the major force behind the adoption of new policies in the city. Individual leaders, usually from the highest ranks of business, bring their policy ideas before the Council for discussion and approval. All resolutions have to be unanimously supported by the Council, a stage of the policy process that sometimes takes years. Backing for the proposal is then solicited throughout the community through the use of luncheons, discussion groups, and the media. Only after all these steps have been completed is the idea presented to Dallas political officials, including the city council and the school board.[47]

Large businesses, banks, and corporate law firms have been very successful in shaping public policy in Houston. A partner in the huge Vinson Elkins law firm suggests that "if you thought something needed to be done in Houston, the managing partners of the big [law] firms would be the logical place to start."[48] More directly, the city's chamber of commerce has been most active in designing public policy, especially in the crucial area of planning the city's growth and development. One report notes that "one had only to study the goals listed by the Chamber of Commerce each year to get a good indication of what City Hall would be working on in years and decades to come."[49]

In dealings with local tax boards, affluent property holders frequently have the resources to outmuscle tax assessors and appraisers. Large corporations usually maintain full-time staff devoted to monitoring their tax obligations. Amoco, for instance, has holdings in 99 percent of the school districts of Texas. The company has a department, complete with a lawyer, an accountant, tax experts, and secretaries, that oversees property tax matters in these districts. According to a Amoco spokesperson, "it's been a very workable system over the years."[50]

In sum, corporate interests are primarily transmitted to local governing officials by influencing the choice of elected officials and by lobbying. At times, other methods are evident. For instance, some of the rich become political officials. For example, Othal Brand, founder of Griffin and Brand (one of the country's largest food processing firms), served as mayor of McAllen between 1978 and 1997. However, this practice is not common since the economically powerful usually avoid actually holding local public office.

Policy Outputs from Local Governments   People associated with big business have generally benefited from the decisions reached by local governments in Texas. The benefits come in many forms, most of them tangible and very obvious.

In San Antonio, the continual annexation of new land to the city has been a concrete benefit to many land developers and real estate agents, and to the institutions (banks, mortgage companies, and savings and loan firms) that financially underwrite the home-building industry.[51] There is some evidence that public services provided by local government have traditionally been better in the affluent northwestern part of San Antonio than in other parts of the city, especially the relatively impoverished west side.[52] Although another study fails to find a social class pattern in the delivery of goods and services in the Alamo City, it is conceded that "the power structure is superordinate with respect to the tax rate, and the revenue rate strongly determines the aggregate level of expenditures."[53] To lure hotels into building their facilities in San Antonio and thus expanding the infrastructure that supports the city's lucrative tourist trade, tax officials have offered tax breaks as incentives. As part of the deal that will bring the Adams Mark to downtown San Antonio, for instance, the hotel was given a 100 percent tax break for ten years, an $8 million reduction that costs the city, the county, and the school districts needed revenue.[54]

Houston's generous annexation of outlying areas has enhanced the fortunes of some economic interests. For instance, many unannexed areas around the city are new housing subdivisions that incur large debts in order to construct sewage lines, flood control projects, and water delivery systems. It is difficult for residents of these areas to pay the loans without substantially increasing their property taxes. Annexation by the city of Houston passes payment of the debts along to all of the city's residents. Among the major beneficiaries of this scheme are the bankers who are guaranteed debt repayment with interest.[55]

The delivery of public services, such as police protection, library facilities, sanitation, and roads, is not, by and large, predicated on the wealth or poverty of a neighborhood in Houston.[56] However, the overall planning of the city, its basic tax rate, and the commitment of local government to regulate social relations and allocate public amenities are largely determined by the business establishment. In accordance with the free enterprise ethic of this group, Houston's government has not been encouraged to expend its resources in the general public interest. Hence people with money are encouraged to spend it as they see fit; people without much income may very well go without many services, such as new roads. Moreover, as summarized by Feagin:

> Houston is indeed the planless city, if by planning we mean significant governmental planning and zoning in the public interest for a broad range of infrastructural and socioeconomic problems of development. Much "public" planning has often been privatized and haphazard. This situation has created serious social and environmental problems. Among these are . . . the excessive freedom for developers whose actions can bring major infrastructural crises for neighborhoods and a city hall often unresponsive to the particular needs of neighborhoods.[57]

By and large, public policy in Dallas has been dictated by the Citizens Council. In effect, decisions affecting taxes, transportation, services, and growth have been tailored to the city's business class.[58]

The corporate bias in local policies leaves few benefits available for other interests. For instance, remarkably small amounts are spent in Houston for public parks. Public transportation in most Texas cities is a low-priority item. Police departments in many of the larger cities are understaffed, and the people who work in these police departments are usually underpaid.

★ ★ ★ ★ ★　## POLITICAL CHANGE AT THE LOCAL LEVEL

City politics in Texas appears to be changing. The primary impetus for this change has been alteration of the selection procedure for electing local officials. Introduction of district elections instead of at-large elections has meant that more candidates must be chosen from specific geographic areas. Gone are the days when virtually all local politicians came from the same middle- to upper-middle-class section of the city and belonged to the same race (non-Hispanic whites). More and more African Americans and Hispanics are found on the governing boards of Texas's major cities these days. A majority of San Antonio's council seats in recent years has been occupied by Mexican Americans. In 1993, several members of Houston's fourteen-person council were from minority groups. In that same year, nearly half the Dallas council was composed of minority group members.

In addition, community groups have emerged from neighborhoods traditionally ignored by the local political process. The foremost example is the rise of COPS (short for Communities Organized for Public Service) in San Antonio. Throughout the 1970s, various organizations from the west side of the city came together with the financial and spiritual backing of the local Catholic church and because of the effective mobilization skills of a few people.[59] The greatest initial successes of COPS included improving city services (drainage, sidewalks, streetlights, and so forth) in poor areas of San Antonio, redesigning the electoral system so that candidates run on a district basis, recruiting some successful candidates for city office, and, along with the voter registration efforts of the Southwest Voter Registration Education Project, increasing the voter turnout of Mexican Americans. By the end of the decade, COPS had become "firmly established in San Antonio as a major political force—some would say *the* major political force."[60]

A COPS-style organization, EPISO, spread to El Paso in the early 1980s. Affiliated organizations can be found in Fort Worth (Allied Communities of Tarrant County), Dallas (Dallas Interfaith Sponsoring Committee), Austin (Austin Interfaith Sponsoring Committee), Houston (The Metropolitan Organization of Houston), and the Rio Grande Valley (Valley Interfaith). Houston's Metropolitan Organization (TMO) is an association of sixty congregations, parishes, and religious institutions. It has been successful in improving city services for the poor, pushing for more equity in school funding, fighting a rate increase for electricity, and establishing a trust fund to help the impoverished buy houses.[61]

In some locales, ad hoc groups have been able to challenge the abuses of large businesses and succeed. For instance, a citizens' group, People Organized in Defense of Earth and its Resources (PODER), emerged from a low-income area of East Austin to accuse major oil companies of operating hazardous storage facilities in their neighborhood. Regulators agreed and seven companies, including Exxon, Mobil, Chevron, and Star, closed their tank farms, leading one of the organizers of PODER to claim, "People have learned that they may not be rich, they may not be politically connected, but they do have a voice—and they can make things happen."[62]

Demographic shifts have also contributed to a climate of political change in Texas. Many of the people who have migrated from other parts of the country have civic values that stress participation in, and awareness of, public affairs. Consequently, hierarchical organizations, such as the Citizens Council, based on pushing a single-purpose business agenda, devised and often implemented without the knowledge of the public, have little appeal for these new arrivals.[63]

Finally, the face of local politics has been altered by the inability of economic power centers to remain monolithic. The Good Government League in San Antonio, for instance, is now defunct. The economic power structures in other cities, including Dallas's seemingly impregnable Citizens Council, have developed internal conflicts. Among other problems, the torch of leadership of the Citizens Council was not passed smoothly from the founders of the organization to the succeeding generation of business leaders, owing to the unwillingness of the latter to put a high premium on civic service.[64]

These problems opened doors for new groups and new faces to move into local politics. Women, for instance, have attained a high profile at the local level in Texas. In recent years, women have been mayors in Houston, Dallas, El Paso, and San Antonio, for example. Hispanics have held the mayor's post in El Paso and San Antonio. An African American is the mayor of Dallas.

A new form of coalition politics has emerged in Texas's cities. Different groups, organizations, and interests must be accommodated for candidates to win office and for decision makers to convert ideas into public policy. Corporate leaders have acknowledged this new situation. For example, James Ketelsen, former chair of Tenneco, said of Kathy Whitmire when she was that city's mayor, "She's managed the city with a broader consensus of groups that have to be taken into consideration. That's the new world of politics in Houston as well as in the nation."[65]

However, the question of whether disunity in local economic elites, new community organizations, and changes in election methods will combine to undo the preeminence enjoyed by business in local politics is problematic for two reasons.

First, economically influential groups can often adjust to challenges and changing times. The demands to run African Americans, Hispanics, and women for office can be met by screening, recruiting, and endorsing just such people. Gender and racial or ethnic background alone does not automatically mean that a person is an opponent of the corporate status quo. Lila Cockrell, San Antonio's first woman mayor, was originally the candidate of that city's Good Government League. Henry Cisneros began his political career with the backing of the League. Kathy Whitmire rarely was at odds with Houston's business establishment. As noted by one student of that city's politics, Whitmire "remained a strong advocate of a probusiness approach to local government and of bringing new companies to the city. She did not alter, in any fundamental way, the dependence of local government on private enterprise; and she did not respond to her voters by calling for expanded women's rights, minority rights, or for more neighborhood participation at City Hall."[66]

Moreover, candidates for city positions, especially for the mayor's post, require funds for their campaigns and members of the business community remain the most likely source of financial assistance. In his campaign to become mayor of Houston, River Oaks millionaire Bob Lanier raised much of his money from the wealthy: "A review of Lanier's contributions, stretching over 54 pages, shows a virtual who's who of Houston's businesses and developers."[67]

A study of leaders in cities that have experienced a change in the social background of elected representatives owing to the implementation of elections by districts finds that "the overwhelming majority of respondents . . . recognize the business community, or some portion of it, as the most powerful force in city politics."[68] Electoral reform has not brought about the demise of existing economic power structures. Community leaders feel that "business and development interests will probably adapt to the new electoral system and will remain the most powerful groups in city politics."[69] Indeed, writing in 1996, the author of a study of Dallas concludes that "although the Charter Association died after a federal court put an end to at-large city council elections, the Citizens Council remains the most powerful policy-oriented group in town."[70]

Second, the newer organizations emerging in local government do not have very radical programs. COPS, for instance, has shied away from extreme ideas that promote Hispanic political power at the direct expense of Anglo political and economic standing. Rather, this group focuses on improving public services to its constituency and on the inclusion of voices from poor neighborhoods in private and governmental discussions of the future of San Antonio. If that future must be based on attracting more corporate business to the Alamo City, than so be it. COPS has worked mostly with, not against, major business groups in the city.[71]

★ ★ ★ ★ ★ CONCLUSION

Texas's local government, like its state government, is greatly influenced by economic leaders. The various forms of local government in the state are easily accessed by these people. Through effectively screening candidates, financing their campaigns, and lobbying them once they are in office, the economically influential exercise a great deal of political clout. The payoff has been public policy beneficial to the business community without its having to foot much of the tax bill that underwrites these amenities.

To be sure, some important changes have been made at the local level of government. New electoral systems, the rise of noneconomic groups, and the influx of new people into Texas have put stress on the once-monolithic local power structures. However, there are no clear signs that the high priority given to the preferences of corporate interests by local decision makers faces any serious threat.

★ ★ ★ ★ ★   **NOTES**

1. *1996–1997 Texas Almanac and Industrial Guide* (Dallas: Dallas Morning News, 1995), p. 505.

2. Ibid, pp. 513–515.

3. Thomas R. Dye, with L. Tucker Gibson, Jr., and Clay Robison, *Politics in America* (Upper Saddle River, NJ: Prentice-Hall, 1997), p. 898.

4. Woodworth G. Thrombley, *Special Districts and Authorities in Texas,* Public Affairs Series, no. 39 (Austin: University of Texas Press, 1959), p. 6.

5. Kenneth R. Mladenka and Kim Quaile Hill, *Texas Government: Politics and Economics,* 2d ed. (Pacific Grove, CA: Brooks/Cole, 1989), p. 272.

6. Final Report of the Select Committee on Tax Equity, *Rethinking Texas Taxes* (Austin: Select Committee on Tax Equity, 1989), pp. 16, 116.

7. Legislative Budget Bureau, *Fiscal Size Up: 1996–97 Biennium Texas State Services* (Austin: Legislative Budget Bureau, n.d.), pp. 2–11.

8. Select Committee on Tax Equity, *Rethinking Texas Taxes,* Chapter 7.

9. Ibid.

10. Ibid., p. 118.

11. Legislative Budget Bureau, *Fiscal Size Up,* pp. 2–8.

12. Ibid.

13. "Study: Taxable Property for Schools," *The Monitor,* February 1, 1997.

14. *Rethinking Texas Taxes,* p. 115.

15. Kenneth R. Mladenka and Kim Quaile Hill, *Texas Government,* p. 230.

16. Ibid., p. 238.

17. Patricia Evridge Hill, *Dallas: The Making of a Modern City* (Austin: University of Texas Press, 1996), Chapter 5.

18. LBJ School of Public Affairs, *Local Government Election Systems* (Austin: LBJ School of Public Affairs, 1984), p. 45.

19. Ibid., p. 44.

20. Ibid., passim.

21. Patricia Evridge Hill, *Dallas: The Making of a Modern City,* p. 111.

22. G. William Domhoff, *The Powers That Be* (New York: Random House, 1978), p. 155. Also see his discussion in *Who Really Rules?* (Santa Monica: Goodyear, 1978), pp. 160–68.

23. Jim Chiles, "Who Owns Texas?" *Texas Monthly,* June 1980, p. 129.

24. Joe A. Feagin, *Free Enterprise City: Houston in Political and Economic Perspective* (New Brunswick, NJ: Rutgers University Press, 1988), p. 120.

25. Ibid., p. 143.

26. From the charter of the Dallas Citizens Council, cited in Carol Thometz, *The Decision Makers: The Power Structure in Dallas* (Dallas: Southern Methodist Press, 1963), p. 123.

27. Ibid., p. 31.

28. Harry Hurt III, "The Most Powerful Texans," reprinted in *Texas Monthly's Political Reader* (Austin: Texas Monthly Press and Sterling Swift Publishing, 1978), p. 112.

29. Robert Lineberry, *Equality and Urban Policy: The Distribution of Municipal Services* (Beverly Hills: Sage, 1976), p. 56.

30. Thomas A. Baylis, "Leadership Change in Contemporary San Antonio," in David R. Johnson, John A. Booth, and Richard J. Harris, eds., "The Politics of San Antonio: Community, Progress, and Power" (Lincoln, NB: University of Nebraska Press, 1983), p. 99.

31. Mitch Green, "Like to Set Your Own Tax Rate?" *Texas Observer,* August 25, 1972, p. 6.

32. *Dallas Morning News,* May 12, 1993, p. D-11.

33. Chair of the Board of Equalization of Dallas County, quoted in House Study Group, *Property Taxes: Relief, Reform . . . Revolt?* (Austin: House Study Group, 1980), p. 130.

34. Tom Curtis, "Who Runs Cowtown?" reprinted in *Texas Monthly's Political Reader,* p. 241.

35. The statement is by Sam Young, Sr., in Paul Sweeney, "The League is Weaker: But Still a Force," *El Paso Times,* December 20, 1978, p. 1. Mr. Young was identified as the most important figure in El Paso by two sources: William V. D'Antonio and William H. Form, *Influentials in Two Border Cities* (Notre Dame, IN: University of Notre Dame Press, 1965), p. 62, and Carey Galernter, "Young's Power: More than a Banker's," *El Paso Times,* December 18, 1978, pp. 1, 12.

36. Quotation in Paul Sweeney, "The League Is Weaker: But Still a Force," p. 15.

37. Bill Crane, "San Antonio: Pluralistic City and Monolithic Government," in *Urban Politics in the Southwest,* Leonard E. Goodall, ed. (Tempe, AZ: Institute of Public Administration, Arizona State University, 1967), p. 134; also see Arnold Fleischmann, "Sunbelt Boosterism: The Politics of Postwar Growth and Annexation in San Antonio," in *Rise of the Sunbelt Cities,* David C. Perry and Alfred J. Watkins, eds. (Beverly Hills, CA: Sage, 1977).

38. Carol Thometz, *The Decision Makers,* p. 39.

39. Kent Tedin, "The 1981 Election for Mayor of Houston," *Texas Business Review 56* (November–December 1982):285.

40. Patricia Evridge Hill, *Dallas: The Making of a Modern City,* pp. 163–165.

41. Paul Sweeney, "The League Is Weaker," p. 15.

42. Thomas A. Baylis, "Leadership Change in Contemporary San Antonio," p. 99.

43. Robert Lineberry, *Equality and Urban Policy,* p. 55.

44. Joe R. Feagin, *Free Enterprise City,* p. 153.

45. Tom Curtis, "Who Runs Cowtown?" p. 241.

46. Wendell M. Bedichek and Neal Tannahill, *Public Policy in Texas* (Glenview, IL; Scott, Foresman, 1982), p. 282.

47. See Carol Thometz, *The Decision Makers,* and Patricia Evridge Hill, *Dallas: The Making of a Modern City.*

48. Griffin Smith, Jr., "Empires of Paper," reprinted in *Texas Monthly's Political Reader,* p. 33. Also see Kenneth J. Lipartito and Joseph A. Pratt, *Baker & Botts in the Development of Modern Houston* (Austin: University of Texas Press, 1996).

49. Quotation in Joe Feagin, *Free Enterprise City,* p. 165.

50. Jim Hightower and Tim Mahoney, "Texas Property Taxes: The Unfair Deal," *Texas Observer,* July 21, 1978, p. 6.

51. For a good history of annexation in San Antonio, see Arnold Fleischmann, "Sunbelt Boosterism: The Politics of Postwar Growth and Annexation in San Antonio," in *Rise of the Sunbelt Cities.*

52. Discussed in Peter A. Lupsha and William J. Siembieda, "The Poverty of Public Services in the Land of Plenty: An Analysis and Interpretation," ibid.

53. Robert Lineberry, *Equality and Urban Policy,* p. 159.

54. Ken Dilanian, "Hotel's Tax Breaks Carry a Price," *San Antonio Express News,* March 10, 1996, pp. 1A, 6A. My thanks to Mark Priewe, University of Texas at San Antonio, for providing this example.

55. See, for an example, Harvey Katz, *Shadow on the Alamo* (Garden City, NY: Doubleday, 1972), Chapter 9.

56. Kenneth R. Mladenka and Kim Quaile Hill, *Texas Government,* pp. 254–258.

57. Joe Feagin, *Free Enterprise City,* p. 173.

58. See Patricia Evridge Hill, Dallas: *The Making of a Modern City,* especially Chapter 5 and the Epilogue.

59. For a discussion of the origins of COPS, see Joseph D. Sekul, "Communities Organized for Public Service: Citizen Power and Public Policy in San Antonio," in *The Politics of San Antonio,* Chapter 9.

60. Paul Burka, "The Second Battle of the Alamo," in *Texas Monthly's Political Reader,* p. 245. [Emphasis in the original.]

61. Betty Ward, "Ten Years of Organizing," *Texas Observer,* October 26, 1990, p. 20.

62. Quotation in Mike Ward, "Citizens Use Voice for Change," *Austin American-Statesman,* February 14, 1993, pp. A1, A18–19.

63. Patricia Evridge Hill, *Dallas: The Making of a Modern City,* Epilogue.

64. Ibid.

65. Quotation in Michelle Kay, "The Prime of Kathy Whitmire," *Texas Monthly,* January 1988, p. 27.

66. Joe Feagin, *Free Enterprise City,* p. 155.

67. Scott Harper, "Lanier Shows That He Can Still Raise Big Bucks," *Houston Post,* July 16, 1992, pp. A-23, A-36.

68. LBJ School of Public Affairs, *Local Government Election Systems,* p. 46.

69. Ibid., p. 47.

70. Patricia Evridge Hill, *Dallas: The Making of a Modern City,* p. 165.

71. See Joseph D. Sekul, "Communities Organized for Public Service."

EPILOGUE

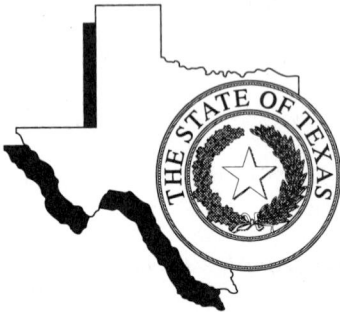

Texas Politics: A Note on Change

If political power is economically structured in Texas, what does this suggest about the possibility of change in the state's political system? What follows is a tentative and clearly incomplete answer to this question; nonetheless, we will pursue the implications of the economic-elite model for the future of Texas politics. Because speculation about the future must be based on an understanding of the present, we will first present a brief summary of this book.

★★★★★ A RECAPITULATION

The economy of Texas is controlled by a relatively small number of corporations. This pattern is evident in the production, conversion, and delivery of agricultural items and petroleum by-products, as well as in the financial exchanges occurring through the state's banks, insurance firms, and savings and loan associations. Large companies dominate the economy of Texas. Wealth is a publicly acceptable sign of success. Deference to those who have succeeded financially has been a core value in Texas culture since the formation of the state.

Many of Texas's dominant businesses are economically interconnected. They share a commitment to growth in profits and recognize that stability within the business community—a stability that can restrain competition among rival businesses—is necessary for such expansion. More directly, social ties, common ownership, mergers, joint ventures, and interlocking boards of directors consolidate the Texas business world.

The crisis that plagued Texas's economy as the petroleum boom of the 1970s turned into the bust of the 1980s sent a shock wave through the higher economic circles. Several leading firms, especially in the financial area, did not survive the economic downturn. As a result, some disintegration of the elite group—at both the state level and the local level—occurred. In particular, many of the state's home-grown large companies, especially its banks and savings and loan associations, collapsed. The holdings of these institutions have been taken over by out-of-state interests. The state's new elite is composed mostly of companies with non-Texan origins and roots. Moreover, new economic options have been pursued in the state, mostly in technology and in business opportunities that were opened with the passage of the North American Free Trade Agreement (NAFTA). In each of these areas, however, large corporations tend to dominate.

The commanding economic position held by a large company is usually sufficient to give it leverage in the Texas political system. In concert, corporations present a formidable opposition in any contest with the government. The hegemony of the business community in society, with its control over valuable resources, including jobs and goods and services, virtually guarantees favorable treatment of business by government officials. In other words, even without direct communication, either in the form of overt promises or threats, political leaders frequently heed the preferences and interests of large corporations. In effect, government has quietly entered into a symbiotic partnership with big business, an agreement in which "government is clearly the junior partner in the . . . combined firm."[1]

This is not to say that business remains aloof from the everyday world of political decision making. Quite the contrary. To maximize the likelihood of achieving their goals and to minimize the political effectiveness of rival groups, dominant economic interests are continually involved in the affairs of the state, through influencing the selection of officeholders and lobbying.

Candidate recruitment begins with the screening of aspirants to electoral office. Influential economic interests or their representatives, such as law firms, play a major role in the selection of candidates. Persons sponsored by the wealthy receive large campaign contributions. The electoral hopes of candidates and parties not in harmony with business preferences are dashed by neglect and, at times, by outright opposition.

To be sure, more competition between the Republicans and the Democrats is evident in Texas elections, thus ostensibly providing the voters more choice. However, the ideological differences between these two parties, at least in Texas, arc not vast. Moreover, winning candidates, regardless of their party affiliations, are remarkably similar in their conservative, probusiness outlook. Consequently, substantive competition in elections is rarely found in Texas. Perhaps as a consequence, voter turnout is extremely low.

The appointment of government officials is also influenced by the business community; indeed, corporate executives and wealthy individuals frequently fill key administrative posts. As a result, most of the people holding elected and appointed offices are very sympathetic to the interests of the state's dominant businesses.

Organized interest groups actively apply pressure to government officials. These groups hire lobbyists—often former members of the state government—to directly contact political leaders. A great deal of money is spent on currying favor with policy makers. Business groups also supply important information to decision makers, the vast majority of whom, at least in the legislature, lack the resources to adequately gather data that is vital to the formulation of public policy. More and more, corporate interest groups rally the public behind their cause.

The organizational design of Texas government enhances the political power of well-organized interest groups. The state constitution creates a generally weak government, which is unable to counter much of the pressure that emanates from the private sector. Moreover, the constitution has been amended to guarantee privileged status to policies that benefit certain corporate interests. Even though the current constitution was intended to prevent the concentration of power in the hands of the corporations and the government, only the latter has been effectively controlled.

The legislature has proven to be very receptive to corporate interests. Legislators work only part-time, without much money or staff assistance. The organization of the legislature is hierarchical; extensive power is vested in the offices of the Speaker and the lieutenant governor. Through their leadership, many corporate interests come to influence the deliberations of the legislature. Once the Speaker and the lieutenant governor are on board the corporate ship, most business-oriented proposals sail through the legislature smoothly.

The executive branch—including the governor, other elected administrators, and a multitude of appointed bureaucrats—is readily accessible to business interests. Most of these offices and agencies are autonomous; each is able to work within its own sphere of influence without much concern about overall coordination or public accountability. This is an ideal setting for well-organized groups to influence the implementation of public policy. Dominant economic interests apply pressure through the exchange of personnel, campaign contributions, and the development of a close working relationship with state agencies. Influential economic interests helped create some of these agencies. They also sit on administrative boards and commissions and provide "expertise and research" to administrators. Finally, economic leaders are often the chief political supporters of administrative units.

Even the courts in Texas are not immune from the influences of the economic elite. Wealthy citizens are in a good position to buy the resources necessary to fully comprehend and master the nuances of the state's multiple-level court system. Furthermore, most of the key participants in the judicial process, ranging from judges to some jurors, are similar in background to economically influential individuals and groups. Again, campaign contributions frequently tie the electoral aspirations of judges to the preferences of economic organizations. The result is an imbalance in the distribution of justice, leaving Texans without wealth at a distinct disadvantage.

Indeed, the whole of public policy in Texas is oriented toward corporate interests. Whether it be in areas budgeted by the state (education, transportation, or welfare) or in activities regulated by government (natural resources, finances, or labor), the corporate sector is the primary beneficiary of governmental action.

The public school system supplies business with a workforce suitable to corporate Texas, a source of investment capital (through the Permanent University Fund and the Permanent School Fund), and research findings and facilities (through universities). The state's magnificent highway system serves the economic interests of automobile, petroleum, construction, and insurance corporations while doing relatively little for the impoverished. The poor are only partially assisted through the state's welfare programs. Welfare policies do, however, provide direct aid to corporations and wealthy individuals. The corporate sector benefits indirectly from the creation of a source of cheap labor and the containment of a potentially hostile mass of impoverished people.

For all the benefits they receive, affluent Texans do not pay their full share of taxes. The overall tax system in the state is very regressive, cutting more into the surplus income of middle- and lower-class Texans than into the earnings of the wealthy.

The consumers of the state, thanks to corporate-oriented government regulation, are faced with high prices for petroleum products, electricity, and insurance. Saving money in state-regulated financial institutions has been risky. People who suffer harm from marketed products find it more difficult to hold businesses responsible these days. Moreover, although they underwrite most of the basic costs of industrialization, consumers often pay a high price to live in an environment polluted by the noxious wastes of big business.

Even labor laws that improve the lot of most of the state's workers greatly assist corporate employers. The state lacks strong unions, does not have full government protection for all employees, and assumes only limited responsibility for the plight of unemployed or injured workers. For these reasons, Texas businesses operate in a labor environment that allows maximization of profits.

Corporate influence in Texas further extends to local politics, especially in the state's largest cities. Through their sheer presence, their selection and sponsorship of local political officials, and their lobbying efforts, members of local economic elites exercise substantial control over local politics. Consequently, policies enacted by local government follow the preferences and interests of the business class.

★★★★★ IMPLICATIONS FOR POLITICAL CHANGE

There are two ways to change the close relationship between corporate and political power in Texas. One involves a fundamental alteration of the economic system. The other is less extreme; it emphasizes opening the political system to more voices and interests, thereby making it more pluralistic.

Fundamental Change

Reordering the economic system would require a major transformation of the institutions that control the means of production and the distribution of goods and services in Texas. The entrenched power of large corporations would have to be uprooted and economic control would have to be transferred to small-scale businesses, to cooperatives composed of average citizens, or to government bodies. For a few reasons, these changes are unlikely to occur.

First, most Texans are quite content with corporate control of their state's economy. They would greatly resist any attempt by government, which they basically distrust, or by other groups and organizations to substantially interfere with or take over the economic power of the private sector.

Second, the economically influential would, of course, resist any efforts to undermine their privileged position. Economic reprisals against persons, groups, or communities seeking fundamental change could easily be arranged. Threats of job layoffs, actual unemployment, cutbacks in the production and delivery of goods, and movement out of locations where conflict is threatened are some of the retaliatory options available to dominant firms. In addition, the government could be expected to suppress calls for fundamental economic change.

Nonfundamental Change

Nonfundamental change means efforts aimed at broadening the base of political power without totally altering the economic and political standing of the wealthy. There are three sources of nonfundamental change.

First, change can come from within the economy. Economic contraction and expansion can cause a restructuring of economic relations. Texas has experienced both. When the economy grows, more people with diverse economic skills must be integrated into the workforce of the state. Although some of these people come from outside of Texas, the economic well-being of the indigenous population also improves. The needs of this new workforce must be accommodated politically. The reemergence of the Republican party in Texas has been, in large part, a response to the political orientations of many new residents who have migrated to the state. The effort by the Democratic party to incorporate more members of minority groups represents a recognition of the improved social and economic status of the state's African American and Hispanic populations.

During the recent period of economic contraction, a somewhat different set of forces was put into motion. At first, crisis led to the pursuit of corporate self-interest (for the sake of organizational survival) and division within the ranks of the business community. Companies had to concentrate on internal matters first. Their forays into the political arena were designed to promote their special interests. It was a good time for new organizations to gain access to political decision makers. The emergence of renewed unity among Texas's businesses portends a closing of political ranks in the corporate community.

Second, change can come from outside political authorities. Policies imposed on Texas by external decision makers have at times led to an increase in the political clout of some groups and individuals. Bans on restrictions on voting (see Chapter 3) and on racial and gender discrimination have improved the status of many Texans. The Voting Rights Act authorizes the U.S. Department of Justice to review the forms of representation used in cities throughout the country. Any time a city with a record of racial discrimination seeks to annex land, change its charter, or alter its laws on voting, it must first secure the approval of the Justice Department. The Department has routinely ruled that municipal plans that deny representation to members of minority groups are in violation of the Voting Rights Act. Consequently, many cities in Texas have had to institutionalize district elections, causing a major shift in the compositions of city councils. Federal courts have also compelled the state to redraw district lines to improve the electoral chances of African Americans and Hispanics.

Third, change can come from the people of Texas. Although Texans are usually apathetic and deferential to authority, there have been times when they have banded together to promote political change. On various occasions, groups such as Hispanics (through organizations such as LULAC, COPS, and the G.I. Forum), consumers, environmentalists, and noncorporate farmers have demanded, and gained, a greater say in decision making. Indeed, a constant theme in Texas's history and culture has been the acceptance of populism, the belief that the people should rule. The Populist movement appeared in the mid-1870s, influenced the writing of the Texas Constitution (see Chapter 1), and has reemerged on several occasions throughout the last one hundred years.

For instance, the liberal-populist theme permeated campaigns during the 1982 statewide election. Several winning candidates made overt appeals to consumers and others who had previously had little power in state politics. Hispanics and African Americans claim, with some justification, that their votes tipped the electoral balance to the advantage of these candidates. After these electoral victories, some changes in public policy could be detected.

In short, the possibility of thoroughly renovating the economic foundation of political power in Texas is very remote. Changes made by people working within the corporate capitalist system seem more achievable. Hard work, political awareness and involvement, and a willingness to join with others will produce some benefits for the relatively powerless—even in a state as dominated by corporate politics as Texas.

★★★★★   **NOTE**

1. Kenneth M. Dolbeare, *Political Change in the United States: A Framework for Analysis* (New York: McGraw-Hill, 1974), p. 26.

★★★★★ INDEX

ABOUT THE AUTHOR

James W. Lamare is Dean of the College of Social and Behavioral Sciences at the University of Texas—Pan American.